The Party's Just Begun

The Party's Just Begun

Shaping Political Parties for America's Future

SECOND EDITION

Larry J. Sabato
University of Virginia

Bruce A. Larson
Fairleigh Dickinson University

With Polling by John McLaughlin and Associates

Longman

New York San Francisco Boston
London Toronto Sydney Tokyo Singapore Madrid
Mexico City Munich Paris Cape Town Hong Kong Montreal

Vice President/Publisher: Priscilla McGeehon
Senior Acquisitions Editor: Eric Stano
Senior Marketing Manager: Megan Galvin-Fak
Senior Production Manager: Eric Jorgensen
Project Coordination, Text Design, and Electronic Page Makeup: Electronic
   Publishing Services Inc., NYC
Cover Design Manager: John Callahan
Cover Designer: Keithley and Associates, Inc.
Cover Photo: AP Wide World Photos, Inc.
Senior Manufacturing Buyer: Dennis J. Para
Printer and Binder: Courier-Stoughton
Cover Printer: Phoenix Color Corp.

For permission to use copyrighted material, grateful acknowledgment is
made to the copyright holders mentioned thoughout the book, which are
hereby made part of this copyright page.

Library of Congress Cataloging-in-Publication Data
Sabato, Larry
      The party 's just begun: shaping political parties for America's
   Future/Larry J. Sabato, Bruce A. Larson; with polling by John McLaughlin
   and Associates. -- 2nd ed.
         p.cm.
      Includes bibliographical references and index.
      ISBN 0-321-08912-X (pbk.)
         1. Political parties--United States. 2. Voting--United States. I. Larson,
   Bruce A., 1960 II. Title.

JK2261 .s22 2001
324.273--dc21   2001022451

Please visit our website at http://www.ablongman.com

ISBN 0-321-08912-X

1 2 3 4 5 6 7 8 9 10—CRS—04 03 02 01

For our dear mothers, Margaret Simmons Sabato and
Lillian Gilmore Larson.
And for the dedicated staff at the UVA Center for
Governmental Studies.

PREFACE TO SECOND EDITION

So much has happened to the American political parties since the publication of *The Party's Just Begun* in 1988. Seemingly permanent Republican control of the presidency ended in 1992 for eight years, just as the first edition had suggested that it might. At the same time, seemingly permanent Democratic control of the House of Representatives yielded to a Republican victory in 1994—a dramatic transformation that lasts until this day, although Democrats have made up some ground in the House and especially in the Senate. On display in this give-and-take is the rhythm of politics, the natural pendulum swing that we have seen in American life since party groupings first emerged around 1800 and became the current Democratic and Republican bipartisan establishment as of 1856–1860.

Within the parties, even more basic shifts and alterations have occurred. The Democrats finally learned after failed presidential bids in 1984 and 1988 that the party needed to shift closer to the center, remaining liberal on social issues, but becoming more moderate on economic matters. Interestingly, the Republicans lost the presidency in 1992 mainly because of a recession, but partly because the party was perceived as having moved too far to the right, due in good measure to the virulent challenge to George H. W. Bush by television commentator Patrick Buchanan. Yet, an invigorated and very conservative Republican party, emboldened by all of the failings of the early Clinton administration, reasserted itself in 1994 and captured both houses of Congress. That very success planted the seeds of failure, as a Republican-led government shutdown turned Americans off to the GOP and, fearing total

Republican control of government, voters reelected President Clinton, in spite of all of his problems. In turn, the next Republican nominee learned a valuable lesson. It is impossible to imagine that Texas Governor George W. Bush could have defeated Vice President Al Gore in the midst of peace and prosperity had he not embraced gender and racial diversity and the slogan "compassionate conservatism." As it was, of course, Vice President Gore won the popular vote by a substantial margin of 540,000 out of 105 million votes cast.

The stresses on the party system are certainly not restricted to the changes within the two major political parties. One of the strongest challenges ever mounted to two-party government occurred in 1992. Businessman Ross Perot rode over the hill on a white horse, wearing a white hat, promising reform of all kinds and, for a while, leading both major party candidates in the polls by a substantial margin. His decision to drop out of the contest in the summer of 1992 may have deprived him of the chance to be president, but his reentry in October was no small matter. To the shock of most pollsters, Perot received nearly one in five ballots in November, the best third-party showing since former President Theodore Roosevelt ran under the "Bull Moose" Progressive party label in 1912. Although the justification for his candidacy and his new party, the Reform Party, lessened considerably in 1996, Perot was still able to secure about 8 percent of the national vote. The party dissolved for all practical purposes in 2000 with the nomination of the ever-controversial Patrick Buchanan, who received well under 1 percent of the total national vote.

Whether the Reform Party stages a comeback or not, it is hard to believe that the two parties will long remain the only major national electoral institutions. Given the generally weak partisan attachments in the American electorate, which was described in great detail in the first edition of this volume, third parties—both weak and strong—are bound to arise in American political life during the 21st century. Ralph Nader's Green Party candidacy in 2000 may have only secured 2.5 percent of the national vote, but that was more than enough to deprive Al Gore of the presidency. In Florida alone, Nader's 97,000-plus votes would have made the difference many times over in delivering a victory to Gore, had Nader not been in the race. There may well be more of these critical tail-waggers as U.S. politics fully adapts to the technological age.

Still, for all of the pregnant possibilities as well as recent electoral history, one is struck by the amazing stability of the two-party system. That stability is reflected both in the enduring nature of the Democratic/Republican split, but also in the continuing effects of the two-party system on American society as a whole. Despite all of our divisions and controversies, the current electoral system, for better or worse, essentially forces most Americans to choose between the nominees of the two major parties if they want to have a voice in the selection of the winner. Perhaps this produces too many "lesser-of-two-evils" elections, but we are as impressed as ever by the contributions the two parties have made and are making in American life.

Although the basic themes and organization of the second edition remain similar to those of the first edition, the new edition includes many changes. To begin with, the survey research presented in the original edition has been completely replaced with data from a new (August 2000) survey conducted exclusively for this book by John McLaughlin and Associates. McLaughlin and Associates also graciously shared with us the data from their post-election survey, to which readers will find references scattered throughout the book. In addition to the new survey data, Chapters Three (on party organizations) and Five (on party realignments) have been completely rewritten for the second edition. Chapter Three describes the enormous changes that have occurred in the world of party organizations since the book's initial publication and includes new sections on topics such as soft money, member-to-candidate campaign assistance, and legislative campaign committees. Chapter Five provides a new narrative on shifts in American party coalitions since the 1960s and addresses the question of whether the United States has undergone a critical realignment during this period. Although these revisions are the most fundamental of the second edition, readers will find new things in every chapter. Throughout the book, we have attempted to integrate the considerable changes that have taken place in American politics since the book's first edition into the enduring themes that make up the study of American political parties.

Another change for the second edition is the addition of co-author Bruce Larson. A friend, colleague, and former Ph.D. student of Professor Sabato's at the University of Virginia, Larson has conducted research on congressional campaign finance, political parties, and statewide ballot initiatives. It has been an enormous pleasure for us to work together on this and other projects, and we hope to work together often in the future.

No book can be completed without the help of others, and we received it in many forms. We want to provide special thanks to pollster John McLaughlin and his firm for agreeing to conduct the book's survey for us—and for fitting the survey in during the heat of the 2000 presidential election season! Chip Mertz of John McLaughlin and Associates deserves particular thanks for his enormous assistance in constructing the poll questions and structuring the survey questionnaire. Despite having more than enough of his own work to do, Chip was always available to lend his unparalleled expertise to our project. Working closely with John McLaughlin and Associates allowed us to experience first-hand why the outfit is considered one of America's premiere polling firms. We should also stress that we take complete and sole responsibility for the interpretation and presentation of the survey data.

Other people also deserve thanks for helping to make the second edition possible. Melissa Northern, Director of Programs at the University of Virginia (UVA) Center for Governmental Studies in Charlottesville, Virginia, was instrumental in coordinating the research assistants and interns who worked on the second edition of the book. Melissa has an unparalleled ability for managing projects effectively, and the completion of this book would not have been possible without her efforts. Other people at the Center for Governmental Studies also merit thanks for their role in facilitating the second edition. Alex Theodoridis, Chief of Staff at the Center, provided enthusiastic support for the project from the start. UVA student Christopher Spillman updated many of the tables and figures for the book's second edition and produced fine research on various topics discussed in the book. In addition, we appreciate the many other interns at the Center who helped in ways large and small with the second edition of the book.

Outside of the Center for Governmental Studies, many people also provided valuable assistance to this project. Alice Carter furnished excellent editorial advice and thoughtful comments on how to improve the manuscript. Marc Hetherington and Suzanne Globetti of Bowdoin College graciously lent their expertise in working with National Election Studies data. Barbara and Steve Salmore provided helpful thoughts on how we might best approach the second edition. Elsie Carter made sure that we always had the most up-to-date information on West Virginia's Mountain Party. We also thank the reviewers of our second edition proposal for their helpful comments: Stephen J. Farnsworth at Mary Washington College; Margaret V. Moody at Auburn University; and Todd M. Schaeffer at Central Washington University. Finally, we would like to thank Eric Stano at Longman Publishers for his enthusiastic support for the book's second edition. It's been a pleasure to work with Eric, and he deserves much credit for making the second edition of *The Party's Just Begun* a reality.

We would also like to recognize again the numerous individuals who lent their assistance for the first edition of the book. Scholars and friends who provided invaluable comments and insight for the first edition include John Bibby, James Ceaser, Mildred and Weldon Cooper, Eric L.

Davis, Robert H. Evans, Steven Finkel, Jeremy Gaunt, Charles O. Jones, Clifton McCleskey, H. G. Nicholas, Barbara Salmore, and Kenneth W. Thompson. At the heart of the first edition were three public opinion polls taken by the late William R. Hamilton and underwritten by the American Medical Association's political action committee, AMPAC. Although new surveys were conducted for the new edition, readers will find references to the original surveys scattered throughout the book. Financial support for the first edition was provided by the Earhart Foundation, the American Philosophical Society, and the University of Virginia. Finally, a small army of research assistants provided assistance on the first edition, and much of their hard work lives on in the second edition.

Surrounded by such competent people, and with no obvious scapegoats available, we accept the customary responsibility for any errors that remain.

Larry J. Sabato
Director, The Center for
Governmental Studies
Robert Kent Gooch Professor
The University of Virginia
Charlottesville, Virginia

Bruce A. Larson
Assistant Professor of Political
Science
Fairleigh Dickinson University
Madison, New Jersey

April, 2001

CONTENTS

TABLES AND FIGURES

1

The Case for Parties

THERE ARE NO more unappreciated institutions in America than the two major political parties. Often maligned by citizens and politicians alike as the repositories of corrupt bosses and smoke-filled rooms, the parties nonetheless perform essential electoral functions for our nation. Not only do they operate (in part) the machinery for nomination to most public offices, but the two parties serve as vital, umbrellalike, consensus-forming institutions that help counteract the powerful centrifugal forces in a country teeming with hundreds of racial, economic, social, religious, and political groups. The parties are often accused of dividing us; on the contrary, they assist in uniting us as few other institutions do. Just as important, they permit leaders to be successful by marshaling citizens and legislators around a common standard that elected executives can use to create and implement a public agenda.

The grand partnership of the Democratic and Republican parties has endured for thirty-six presidential elections, much longer than most of the regimes around the world that existed when the association began. Yet the parties command precious little respect in some quarters. Many members of the press frequently deride the parties and characterize them as archaic, undemocratic institutions. The judiciary has sometimes treated them as political outcasts and legal stepchildren. Presidents have frequently ignored them, choosing to run their election campaigns

TABLE 1.1. MOST IMPORTANT REASON FOR 2000
PRESIDENTIAL ELECTION VOTE.

Question: This year, which of the following was the most important factor in deciding your vote for president?[a]

The issue differences between the candidates	48%
The personality and character of each candidate	25%
The philosophy of your political party	23%

Source: Post-election survey of voters conducted by John McLaughlin and Associates. See Appendix.
[a]Percentages do not add up to 100 percent because "don't know" and "refused" responses are not included.

wholly apart from the party organization. Many congressional and gubernatorial contenders have run *against* the party, presenting themselves as worthy of public office precisely because they lacked party endorsement or experience. But the greatest scorn for parties—and the residual source of all the other indignities borne by the parties—has been expressed by the American electorate. Politics in general is held in low regard by the voters, and party politics lower still.[1] As Table 1.1 suggests, most voters don't perceive party as playing much of a role in their voting decisions. In a post-election survey following the 2000 presidential election, only 23 percent of voters surveyed reported that the philosophy of their political party was the most important factor in casting their vote for president. Put differently, the table reveals that 73 percent of voters viewed factors *other than party* as most important in making their selection for president.[2] Yet political scientists have found repeatedly that an individual's party identification is a powerful predictor of his or her vote choice in presidential elections.[3] In truth, the puzzle is easily explained. Although issues and candidate attributes surely matter to voters, partisan affiliation just as surely colors how voters *perceive* the issues and candidates.[4]

PARTY AS A VOTING AND ISSUE CUE

Whether most voters appreciate it or not, their partisan identification acts as an invaluable filter for information, a perceptual screen that affects how they digest the political news that manages to reach them. The party filter often is much more effective and encompassing than is realized, since it colors a wide range of voters' views on public issues and ideas. For instance, Table 1.2 presents the opinions of party identifiers on two topics. One would certainly expect a president's job approval rating to be a function of a citizen's party affiliation, and indeed it is: 86 percent of the Democrats gave President Clinton high

TABLE 1.2. PARTY IDENTIFICATION AS AN INTERPRETIVE FILTER.

		Percent of	
Questions	Democrats	Independents	Republicans
Clinton Job Approval			
"Overall, how would you rate Bill Clinton's job as President? Would you say he has done an excellent job, a good job, a fair job, or a poor job?"			
Excellent or Good	86%	56%	33%
Fair or Poor	13%	44%	66%
Bush Tax Cut			
"Do you approve or disapprove of George W. Bush's proposal for an across-the-board federal income tax cut?"			
Approve	25%	48%	82%
Disapprove	65%	43%	13%

Source: Post-election survey of voters conducted by John McLaughlin and Associates. See Appendix.
Totals do not add up to 100 percent since "don't know" and refused responses are not listed in table.

marks in November 2000 while only 33 percent of the Republicans did so. The party perceptual screen also extends to issues. As Table 1.2 illustrates, Republicans approved of George W. Bush's across-the-board tax cut proposal by wide margins (82 percent), while only a quarter of Democrats did. Not surprisingly, partisanship also greatly colored Americans' sense of fairness during the protracted struggle for Florida's 25 electoral votes following the 2000 presidential election: whereas large majorities of Democrats deemed Florida's certified election results as unfair and inaccurate, large majorities of Republicans believed exactly the opposite.[5] From vague, generalized feelings to specific evaluations of candidates, there is no better or more consistent indicator of survey results than partisan affiliation.

Thus, party affiliation provides a useful cue for voters, particularly the least informed and interested, who can use party as a shortcut or substitute for interpreting issues and events they may little comprehend. But even better educated and more involved voters find party identification an assist. After all, no one has the time to study every issue carefully or to become fully knowledgeable about every candidate seeking public office. In an August 2000 survey conducted for this book, at least some of our respondents recognized the parties' role as a voting cue: 53 percent agreed with the statement that "If I don't know anything else about a candidate for public office, knowing the candidate's political party helps me decide whether or not to vote for him or her."[6]

MOBILIZING SUPPORT AND AGGREGATING POWER

The effect of the party cue is enormously helpful to elected leaders. They can count on disproportionate support among their partisans in times of trouble, and in close judgment calls they have a home court advantage. The party perceptual screen even draws together ideologically diverse elements to the benefit of leaders; both conservatives and liberals within each party adjust their perceptions so that they see their chosen party as being in basic agreement with their beliefs (even if it's not true).[7] Thus, the parties aid officeholders by giving them maneuvering room and by mobilizing support for their policies. Because there are only two major parties, pragmatic citizens who are interested in politics or public policy are mainly attracted to one or the other standard, creating natural majorities or near-majorities for party officeholders to command. The party creates a community of interest that bonds disparate groups together over time—eliminating the necessity of creating a coalition anew for every campaign or every issue. Imagine the chaos and mad scrambles for public support that would constantly ensue without the continuity provided by the parties.

Besides mobilizing Americans on a permanent basis, then, the parties convert the cacophony of hundreds of identifiable social and economic groups into a two-part (semi)harmony that is much more comprehensible, if not always on key and pleasing to the ears. The simplicity of two-party politics may be deceptive given the enormous variety in public policy choices, but a sensible system of representation in the American context might well be impossible without it. And those who would suffer most from its absence would not be the few who are individually or organizationally powerful—their voices would be heard under almost any system. As Walter Dean Burnham has pointed out, the losers would be the many individually powerless for whom the parties are the only effective devices yet created that can generate countervailing collective power on their behalf.[8]

A FORCE FOR STABILITY

This last argument may have the faint odor of revolution to it, but nothing could be further from the truth. As mechanisms for organizing and containing political change, the parties are a potent force for stability. They represent continuity in the wake of changing issues and personalities, anchoring the electorate as the storms that are churned by new political people and policies swirl around. Because of its unyielding, pragmatic desire to win elections (not just contest them), each party in a sense acts to moderate public opinion. The party tames its own extreme elements by pulling them toward an ideological center in order to attract a majority of votes on election day. Liberal Democrats, for example, rallied around the 1992 and 1996 general election campaigns of centrist Bill Clinton, and firebrand GOP conservatives were willing to support the relatively moderate George W. Bush in 2000 as an alternative to being shut out of the White House for another four years.[9] Parties serve as forces for stability even when relatively radical candidates win party nominations. The general election campaigns of Barry Goldwater in 1964 and George McGovern in 1972 stressed primarily mainstream issues and concerns, even though this may not coincide with our memories of them since neither candidate was ever able to escape from torrid prenomination records and rhetoric. Yet even most Goldwater diehards in the GOP and passionate McGovernites among the Democrats understood the need for and approved the candidate's move to the moderate center. The election process itself, acting through the medium of the parties, "mainstreams" many of the malcontents and firebrands.

This stabilizing process occurs with groups as well as individuals. The pragmatic nature of each American party sends it scurrying to attract each new politically active organization or element in the population. The newly enfranchised 18–21-year-olds were fought over and assiduously courted in the early 1970s, with the Democrats winning the bulk of the new adherents, thanks to their developing opposition to the Vietnam war.[10] Later in the same decade, fundamentalist Christians awakened politically. While first drawn to Democrat Jimmy Carter's "born again" personality, a substantial majority of the white evangelicals succumbed to Republican Ronald Reagan's charms in 1980 and 1984, partly on the basis of his party's conservative stands on defense and "family issues" (abortion, the Equal Rights Amendment, and the like). Since then, the religious right has become a key component of the GOP coalition, mobilizing scores of voters on behalf of Republican candidates.[11]

Another aspect of the stability the parties provide can be found in the nature of the coalitions they forge. There are inherent contradictions in these coalitions that, oddly enough, strengthen the nation even as they strain party unity. The Democratic New Deal majority, for example, included many blacks and most Southern whites—contradictory elements nonetheless joined in common political purpose. This party union of the two groups, as limited a context as it may have been, surely provided a framework for acceptance and reconciliation in the civil rights era. Nowhere can this be more clearly seen than in the South, where most state Democratic parties remained predominant after the mid-1960s by building on the ingrained Democratic voting habits of both whites and African Americans to create a new, moderate, generally integrated politics. In a more recent example, the inclusion of white fundamentalist Christians into GOP party affairs has served to lessen their alienation from mainstream American society by giving them a home in the American political system.

UNITY, LINKAGE, ACCOUNTABILITY

Parties provide the glue to hold together the disparate parts of the fragmented American governmental and political apparatus. The Framers of the Constitution designed a system that divides and subdivides power, making it possible to preserve individual liberty but difficult to coordinate and produce timely action. Parties help to compensate for this drawback by linking all the institutions and loci of power one to another. While rivalry between the executive and legislative branches of American government is inevitable, the partisan affiliations of the leaders of each branch constitute a common basis for cooperation, as any president and his fellow party members in Congress usually demonstrate daily. Even within each branch, there is intended fragmentation, and party once again helps to narrow the differences between the House of Representatives and the Senate, or between the president and his chiefs in the executive bureaucracy. Similarly, the federalist division of national, state, and local governments, while always an invitation to conflict, is made more workable and easily coordinated by the intersecting party relationships that exist among officeholders at all office levels. Party affiliation, in other words, is a sanctioned and universally recognized basis for mediation and negotiation laterally among the branches and vertically among the layers.

The party's linkage function does not end there, of course. Party identification and organization is a natural connector and vehicle for communication between the voter and the candidate as well as between the voter and the officeholder. The party connection is one means to ensure or increase accountability in election campaigns and in government. Candidates on the campaign trail and elected party leaders in office are required from time to time to account for their performance at party-sponsored forums and in party nominating primaries and conventions.

Political parties, too, can take some credit for unifying the nation by dampening sectionalism. Since parties must form national majorities to win the presidency, one region is guaranteed permanent minority status unless ties are established with other areas. The party label and philosophy is the bridge enabling regions to join forces, and, in the process, a national interest is created and served rather than a merely sectional one.

THE ELECTIONEERING FUNCTION

The election, proclaimed H. G. Wells, is "democracy's ceremonial, its feast, its great function," and the political parties assist this ceremonial in essential ways. First, the parties funnel talented (and, granted, some not-so-able) individuals into politics and government. Hundreds of candidates are recruited each year by the two parties, and many of them are party-trained and briefed for their responsibilities on the hustings. Furthermore, many of their staff members—the ones who manage the campaigns and go on to serve in key governmental positions once the election is over—are also brought into politics by way of party involvement. Both parties now provide campaign "training schools" for staffers as well as candidates. Perhaps most importantly, the parties are directly contributing to their nominees' elections more than ever before in the modern era. As Chapter Three will discuss, the parties have become major providers of money and campaign services at all levels of politics.

Elections can only have meaning in a democracy if they are competitive, substantive, focused, and comprehensible to the average voter. These criteria probably could not be met in America without the parties. Even in the South, once the least competitive American region, the parties today regularly produce vigorous contests at the state (and increasingly, the local) level.[12] The rivalry between the parties promotes the competition necessary for the system's health even in basically homogeneous communities. Through national platforms and advertising campaigns, the parties assist in framing and defining the issues. Because they are a mechanism for accountability, they force their candidates to pay some attention to central party ideas and values. The simplicity of the labels themselves, and the voting cues they provide, keep elections somewhat understandable for the least involved citizens. In fact, the parties' duopoly in American politics assures simplicity by providing only two leading candidates for each office.

POLICY FORMULATION AND PROMOTION

Senator Huey Long of Louisiana, the premiere populist demagogue of the twentieth century, was usually able to capture the flavor of the average man's views about politics. Considering an Independent bid for president before his assassination in 1935, Long liked to compare the Democratic and Republican parties to the two patent medicines offered by a traveling salesman. Asked the difference between them, the salesman explained that the "High Populorum" tonic was made from the bark of the tree taken from the top down, while "Low Populorum" tonic was made from bark stripped from the root up. The analogous moral, according to Long, was this: "The only difference I've found in Congress between the Republican and Democratic leadership is that one of 'em is skinning us from the ankle up and the other from the ear down!"[13]

Long would certainly have insisted that his fable applied to the national party platforms, the most visible instrument by which parties formulate, convey, and promote public policy. Most citizens in our own era undoubtedly still believe that party platforms are relatively undifferentiated, a mixture of pablum and pussyfooting (as a more modern demagogue, George Wallace, might have phrased it in one of his presidential campaigns). Yet, examine for a moment some excerpts from the 2000 Democratic and Republican national platforms, presented in Table 1.3. On a host of issues, the two parties could not have taken more

TABLE 1.3. COMPARISON OF THE 2000 DEMOCRATIC AND REPUBLICAN PLATFORMS ON SELECTED ISSUES.

Democratic	*Republican*
Taxes	
"Democrats seek the right kind of tax relief—tax cuts that are specifically targeted to help those who need them the most. These tax cuts would let families live their values by helping them save for college, invest in their job skills and lifelong learning, pay for health insurance, afford child care, eliminate the marriage penalty for working families, care for elderly or disabled loved ones, invest in clean cars and clean homes, and build additional security for their retirement."	"When the average American family has to work more than four months out of every year to fund all levels of government, it's time to change the tax system, to make it simpler, flatter, and fairer for everyone. It's time for an economics of inclusion that will let people keep more of what they earn and accelerate movement up the opportunity ladder."
Abortion	
We support contraceptive research, family planning, comprehensive family life education, and policies that support healthy childbearing... The Democratic party stands behind the right of every woman to choose, consistent with *Roe v. Wade*, and regardless of ability to pay."	"We renew our call for replacing 'family planning' programs for teens with increased funding for abstinence education, which teaches abstinence until marriage as the responsible and expected standard of behavior... We support a human life amendment to the Constitution and we endorse legislation to make clear that the Fourteenth Amendment's protections apply to unborn children. We support the appointment of judges who respect traditional family values and the sanctity of innocent human life."
Gun Control	
"We need mandatory child safety locks to protect our children. We should require a photo license I.D., a full background check, and a gun safety test to buy a new handgun in America. We support more federal gun prosecutors, ATF agents and inspectors, and giving states and communities another 10,000 prosecutors to fight gun crime."	"We defend the constitutional right to keep and bear arms, and we affirm the individual responsibility to safely use and store firearms. Because self-defense is a basic human right, we will promote training in their safe usage, especially in federal programs for women and the elderly."

(continued)

TABLE 1.3. *CONTINUED*

Democratic	*Republican*

Religion

"Democrats believe that partnerships with faith-based organizations should augment—not replace—government programs, should respect First Amendment protections, and should never use taxpayer funds to proselytize or to support discrimination."

"We assert the right of religious leaders to speak out on public issues and will not allow the EEOC or any other arm of government to regulate or ban religious symbols from the workplace. We condemn the desecration of places of worship and objects of religious devotion, and call upon the media to reconsider their role in fostering bias through negative stereotyping of religious citizens... We strongly disagree with the Supreme Court's recent ruling, backed by the current administration, against student-initiated prayer."

Education

"The Democratic Party supports expansion of charter schools, magnet schools, site-based schools, year-round schools, and other nontraditional public school options. What America needs are public schools that compete with one another and are held accountable for results, not private school vouchers that drain resources from public schools and hand over the public's hard-earned tax dollars to private schools with no accountability."

"Governor Bush's education reforms will...assist states in closing the achievement gap and empower needy families to escape persistently failing schools by allowing federal dollars to follow their children to the school of their choice. We advocate choice in education, not as an abstract theory, but as the surest way for families, especially low-income families, to free their youngsters from failing or dangerous schools and put them onto the road to opportunity and success."

Energy and the Environment

"Democrats believe we must give Americans incentives to invest in driving more fuel-efficient cars, trucks, and sport utility vehicles; living in more energy-efficient homes, and using more environmentally-sound appliances and equipment... Democrats believe that with the right incentives to encourage the development and deployment of clean energy technologies, we can make all our energy sources cleaner, safer, and healthier for our children. And we

"Republicans [will] enact their National Energy Security Act. That strategy will: Increase domestic supplies of coal, oil, and natural gas; Provide tax incentives for production; Promote environmentally responsible exploration and development of oil and gas reserves on federally-owned land, including the Coastal Plain of Alaska's Arctic National Wildlife Refuge; Advance clean coal technology; Maintain the ethanol tax credit. Provide a tax incentive for residential use of solar

(continued)

TABLE 1.3. CONTINUED

Democratic	Republican
must dramatically reduce climate-disrupting and health-threatening pollution in this country, while making sure that all nations of the world participate in this effort."	power... Our country does have ample energy resources waiting to be developed, and there is simply no substitute for an increase in their domestic production... Complex and contentious issues like global warming call for a far more realistic approach than that of the Kyoto Conference. Its deliberations were not based on the best science..."

Civil Rights and Affirmative Action

"The Democratic Party has always supported the Equal Rights Amendment and will continue to do so, and we are committed to ensuring full equality for women and to vigorously enforcing the Americans with Disabilities Act. We support continuation of the White House initiative on Asian Americans and Pacific Islanders.... We support continued efforts, like the Employment Non-Discrimination Act, to end workplace discrimination against gay men and lesbians... Al Gore has strongly opposed efforts to roll back affirmative action programs."	"We believe rights inhere in individuals, not in groups. We will attain our nation's goal of equal opportunity without quotas or other forms of preferential treatment. It is as simple as this: No one should be denied a job, promotion, contract, or chance at higher education because of their race or gender. Equal access, energetically offered, should guarantee every person a fair shot based on their potential and merit."

National Missile Defense

"We reject Republican plans to endanger our security with massive unilateral cuts in our arsenal and to construct an unproven, expensive, and ill-conceived missile defense system that would plunge us into a new arms race. Al Gore and the Democratic Party support the development of the technology for a limited national missile defense system that will be able to defend the U.S. against a missile attack from a state that has acquired weapons of mass destruction despite our efforts to block their proliferation."	"We will deploy defenses against ballistic missiles and develop the weapons and strategies needed to win battles in this new technological era...The ballistic missile threat to the United States has been persistently dismissed, delaying for years the day when America will have the capability to defend itself against this growing danger... The new Republican president will deploy a national missile defense for reasons of national security; but he will also do so because there is a moral imperative involved: The American people deserve to be protected."

divergent substantive positions—and there is nothing mushy or tepid about the rhetoric employed, either.

The 2000 platforms were not exceptional in this regard. Gerald Pomper's study of party platforms from 1944 through 1976 demonstrated that each party's pledges were consistently and significantly different, a function in part of the varied groups in their coalitions.[14] Other research has also found meaningful differences between the two parties' platforms.[15] Interestingly, Pomper's study revealed that some 69 percent of the specific platform positions were taken by one party but not the other. Such was also the case in 2000, when each side dwelt on some subjects that the other mostly or totally ignored. For Democrats, these topics included community investment, suburban sprawl ("livable communities"), racial profiling, and hate crimes. The Republican platform, in contrast, was more interested in judicial excesses, litigation reform, and shifting power back to the states.

Granted, then, that party platforms are quite distinctive. Does this elaborate party exercise in policy formulation mean anything? One could argue that the platform is valuable, if only as a clear presentation of a party's basic philosophy and a forum for activist opinion and public education. But platforms have much more impact than that. Cynics will be amazed to discover that a significant portion of the promises in the victorious party's presidential platform have been completely or mostly implemented; even more astounding, many of the *losing* party's pledges find their way into public policy (with the success rate depending on whether the party controls one, both, or neither house of Congress).[16] The party platform also has great influence on a new administration's legislative program and the president's State of the Union address. And while party affiliation is normally one of the most important determinants of voting in Congress (and in some state legislatures), the party-vote relationship is even stronger when party platform issues come up on the floor of Congress.[17] As Gerald Pomper concludes, "We should therefore take platforms seriously—because politicians appear to take them seriously."[18]

PROMOTION OF CIVIC VIRTUE

In devising policy and platforms on the public stage, the parties assist in informing and educating the citizenry about vital issues. But the parties' promotion of civic virtue goes far beyond this. Because identification with a party is at the core of many Americans' political lives, the prism through which they see the world, many voters accept and adopt the parties' values and view of responsible citizenship. These values include involvement and participation, work for the "public good" (as conceived in partisan terms, naturally), and trust in America's fundamental institutions and processes. The parties teach people to accept these values even if, as individual citizens, they fail to live up to them. For example, parties honor the act of voting as the irreducible minimum responsibility of a good citizen. Most citizens do not vote regularly, but, because of political socialization by the parties, their families, and their schools, they know they *should* vote. Perhaps that is why, in the August 2000 survey conducted for this book, 79 percent reported they had cast a ballot in the 1996 presidential election, when in fact a paltry 49 percent had actually gone to the polls![19] At least people believe in voting in theory if not in practice.

Party identification can also encourage belief and confidence in a society's institutions. Seymour Martin Lipset and William Schneider found that Democratic and Republican identifiers have the highest confidence in American institutions while self-described Independents have the lowest, leading to their conclusion that "general confidence seems to be associated with partisanship *per se*."[20] Interestingly, research also suggests that citizens who depend heavily on the perceptual screen of partisanship to evaluate politics tend to feel more politically efficacious than do individuals who see the political world in terms of issues, processes, and public officials.[21]

A WORLD WITHOUT PARTIES

If these are the roles parties play in American life, what would that life be like without a strong two-party system? Surely, even the parties' severest critics would agree that our politics will be the poorer for any further weakening of the party system. We have only to look at who and what gains as parties decline.

- *Special Interest Groups Gain.* Their money, labels, and organizational power can serve as a substitute for the parties' own. Yet, instead of fealty to the national interest or a broad coalitional party platform, the candidates' loyalties would be pledged to narrow, special interest agendas instead. "Pressure groups may destroy party government but they cannot create a substitute for it," observed E. E. Schattschneider.[22]

- *Wealthy and Celebrity Candidates Gain.* Their financial resources or fame can provide name identification to replace party affiliation as a voting cue. The number of millionaires willing to finance their own campaigns has surely grown during the past few decades. New Jersey Senate candidate Jon Corzine—who broke all records in 2000 by spending more than $60 million of his own money on his Senate campaign—brought the political advantages of wealth to new heights. The number of inexperienced but successful candidates drawn from the entertainment and sports worlds also seems to grow each year.

- *Incumbents Gain.* The value of incumbency increases where party labels are absent or less important, since the free exposure incumbents receive raises their name identification level. There would also be extra value for candidates endorsed by incumbents or those who run on slates with incumbents.

- *The News Media, Particularly Television News, Gains.* Party affiliation is one of the most powerful checks on the news media, not only because the voting cue of the party label is in itself a countervailing force but also because the "perceptual screen" erected by party identification filters media commentary. (People tend to hear, see, and remember the news items that reinforce their party attitudes and biases.)[23]

- *Political Consultants Gain.* The entrepreneurs of campaign technologies (such as polling, television advertising, and direct mail) secure more influence in any system of party decline. Although political parties and political consultants have gradually arrived at something of a symbiotic partnership[24]—where each side benefits from the other—consultants will always be more concerned with winning the election at hand than with helping parties build long-term ties in the electorate.[25] Without the broader perspective (ideally) provided by parties, electoral politics would be colored more than ever by consultants' short-term goals (favorable win-loss records).

Citizens should be deeply troubled by these prospects. Most Americans are concerned about the growth in single-issue politics and special interest financing of political campaigns, and most want public office available to able citizens of modest means and those who are respected for knowledge more than fame. Few average voters, or anyone else, favor empowering the news media still further, and with good reason. The news industry's influence is already overweening, and government conducted through the media is inherently dangerous without the unifying and stabilizing influence of party identification. Moreover, is there anyone in or around politics who would not cringe at the assertion made by the late Democratic political consultant Robert Squier, "The television set has become the political party of the future."[26] The personality-cult politics encouraged by television is unaccountable, aloof from average voters, and prone to stylistic gimmickry, and it has been lovingly patterned by the very consultants who hail the medium of television and advance their interests at the parties' expense. The consultants' main alliance, of course, is with incumbent officeholders whose power they help preserve and who also electorally benefit in some ways from party woes. With 80 to 90 percent of incumbent officeholders at all levels regularly reelected, the last trend we ought to encourage is any weakening of party. Vigorous parties help to produce competition which, to judge from the troublingly high incumbent reelection rates, our politics desperately needs.

There are many other unfortunate and debilitating side effects to party decline. Without the linkage provided by political parties, the federalist division and the separation of powers in the American system leads to gridlock among the competing branches and layers of government. As political scientist Clifton McCleskey writes, "Dividing political power to prevent its abuse is the heart of constitutionalism, but it is as well an invitation to immobilism, endangering the capacity of government to act at all unless some bridging mechanisms can be found."[27] Only the political parties, says McCleskey, are "capable of generating political power from the people and transmitting it to public officials, so as to overcome the fragmentation within the government."[28]

With atrophied parties, public officials have more difficulty developing popular support for their programs, and they have to expend more energy to do it. The most vital connection they have to voters and to other officeholders is devalued. Compromise becomes more elusive, both in government and among political groups in elections. Consensus is forged less easily, and effective action to combat whatever problems are plaguing society cannot be taken. If serious inadequacies persist for too long, dissatisfaction and instability would inevitably grow, perhaps producing the volatility and divisive fragmentation of a multiparty system that features transient, emotional issues and colorful personalities but little hope of competent, successful government.

Citizens lose mightily under such conditions, and in fact suffer whenever parties are incapacitated to any great degree, since they cannot use the parties as a tool to influence officeholders. Accountability without parties is impossible in a system as multifaceted as America's. After all, under the separation of powers arrangement, no one—not even the president—can individually be held responsible for fixing a major problem because no one alone has the power to do so. Collective responsibility by means of a common party label is the only way for voters to ensure that officials are held accountable for the performance of the government.

Any diminution of party strength is also likely to lead to a further decline in voter turnout, something the United States can hardly afford since it already has one of the lowest voter participation rates in the democratic world. The parties currently provide the organizational stimulus for the volunteer involvement of millions. Additionally, their get-out-the-vote efforts on election day surely increase turnout,[29] amounting to several million extra voters in national contests. Without the parties' work, many fewer citizens would cast a ballot and take an interest in politics. Those who did would be more easily swept up by the political tides of the moment, and a necessary element of stability would be removed from the electoral system.

Already, as party ties weaken, increasing volatility can be observed in the electorate. Voters are making their voting choices later and later in the campaign season. Whereas, in elections in the 1950s, a majority of the voters had already chosen their candidates *before* the general election campaign began, by the 1980s, a large majority was delaying making a decision until September or later.[30] In a postelection survey for the 2000 election, 37 percent of voters reported deciding their presidential vote after Labor Day, and 11.5 percent reported making their decision in the last week of the campaign.[31] At times, these later deciders vote heavily in one direction, depending on last-minute events and the final twists of a campaign.[32] It can be dangerous when important elections hinge on one or two developments in a campaign's waning hours; the vote should be based on a broad evaluation of individual and national interest, coupled with retrospective judgment of a party's performance in office and speculation on the promise of party candidates. Strong party identification once prevented this pronounced volatility by anchoring a voter during late-developing political storms.

FORCES OF DECLINE AND REVIVAL

If these are the increasingly visible results of party decline, what forces arrayed against the parties have produced the deterioration? Perhaps the problem stems from the individualism that is so much a part of the American character. This "don't fence me in" attitude held by most voters is supplemented by a natural suspicion of aggregated power in big organizations. In one of the polls conducted for the first edition of this book, respondents were asked how they viewed the "many large institutions such as government, labor unions, corporations, and utilities in America today." Only 24 percent agreed with the statement "Being big is *good* because it allows these institutions to work better and get more done," while 58 percent chose the alternate position, "Big is *bad* because these institutions are wasteful and have too much power."[33]

Many social, political, technological, and governmental changes (which will be discussed more thoroughly in the concluding chapters) have also contributed to party woes. Historically, the government's assumption of important functions previously performed by the parties, such as printing ballots, conducting elections, and providing social welfare services, had a major impact. In the large cities, particularly, party organizations once were a central element of life for millions, sponsoring community events and entertainment, helping new immigrants to settle in, giving food and temporary housing to those in immediate need—all in exchange for votes, of course. But as these social services began to be seen as a right of citizenship rather than a privilege extended in exchange for a person's support of a party, and as the flow of immigrants slowed dramatically in the 1920s, party organizations gradually withered in most places.

Simultaneously, the Progressive-inspired direct primary usurped the power of nomination from party leaders and workers, giving it instead to a much broader and more independent electorate and thus loosening the tie between the party nominee and the party organization. Progressive civil service laws also removed much of the patronage used by the parties to reward their loyal followers.

In the post-World War II era, extensive social changes fed the movement away from strong parties. Broad-based education emancipated many voters from complete reliance on the cue of party label. Education also fed the growing issue-oriented politics, which tends to cut across party lines and encourage the party-straying habit of ticket-splitting.[34] At the same time, millions of people began to move out of the cities, which are easily organizable because of population density, and into the sprawling suburbs, where a sense of privacy and detachment can often deter the most energetic of organizers. Electorally, as we have already reviewed, the trends were almost all antiparty: the preeminence of television and the personality politics it brings, the rise of political consultants, the growth of PACs and interest groups, and the development of a cadre of independent-minded candidates and officeholders who had reached their posts without the help of their parties and wanted to remain as free as possible of party restraints.

Fortunately for those who see the compelling need for stronger parties, there are also winds at the parties' backs today, forces that have helped reverse decades of decline. None may be more important than the growing realization of the worth of political parties by many journalists and officeholders, as well as the continued advocacy of party-building reforms by many academics and political practitioners. The resolve of recent national party leaders, such as Republican National Committee Chairmen William Brock, Frank Fahrenkopf, and Haley Barbour and Democratic National Committee chairs Paul Kirk and Ron Brown, has been of paramount significance to the ongoing revival of political party organizational and financial might.[35] Additionally, the application of modern campaign technologies to help parties (not just individual candidates) raise money, advertise, and contact supporters has been a healthful if insufficient tonic, with potential for even greater good, as later chapters will suggest and propose.

THE DEFINITIONS OF PARTY

So far, we have avoided defining the object of our attentions, and with good reason. Political scientists and other observers differ significantly in their precise descriptions of the term "political party." In 1770 the great British parliamentarian Edmund Burke began to develop the classic model of the responsible, centralized, disciplined, and issue-oriented political party when he called it "a body of men united, for promoting by their joint endeavors the national interest, upon some particular principle in which they are all agreed."[36] It was really Burke's conception that was expanded upon in the late 1940s by the Committee on Political Parties of the American Political Science Association in their landmark report, *Toward a More Responsible Two-Party System*.[37] The APSA Committee urged the American parties to be more concerned with policies and issues by offering the voters a clear ideological choice and following up to ensure that their successful candidates enacted those policies once in office. The APSA Committee-preferred model, of course, is far removed from both the traditional American party "machine," which was highly disciplined but deemphasized issue politics, and the conventional modern state and national party, which is relatively decentralized (if less so than a few decades ago), permeable, centrist, and without much authority to enforce election mandates.[38] As we have seen, though, the party platforms are more sharply issue-defined and divergent than is commonly believed, and they find their way into law to a surprising extent. The parties have become more "responsible" than many reformers would have dreamed possible at the turn of the century.

Other political scientists, such as Joseph Schlesinger, have chosen to focus in recent years on the pragmatic essence of parties by defining the party as "a group organized to gain control of government in the name of the group by winning election to public office."[39] This model concentrates exclusively on office-seekers and excludes both their non-office-seeking supporters and the voters who elect them and who may identify with the group.[40]

Our own definition is at once pragmatic—how could it be otherwise in the American mold?—and inclusive: *A political party is a group of office-holders, candidates, activists, and voters who identify with a group label and seek to elect individuals to public office who run under that label.* Our model is not a disciplined, "responsible party" one, but neither should it imply that parties are unprincipled. Pragmatism does not require the abandonment of principle; it demands merely that principle be tested by practical results. While pragmatic in this sense, the American parties have adopted discernibly distinctive philosophies and have taken generally different approaches to governing, especially in recent times. Our definition also emphasizes the *raison d'être* of American parties (contesting elections), as well as the trinity of groups necessary to produce a true political party rather than simply an interest group: the party in office or seeking office, the party activists who comprise the organization, and the party in the electorate (voters who, to varying degrees, identify with the party label).

In this volume, we are particularly concerned with the party in the electorate. There will always be plenty of ambitious individuals to seek office under a major party's standard. There will likely always be an adequate (though perhaps not ample) number of activists attracted by specific issues and personalities to hold the key positions in the party organization. What is no longer certain, though, is whether there will be sufficient support for, and loyalty to, the major parties among the uninvolved pool of voters to prevent fragmentation and sustain the current political arrangement that so clearly benefits the United States. Some modern definitions of party, while useful for certain kinds of analysis, are deficient precisely because they exclude the essential band of party identifiers found in the general electorate. Political parties without people, without a firm and extensive foundation of support drawn from the ranks of average voters, are lifeless shells incapable of performing some of their indispensable functions. As this chapter has tried to make clear, the country's future depends upon vibrant parties, and developing vibrant parties calls for strengthening the tie between party and voter and for bringing the organizations to life with a broader base of committed individuals rather than just more money and dazzling technologies.

Later on, in Chapters Four and Five, we will explore at length the perceptions of party that voters currently possess, with an eye to using that information to build the party in the electorate. Before that, however, we need to sketch the history of party development in the United States and to examine the substantial changes that have occurred in both the party in office and the party organization.

NOTES

1. See Paul Allen Beck, *Party Politics in America*, 8th ed. (New York: Addison Wesley Longman, 1997), 28; and Jack Dennis, "Trends in Support for the American Party System," *British Journal of Political Science* 5 (April 1975): 229.
2. Postelection survey conducted by John McLaughlin and Associates. See Appendix. Even when self-described independents are removed from the analysis, only 23.5 percent considered their party's philosophy as the most important reason for their vote.
3. See Warren Miller and Merrill Shanks, *The New American Voter* (Cambridge, Mass.: Harvard University Press, 1996). See also Paul Abramson, John Aldrich, and David Rohde, *Change and Continuity in the 1996 Elections* (Washington, D.C., Congressional Quarterly Press, 1998), 172–174. See also Angus Campbell et al., *The American Voter* (New York: Wiley, 1960); and Norman H. Nie, Sidney Verba, and John R. Petrocik, *The Changing American Voter* (Cambridge, Mass.: Harvard University Press, 1976).
4. Richard Brody and Benjamin I. Page, "Comment: The Assessment of Policy Voting," *American Political Science Review* 66 (1972): 450–458; Richard Brody and Benjamin I. Page, "Policy Voting and the Electoral Process," *American Political Science Review* (1972), 979–995. See also Abramson, Aldrich, and Rohde, *Change and Continuity in the 1996 Elections*, 174.
5. Richard L. Berke and Janet Elder, "Public Splits Along Party Lines Over Vote and Long Delay," *New York Times* (30 November 2000): A1, A30.
6. August 2000 survey conducted for this book by John McLaughlin and Associates. See Appendix.
7. Brody and Page, "Comment: The Assessment of Policy Voting, " Gregory B. Markus and Philip E. Converse, "A Dynamic Simultaneous Model of Electoral Choice," *American Political Science Review* 73 (1979): 406–423.
8. Walter Dean Burnham, *Critical Elections and the Mainsprings of American Politics* (New York: Norton, 1970), 132–133.
9. Emily Pierce, "Bush's Center Strategy," *Congressional Quarterly 2000 Republican National Convention Guide* (29 July 2000): 21–24.
10. Actually, most of the 18–21-year-olds never even registered to vote, but of those who did, George McGovern won a narrow majority of them in his 1972 presidential bid—the only age group he carried in his landslide loss.
11. James L. Guth, Lyman A. Kellstedt, Corwin E. Schmidt, and John C. Green,"Thunder on the Right? Religious Interest Group Mobilization in the 1996 Election," in Allan J. Cigler and Burdett Loomis, *Interest Group Politics*, 5th ed. (Washington, D.C.: Congressional Quarterly, 1998.)
12. John H. Aldrich, "Southern Parties in State and Nation," *Journal of Politics* 62 (August 2000): 643–670, 647.

13. As quoted in Ken Bode, "Hero or Demagogue?" *The New Republic* 195 (3 March 1986): 28.

14. Gerald M. Pomper with Susan Lederman, *Elections in America*, 2nd ed. (New York: Longman, 1980), 145–150, 167–173. A 1983 study by Alan Monroe also shows that Democratic and Republican platforms agree on very little. Alan Monroe, "American Party Platforms and Public Opinion," *American Journal of Political Science* 27 (February 1983): 27–42. On the influence of interest groups see also Kelly D. Patterson, *Political Parties and the Maintenance of Liberal Democracy* (New York: Columbia University Press, 1996), 31; L. Sandy Maisel, "The Platform Writing Process: Candidate-Centered Platforms in 1992," in Daniel M. Shea and John C. Green, eds., *The State of the Parties: The Changing Role of Contemporary American Parties,* 2nd ed. (Lanham, Md.: Rowman & Littlefield, 1996).

15. See Ian Budge and Richard I. Hofferbert, "Mandates and Policy Outputs: U.S. Party Platforms and Federal Expenditures," *American Political Science Review* 84 (1990): 111–132.

16. See David E. Price, *Bringing Back the Parties* (Washington, D.C.: Congressional Quarterly Press, 1984), 284–288. About two-thirds of the promises in the victorious party's presidential platform have been completely or mostly implemented. See also Jeff Fishel, *Presidents and Promises: From Presidential Pledge to Presidential Performance* (Washington, D.C.: Congressional Quarterly Press, 1985).

17. Pomper, *Elections in America*.

18. Ibid.

19. August 2000 survey conducted for this book by John McLaughlin and Associates. See Appendix.

20. Seymour Martin Lipset and William Schneider, *The Confidence Gap* (New York: The Free Press, 1983), 103–104. See also Stephen C. Craig, *The Malevolent Leaders: Popular Discontent in America* (Boulder: Colo.: Westview Press, 1993), 40. Craig reports that political independents often (though not always) have lower levels of trust in government and external political efficacy than do partisan identifiers.

21. John R. Hibbing and Elizabeth Theiss-Morse, *Congress as Public Enemy: Political Attitudes Toward American Political Institutions* (New York: Cambridge University Press, 1995), 130–131.

22. E. E. Schattschneider, *Party Government* (New York: Rinehart, 1942), 208–209.

23. See, for example, Doris A. Graber, *Mass Media and American Politics*, 5th ed. (Washington, D.C.: Congressional Quarterly Press, 1996); Larry J. Sabato, *Feeding Frenzy: How Attack Journalism Has Transformed American Politics* (New York: The Free Press, 1991); Shanto Iyengar and Donald Kinder, *News That Matters* (Chicago: University of Chicago Press, 1987).

24. Robin Kolodny, "Electoral Partnerships: Political Consultants and Political Parties," in James Thurber and Candice J. Nelson, *Campaign Warriors: Political Consultants and Elections* (Washington, D.C.: Brookings, 2000), 110–132.

25. Ibid. See also Sabato, *The Rise of Political Consultants: New Ways of Winning Elections* (New York: Basic Books, 1981).

26. As quoted in *The Washington Post*, November 10, 1986, Al.

27. Clifton McCleskey, "Democratic Representation and the Constitution: Where Do Political Parties Fit In?" *University of Virginia Newsletter* 60 (July 1984): 61–64, at 61.

28. Ibid., 63.

29. Peter W. Wielhouwer and Brad Lockerbie, "Party Contacting and Political Participation, 1952–1990," *American Journal of Political Science* (1994) 38: 211–229; Peter W. Wielhouwer, "The Mobilization of Campaign Activists by the Party Canvass," *American Politics Quarterly* 27 (1999): 177–200.

30. Martin P. Wattenberg, *The Decline of American Political Parties, 1952–1994* (Cambridge, Mass.: Harvard University Press, 1996), 130–131. In 1952 and 1956, half or more of the voters made a presidential choice before the start of the general election campaign, but, in 1980, half decided during the general election and 9 percent on election day itself (compared to just 2 percent on election day in both 1952 and 1956).

31. Postelection survey conducted by John McLaughlin and Associates, November 7, 2000. See Appendix.

32. See Wattenberg, ibid., who cites the case of the 1980 presidential election.

33. Ten percent volunteered that "it depends" and 8 percent had no opinion. See Larry J. Sabato, *The Party's Just Begun: Shaping Political Parties for America's Future* (Glenview, Ill.: Scott, Foresman and Company, 1988), 24.

34. Nie, Verba, and Petrocik, *The Changing American Voter.*

35. Brock, a former United States Senator from Tennessee, was RNC chairman from 1977 to 1981; Fahrenkopf was RNC chairman from 1983 to 1989; Barbour served as RNC chair from 1993 through 1996. On the Democratic side, Kirk served as DNC chair from 1985 to 1989 and Brown served from 1989 to 1993.

36. From Burke's *Thoughts on the Cause of the Present Discontents.* See also the discussion in Giovanni Sartori, *Parties and Party Systems: A Framework for Analysis*, Vol. 1 (New York: Cambridge University Press, 1976), 1–29.

37. The report was published by Rinehart of New York in 1950.

38. See Price, *Bringing Back the Parties*, 107–109; see also Paul Allen Beck, *Party Politics in America*, 8th ed. (New York: Addison Wesley Longman, 1997), chap. 16.

39. Joseph A. Schlesinger, "The New American Political Party," *American Political Science Review* 79 (1985): 1153. See also Joseph A. Schlesinger, *Political Parties and the Winning of Office* (Ann Arbor, Mich.: University of Michigan, 1991), 6. Schlesinger's definition follows that in Anthony Downs, *An Economic Theory of Democracy* (New York: Harper and Row, 1957), 25.

40. A few other social scientists have relied on Schlesinger's definition or some variant of it. See, for example, John Frandeis, "Voters, Government Officials, and Party Organizations: Connections and Distinctions," in Daniel M. Shea and John C. Green, eds., *The State of the Parties: The Changing Role of Contemporary American Parties*, 2nd ed. (Lanham, Md.: Rowman & Littlefield, 1996), 388. See also Mildred A. Schwartz, *The Party Network: The Robust Organization of Illinois Republicans* (Madison, Wisc.: University of Wisconsin Press, 1990), 12. John Aldrich begins with Schlesinger's definition and then builds on it. See John H. Aldrich, *Why Parties? The Origin and Transformation of Party Politics in America* (Chicago: University of Chicago Press, 1995), 283–284.

2

The Evolving Party

DESPITE THE ABSENCE of any constitutional sanction for political parties, and the open hostility of many of the nation's early leaders toward the emerging political parties in the 1790s, parties have been a remarkable constant of American political life over more than a century and a half. But while the institutions have symbolized continuity, their form and substance have changed radically with the passage of time, reflecting the conditions of politics and government in each age. Like the Constitution itself, political parties have proven to be pragmatic and flexible, altering their identities, structures, and operations to suit the needs of the contemporary electorate in every era. Particular parties have come and gone; even the enduring Democratic and Republican parties have been utterly transformed several times in all but name. Parties have based themselves in small caucuses of elites, mass movements generated by geography and issues, big-city machines of service delivery and feudal loyalties, and, most recently, the technological innovations of modern communications. For all of these diverse manifestations, the essence of the party idea has remained the same, even as the functions performed by the parties have changed. In this chapter we will first sketch the evolution of the party—idea and reality—as it has developed in the United States. Then we will concentrate on how political parties influence and define the government at state and national levels and on how the parties are, in turn, shaped by their interaction with the fundamental processes and institutions of American government.

THE INEVITABILITY OF PARTY

Many of the Republic's leading statesmen in the late eighteenth century feared that parties would upset the delicate consensus that existed in the new nation. To their great credit, they were unwilling to sacrifice individual liberty to prevent the formation of parties. At the same time, they were convinced that the American system would effectively strangle the influence of parties by dividing power in an intricate and elaborate fashion, frustrating any party's attempt to dominate and control the government.[1] Thus, while liberty would give rise to parties, the parties' subsequent failures would cause them to wither away, reasoned James Madison and others. But as Schattschneider surmised:

> The scheme, in spite of its subtlety, involved a miscalculation. Political parties refused to be content with the role assigned to them. The vigor and enterprise of the parties have therefore made American political history the story of the unhappy marriage of the parties and the Constitution, a remarkable variation of the case of the irresistible force and the immovable object, which in this instance have been compelled to live together in a permanent partnership.[2]

Thanks to the nearly universal support and admiration for George Washington, the nation's first years were marked by relative harmony and the absence of any clearly defined organizational factions, though the early clashes between Alexander Hamilton and Thomas Jefferson (and their respective supporters) portended the partisan divisions to come. For his part, Washington made warnings about the evils of parties a centerpiece of his Farewell Address in 1796:

> Let me now ... warn you in the most solemn manner against the baneful effects of the spirit of party generally.... It exists under different shapes in all governments, more or less stifled, controlled, or repressed; but in those of the popular form it is seen in its greatest rankness and is truly their worst enemy.... It serves always to distract the public councils and enfeeble the public administration. It agitates the community with ill-founded jealousies and false alarms; kindles the animosity of one part against another; foments occasionally riot and insurrection. It opens the door to foreign influence and corruption.... There is an opinion that parties in free countries are useful checks upon the administration of the government, and serve to keep alive the spirit of liberty. This within certain limits is probably true; and in governments of a monarchical cast patriotism may look with indulgence, if not with favor, upon the spirit of party. But in those of the popular character, in governments purely elective, it is a spirit not to be encouraged.[3]

Ironically, though, Washington's personal farewell also marked the departure of partyless politics in the United States.[4] By the presidential election of 1800, two congressional party caucuses composed of like-minded members had organized around the competing standards of Hamilton—the Federalists, supporters of strong central government—and Jefferson and Madison—the Republicans, who preferred empowering states rather than the federal government. The caucuses nominated presidential candidates, and the Republicans' Jefferson defeated incumbent President John Adams, who had become identified with the Federalists. Jefferson, then, became the first president elected as the nominee of a political party. At about the same time, the legislative caucuses began communications with supporters in the states, and "committees of correspondence" formed sporadically as the first manifestations of local party organization.

Resistance to the party system was still great, however. Even the congressional caucus leaders viewed their activities as merely a necessary evil, required by the subversion and maneuvering taking place on the other side. This discomfort eventually resulted in the virtual disintegration of the presidential caucus system. The Federalists were repeatedly unsuccessful in their presidential efforts, and by 1816 they ceased to nominate a candidate. From 1816 to 1824, during James Monroe's presidency, America experienced a relatively party-free period at the national level, the so-called Era of Good Feelings, when personalities, not party, held sway. (The television age is not the first candidate-centered era in our country's history!)

The absence of party conflict proved brief and unnatural, though. Even during Monroe's tenure, many state party organizations thrived, and inevitably, new national factions formed, fueled in part by the enormous increase in the electorate that took place between 1820 and 1840, when property requirements as a condition of suffrage were abolished in most states. Also, by the 1820s, all the states, save for South Carolina, that had selected presidential electors indirectly (by vote of the state legislature) shifted to popular election of Electoral College slates, thus transforming presidential politics. Caucus nominations, criticized as elitist and antidemocratic, gave way to selection at large party conventions. The new Democratic party, formed around the charismatic populist President Andrew Jackson, combined much of the old Republican party and most newly enfranchised voters. It held the country's first major national presidential nominating convention in 1832.[5] Jackson's strong personality helped to polarize politics, and opposition to the president coalesced into the Whig party, whose early leaders included Henry Clay. The incumbent Jackson defeated Clay in the 1832 presidential contest and became the first chief executive nominated and elected by a truly national, popularly based political party.

The Whigs and the Democrats continued to strengthen after 1832, establishing state and local organizations almost everywhere. Their competition was usually fierce and closely matched, and they brought the United States the first broadly supported two-party system in the Western world.[6] Unfortunately for the Whigs, the issue of slavery sharpened many already present and divisive internal party tensions, and these led to its gradual dissolution and replacement by the Republican party. Formed in 1854, the Republican party set its sights on the abolition (or at least the containment) of slavery, and it was able to assemble enough support from the Whigs, antislavery Northern Democrats, and others to win the presidency for Abraham Lincoln in a fragmented 1860 vote.

From that election to this day, the same two great parties—the Republicans (GOP) and the Democrats—have dominated American elections. Control of an electoral majority has seesawed back and forth between the two parties. The dominance of the Republicans in the Reconstruction era eventually gave way to a highly competitive system from 1876 to 1896. In the latter year, however, the GOP skillfully capitalized on fears of the growing agrarian populist sentiment in the Democratic party to fashion a dominant and enduring majority of voters that essentially lasted until the early 1930s, when the Great Depression created the conditions for a Democratic resurgence. Franklin Roosevelt's New Deal coalition of 1932 (the South, ethnics, organized labor, farmers, liberals, and big city machines) basically characterized both the Democratic party and the prevailing national majority until at least the late 1960s. The period since 1970 has seen neither party clearly dominant, and by the century's end, the two parties would be highly competitive. (This development will be a major subject of discussion in Chapter Five.)

The modern era seems very distant from the "Golden Age" of parties from the 1870s to the 1920s. Immigration from Europe (particularly Ireland, Italy, and Germany) fueled the development of big city party organizations that ruled with an iron hand in their domains. Party and government were virtually interchangeable in those instances. The parties were the providers of needed services, entertainment, and employment. The devotion they engendered among their supporters, voters, and officeholders helped to produce startlingly high voter turnout—75 percent or better in all presidential elections from 1876 to 1900 compared to about 50 percent today[7]—as well as the greatest legislative discipline ever achieved among party contingents in Congress and many state legislatures![8]

As we reviewed in Chapter One, the heyday of the party—at least a certain *kind* of party—has passed. The reduction in patronage, the direct primary, the spread of nonpartisan elections, the substitution of the Australian (or secret) ballot for the party-sponsored ballot,[9] the cut-off of immigration in the 1920s by Congress, and the growth of the social welfare state—where services became governmental rights and not party privileges—all took a toll. This decline can be exaggerated, though, and it often is. Viewing parties in the broad sweep of American history, several things become clear. First, while political parties have evolved considerably and changed form from time to time, they have more often than not been reliable vehicles for mass participation in a representative democracy. In fact, the gradual but steady expansion of suffrage itself was orchestrated by the parties. Just as Schattschneider insisted, "In the search for new segments of the populace that might be exploited profitably, the parties have kept the movement to liberalize the franchise well ahead of the demand.... The enlargement of the practicing electorate has been one of the principal labors of the parties, a truly notable achievement for which the parties have never been properly credited."[10] Second, the parties' journey through American history has been characterized by the same redoubtable ability to adapt to prevailing conditions that is often cited as the genius of the Constitution. Flexibility and pragmatism mark both—and help to ensure both their survival and the success of the nation they serve. Third, despite massive changes in political conditions and frequent dramatic shifts in the electorate's moods, the two major parties have not only achieved remarkable longevity, they have almost consistently provided strong competition for one another and the voters at the national level. Of the thirty presidential elections from 1884 to 2000, for instance, the Republicans won sixteen and the Democrats fourteen. Even when calamity has struck the parties—the Great Depression or Watergate for Republicans, the Civil War, McGovernism, or the 1994 congressional rout for Democrats—they have proven tremendously resilient, sometimes bouncing back from landslide defeats to win the next election. Perhaps most of all, history teaches us that the development of parties in the United States was an inevitability. Human nature alone guarantees conflict in any society; in a free state, the question is simply how to contain and channel conflict productively without infringing on individual liberties. The Founders' hopes for the avoidance of faction have given way to an appreciation of the parties' constructive contribution to conflict definition and resolution during the years of the American republic.

ONE-PARTYISM IN AMERICAN POLITICS

The two-party system has not gone unchallenged, of course. At the state level, two-party competition was once severely limited or nonexistent in much of the country.[11] Especially in the one-party Democratic states of the Deep South and the rock-ribbed Republican states of Maine, New Hampshire, and Vermont, the dominant party's primary nomination was considered tantamount to election, and the only real contest was an unsatisfying intraparty one where factions were fluid and the multiplicity of candidacies proved confusing to voters.[12] Even in most two-party states, there existed dozens of cities and counties that had a massive majority of voters aligned with one or the other party, and thus were effectively one-party in local elections. Obviously, historical, cultural, and sectional forces primarily accounted for the concentration of one party's supporters in certain areas. The Civil War's divisions, for instance, were mirrored for the better part of a century in the Democratic predisposition of the South and the Republican proclivities of the Yankee northern states. Whatever the combination of factors producing one-partyism, the condition has certainly declined precipitously in the last quarter-century.[13]

The spread of two-party competition, while still uneven in some respects, is one of the most significant political trends of recent times, and virtually no one-party states are left. There are no purely Republican states anymore, and significant two-party competition has even spread to the formerly Democratic South. Ironically, as Chapters Four and Five will explore, the growth of two-party competition has probably been spurred as much by the decline in partisan loyalty among voters as by the increasing organizational strength of the party units. In other words, citizens are somewhat more inclined to cross party lines to support an appealing candidate regardless of party affiliation, thus making a victory for the minority party possible whether or not it has earned the win through its own organizational hard work. It should also be noted that the elimination of pockets of one-party strength adds an element of instability to the system, since even in lean times of national electoral disaster each party was once assured of a regional base from which a comeback could be staged.[14] Nonetheless, the increase in party competitiveness can be viewed positively, since it eliminates the odious effects of one-partyism and guarantees a comprehensible and credible partisan choice to a larger segment of the electorate than ever before.

THIRD PARTIES IN AMERICA

Third-partyism has proven more durable than one-partyism, though no third party in the twentieth century has been able to wage a sustained challenge against the two dominant parties.[15] Minor party electoral victories have been especially sparse in the United States. Indeed, not a single minor party has ever come close to winning the presidency, and only seven minor parties have won so much as a single state's Electoral College votes.[16] Just five third parties (the Populists in 1892, Theodore Roosevelt's Bull Moose party in 1912, the Progressives in 1924, George Wallace's American Independent party in 1968, and Ross Perot's independent bid in 1992) have garnered more than 10 percent of the popular vote for president.[17] At the subpresidential level, very few minor party or independent candidates have been elected to Congress, and the overwhelming majority of governors and state legislators have belonged to the major parties. Successful third party candidates do emerge from time to time, of course. The most recent (and colorful) example is the victory of former professional wrestler Jesse "The Body" Ventura in Minnesota's 1998 gubernatorial contest. Running on the Reform Party label, Ventura beat two high-profile major party candidates (one of whom was Hubert Humphrey III, son of the late senator and vice president). Still, minor party victories have been few and far between, and the victories haven't typically translated into new *parties*. Indeed, by early 2000—less than two short years after his 1998 victory—Ventura had already abandoned the Reform Party. And, while he did so to establish his own Independence Party, few believe that Ventura has the determination to create an enduring infrastructure for an organization that revolves largely around himself.[18]

Yet even without winning elections, minor parties sometimes have an electoral impact in the United States by spoiling the electoral prospects of one of the two major parties. By capturing 27 percent of the popular vote on the Progressive Party label in 1912, Theodore Roosevelt—Republican president from 1901 to 1909—helped secure Democrat Woodrow Wilson's victory over Republican incumbent William H. Taft. And while analysts show that the outcome of the 1992 presidential election would have been the same without Perot in the race,[19] Green Party presidential candidate Ralph Nader surely siphoned crucial votes from Al Gore in the historically close 2000 presidential election. Indeed, Nader received 97,000 votes in Florida—a state George W. Bush won by fewer than 600 votes and on which the outcome of the presidential election hinged. Of course, not all of Nader's votes would have gone to Gore had Nader not been on the ballot; some Nader supporters surely would have stayed home, and others might have even supported Bush. But without Nader in the contest, Gore would have almost certainly captured the small number of votes he needed to win Florida (and the presidency).[20] Minor party and independent candidates can also have an impact on the electoral fortunes of major party candidates below the presidential level. Nearly 600 minor party and independent candidates ran for U.S. House and Senate seats in 1996,[21] and political scientist Paul Herrnson estimated that significant minor-party candidates cost House incumbents an average of 10 percent of the vote in the 1992 elections.[22] An unusual type of coattails effect appears to be at work in the world of minor parties. Congressional districts that provide high levels of support for minor party presidential candidates typically also give high levels of support to minor party congressional candidates—even if the minor party candidate for Congress is of a different party than the minor party presidential candidate.[23]

Third parties find their roots in sectionalism (as did the South's Dixiecrats in 1948), in specific issues (such as the agrarian revolt that fueled the Populists), and in appealing charismatic personalities (Theodore Roosevelt is perhaps the best example, though Jesse Ventura provides a more recent illustration). Many of the minor parties have drawn strength from a combination of these sources. The American Independent party enjoyed a measure of success because of a dynamic, demagogic leader (George Wallace), a firm geographic base (the South), and an emotional issue (civil rights). Above all, third parties make electoral progress in direct proportion to the failure of the two major parties to address important issues, incorporate alienated groups, or nominate attractive candidates as their standard-bearers. John Anderson's 1980 Independent presidential bid was spurred not by geography or specific issues or Anderson's persona but by intense dissatisfaction among some voters with the major party nominees (Jimmy Carter and Ronald Reagan).[24] Ross Perot's 1992 presidential bid was fueled by a combination of voter dissatisfaction with the major party candidates[25] and the failure of the two parties to craft a plan for reducing chronic federal budget deficits. Perot, of course, also had an unparalleled capacity to bankroll his campaign using his own money, which helped him surmount the many obstacles that typically face third-party and independent candidates.[26] (We address these obstacles below.) Nader's 2000 Green Party candidacy found its strength in the relatively centrist course charted by the Democratic party under the Clinton-Gore leadership[27]—a course which, according to Nader, left progressives without a party. Nader argued that little difference existed between the two major parties, and he pointed to the large soft money contributions (see Chapter 3) accepted by both parties as evidence of his argument.[28] On a more basic level, Nader's campaign found support among voters who simply disliked both major party candidates.[29]

In some ways, third parties are akin to shooting stars that may appear briefly and brilliantly but do not long remain visible in the political constellation. The United States is the only major Western nation that does not have at least one significant, enduring third party, and there are a number of explanations for this. Unlike many European countries that use proportional representation and guarantee parliamentary seats to any faction securing even as little as 5 percent of the vote, the United States has a "single member, plurality" electoral system that requires a party to get one more vote than any other party in a legislative constituency or in a state's presidential election in order to win. To paraphrase Vince Lombardi, finishing first is not everything, it is the only thing in American politics; placing second, even by a smidgen, doesn't count, and this condition obviously encourages the aggregation of interests into as few parties as possible (the democratic minimum being two).

Other institutional factors undergird the two-party system as well. The laws in most states make it difficult for third parties to secure a place on the ballot, while the Democratic and Republican parties are often granted automatic access.[30] And, although new evidence suggests that ballot access requirements may discourage minor party candidacies less than commonly thought,[31] Democrats and Republicans in the state legislatures continue to team up to ensure that the political pie is cut into only two sizeable pieces, not three or more smaller slices.[32] The public funding of campaigns, where it exists, is far more generous for the two major parties. At the national level, for instance, new third-party presidential candidates receive money only *after* the general election *if* they have amassed more than 5 percent of the vote, and only in proportion to their total vote; the major-party candidates, by contrast, get large, full general election grants immediately upon their summer nominations. By allowing outsider candidates to capture the party label, primary elections may also help to discourage minor party candidacies.[33] The news media, too, are biased against minor parties, which are given relatively little coverage compared to major-party nominees. The media are only reflecting political reality, of course, and it would be absurd to expect them to offer equal time to all comers. Still, it is a vicious cycle for the minor candidates: a lack of broad-based support produces slight coverage, which minimizes their chances of attracting more adherents. Perhaps also hindering third party success is the unwillingness of voters to "waste" their vote on a candidate with little chance of actual electoral victory. Our own survey suggests that not all voters think this way, however. Fifty-seven percent of our survey respondents disagreed with the statement that "It's wasting my vote to vote for a candidate that is not a Republican or Democrat, since Republicans and Democrats almost always win anyway."[34]

Beyond the institutional explanations are historical, cultural, and social theories of two-partyism in America.[35] The dualist approach, frequently criticized as overly simplistic, suggests that there has always been an underlying binary nature to United States politics. Whether it was the early conflict between eastern financial interests and western frontiersmen, the sectional division of North and South, the more current urban versus rural or urban versus suburban clashes, or even the natural tensions of democratic institutions (the government against the opposition, for instance), dualists see the processes and interests of politics inevitably reducing the players into two great camps. Others emphasize the basic social consensus existing in American life. Whatever their ideological leanings, and despite great diversity in heritage, the vast majority of Americans accept without serious question the fundamental structures of our system: the Constitution, the governmental setup, a lightly controlled free enterprise economy, and so on. This consensus, when allied with certain American cultural characteristics developed over time (pragmatism, acceptance of the need for compromise, a lack of divisive social class consciousness), produces the conditions necessary for a relatively nonideological, centrist politics that can naturally support two moderate alternative parties that offer change when it is wanted, but continuity even then. This suggests again the extra-Constitutional genius of the two-party system and the secret of the two parties' success in shutting out third parties before they establish a long-term beachhead. The essential pragmatism, centrism, and flexibility of the major parties allows them to absorb the acceptable, reasonable elements and issues of prominent minor parties, quickly depriving third parties of their raison d'être. For example, President Clinton assembled an economic summit almost immediately upon assuming office in 1993; its purpose was to consider solutions to some of the economic problems effectively broached by independent candidate Ross Perot during the 1992 election.[36] The passion for power and victory that drives both Democrats and Republicans overrides ideology and prevents rigidity. Unless a kind of rigor mortis takes hold in the future in one or both major parties—with, say, the capture of party machinery by unyielding extremists of right or left—it is difficult to imagine any third party becoming a major, permanent force in American politics. The corollary of this axiom, though, is that the major parties must be eternally vigilant to avoid such ideologically inspired takeovers, and the best preventative medicine is to expand participation in party activities to as broad-based a group of voters as possible.

Of course, third parties can emerge for reasons other than ideology *per se*; a significant component of both the Perot and Nader candidacies was a reform-driven rejection of Washington politics-as-usual. Still, if reform-based challenges to the two parties were to become strong enough, the major parties could be expected to absorb the reform impulse. Indeed, by 2000 each party's presidential primary included what might be considered a reform candidate—John McCain on the GOP side and Bill Bradley for the Democrats. Such candidacies will likely become more successful if third party challenges based on political reform become stronger. This would be similar to what occurred at the turn of the last century, when calls for political reform galvanized progressive wings in both major parties.

Third parties are limited in their ability to win office in the United States, but they are nevertheless an important piece of the American political landscape. For the foreseeable future, third parties likely will continue to play useful supporting roles similar to their historically sanctioned ones. They can popularize ideas that might not receive a hearing otherwise. They can serve as vehicles of popular discontent with the major parties and thereby induce change in major party behavior and platforms. They may well presage and assist future party realignments as they have sometimes done in the past. In a few states, third parties will also continue to take a unique part in political life, as the Conservative and Liberal parties of New York do.[37] But in an open, permeable two-party system that is supplemented by generous means of expressing dissent and registering political opposition in other ways (court challenges, interest group organizing, primary elections, and even—sadly—the all too well-accepted practice of nonvoting), third parties will likely continue to play second fiddle to the major parties in the United States.

THE BASIC STRUCTURE OF AMERICAN POLITICAL PARTIES

The early organizational structures of the two major parties could hardly be characterized as elaborate. The first national party committees were skeletal and formed some years after the creation of the presidential nominating conventions in the 1830s.[38] First the Democrats in 1848, and then the Republicans in 1856, established national governing bodies (the Democratic National Committee, or DNC, and the Republican National Committee, or RNC) to make arrangements for the quadrennial conventions and to coordinate the subsequent presidential campaigns. The DNC and RNC were each composed of one representative from each state—expanded to two in the 1920s after the post of state committeewoman was established—and the states had complete control over the selection of their representatives. In addition, the congressional party caucuses in both houses organized their own national committees, loosely allied with the DNC and RNC. First, the National Republican Congressional Committee (NRCC) was started in 1866 when the congressional GOP was feuding with Abraham Lincoln's successor, President Andrew Johnson, and wanted a counterweight to his control of the RNC. Almost immediately, House Democrats set up a similar committee—the Democratic Congressional Campaign Committee (DCCC). After the popular election of United States senators was initiated in 1913 with the ratification of the Seventeenth Amendment to the Constitution, both parties organized separate Senate campaign committees—the Democratic Senatorial Campaign Committee (DSCC) and National Republican Senatorial Committee (NRSC). Interestingly, this tripartite arrangement of national, House, and Senate committee[39] has persisted in both parties until the present day, and each party's committees are housed together in Washington. Generally, the relationship among the three committees in each party is cooperative, although some rivalry and competition are understandably apparent from time to time in these siblings.

The memberships of both the RNC and DNC have grown considerably in size over the decades, but the DNC's expansion has been much greater, and it is now more than twice the size of the RNC—443 DNC members to just 165 for the RNC as of 2000.[40] Since 1972, the Democrats have also abandoned the principle of equal DNC representation for all states and have assigned the number of committee persons on the basis of each state's population and its past voter support for the party's candidates. While the national conventions formally ratify all national committee members, the real choices are still made in the states, with selection methods varying widely (from election at state party conventions—the most common means—to primary election, selection by state central committees, or designation by the party delegation to the national presidential convention).

The key national party official is the chairperson of the DNC or RNC. While the chair is formally elected by the national committee, he or she is usually selected by the sitting president or newly nominated presidential candidate, who is accorded the right to name the individual for at least the duration of his or her campaign. Only the post-campaign, out-of-power party committee actually has the authority to appoint a chairperson independently. Oddly enough, it is those committee-crowned chairpersons who generally have the greatest impact, because they come to the post at times of crisis when a leadership vacuum exists.[41] A defeated presidential candidate is technically the head of the national party until the next nominating convention, but the reality is naturally otherwise as a party attempts to shake off a losing image. The chair often becomes the prime spokesperson and arbitrator for the party during the interregnum, and he or she is called upon to damp down factionalism, negotiate candidate disputes, raise money, and prepare the machinery for the next presidential election. Balancing the interests of all potential White House contenders is a particularly difficult job, and strict neutrality is normally expected from the chair. Both parties have benefited from adept leadership while out of power. RNC Chairman William Brock during the Carter presidency and DNC Chairman Paul Kirk during the second Reagan term both skillfully used their positions to strengthen their parties organizationally and to polish the party images. More recently, out-party chairs Ron Brown (DNC, 1989–1992) and Haley Barbour (RNC, 1993–1996) fortified their respective parties considerably while the other party held the presidency. By contrast, party chairpersons selected by incumbent presidents and presidential candidates tend to be close allies of the presidents or candidates and often subordinate the good of the party to the needs of the campaign or White House. During the Carter presidency, for example, DNC Chairmen Kenneth Curtis and John White were creatures of the White House who acted as cheerleaders for their chief executive but did little to keep the Democratic party competitive with the then-strengthening GOP organization. David Wilhelm, Clinton's choice for DNC chair from 1992 to 1994, angered congressional Democrats by using DNC funds—traditionally spent on election-related activities—to pay for an advertising campaign promoting Clinton's health care legislation. By 1996, moreover, the Clinton-Gore campaign evidently had crucial control over DNC campaign spending,[42] no doubt with the assent of DNC chair Donald Fowler.[43] Because of their command of presidential patronage and influence, a few national party chairpersons selected by presidents have become powerful and well known, such as Republican Mark Hanna during the McKinley presidency and Democrat James Farley under President Franklin Roosevelt. Most presidentially appointed chairs, however, have been relatively obscure; the chance for a chairperson to make a difference and cut a memorable figure generally comes when there is no competition from a White House nominee or occupant.

The most recent DNC chair, Terry McAuliffe, provides an exception to the rule that out-of-power parties enjoy independent authority to appoint a national chair. In an attempt to extend his influence in party affairs beyond his presidency, Bill Clinton pushed to have McAuliffe—his top fundraiser—installed as DNC chair shortly after Al Gore conceded defeat in the 2000 election. Not all Democrats were happy about the selection of a national chair with such close ties to the controversial Clinton.[44] At least some Democrats believe that Clinton's extramarital affair with White House intern Monica Lewinsky and his subsequent impeachment by the House contributed to Gore's defeat in 2000, and new controversies over gifts and pardons swirled around Clinton as he departed from office at the end of his term. Nevertheless, McAuliffe's fundraising prowess may hold significant appeal for Democrats as the party attempts to regain power in Washington.

Much of any party chairperson's efforts are directed at planning the presidential nominating convention, the most publicized and vital event on the party's calendar. Until 1984, gavel-to-gavel coverage had been standard practice on all national television networks, and even after the recent cutbacks on some channels, a substantial block of time is still devoted to the conventions. Recently, however, several 24-hour cable news channels and some Internet sites have begun providing the gavel-to-gavel coverage once offered by the major networks.[45] The nomination of the presidential ticket naturally receives the lion's share of attention, but the convention is also the ultimate governing body for the party itself. The rules adopted and the platform passed at the quadrennial conclave are durable guideposts that steer the party for years after the final gavel has been brought down. Most of the recent party chairpersons, in cooperation with the incumbent president or likely nominee, have tried to orchestrate carefully every minute of the conventions in order to project just the right image to voters at home. By and large, they have succeeded, though at the price of draining some spontaneity and excitement from the process. Indeed, record-low numbers of Americans tuned into the televised Democratic and Republican national conventions in August 2000.

From 1974 to 1982, the Democratic party also held a midterm convention (also called a mini-convention).[46] Designed to provide party activists a chance to express themselves on policy and presidential performance (whether the chief executive was a Democrat or a Republican), the midterm convention, instead, mainly generated worry among the party leadership and elected officials about the factional infighting and ideological posturing that might be on display before a national audience. While none of the midterm gatherings was a disaster (and none a roaring success, either), by 1986, the Democrats had decided to avoid potential divisiveness and save the $2 million necessary to hold the convention, and it was canceled.

A less expensive programmatic alternative, the policy council, has been used extensively by both parties during their out-of-power years in recent decades.[47] The councils generally have been composed of elected officials (particularly members of Congress) and party leaders, with the councils divided into task forces and study groups in key issue areas. Critiques of administration policies have been released with some regularity, though the reports have usually been longer on criticisms than proposals of specific alternatives. The two most famous and successful of these programmatic bodies were the National Democratic Advisory Council, which operated during some of the Eisenhower years (1956–1961) under the direction of DNC Chairman Paul Butler, and the Republican Coordinating Committee of RNC Chairman Ray Bliss during Lyndon Johnson's administration (1965–1968). These policy groups were not always well received, especially by party congressional leaders who believed that the councils encroached on their territory and prerogatives. The Democratic Policy Commission, created by DNC chair Paul Kirk in 1985, provides a useful model of an inoffensive yet productive policy council. The Commission's mandate was to provide a mainstream, moderate policy foundation for Democratic presidential candidates to use in 1988. Chaired by former Utah Governor Scott Matheson, the Commission held open public hearings and debates for a year around the country before writing and publishing a thoughtful report in 1986.[48] The parties continue to experiment with policy councils. While Ron Brown chose not to establish an official policy council during his tenure as DNC chair,[49] RNC chair Haley Barbour created the National Policy Forum—a set of twenty policy councils designed to foster policy discussions among elected Republican officials nationwide.[50]

While national committee activities of all kinds attract most of the media attention, the party is structurally based not in Washington but in the states and localities. Except for the campaign finance arena, virtually all governmental regulation of political parties is left to the states, for example, and most elected officials give their fealty to the local party divisions they know best. Most importantly, the vast majority of party leadership positions are filled at subnational levels. The pyramidal arrangement of party committees at least theoretically provides for a broad base of support. The smallest voting unit, the precinct, is also the fundamental building block of the party, and each of the more than 100,000 precincts in the United States potentially has a committeeman or woman to represent it in each party's councils. (Sadly, the reality is that too many of these posts go unfilled or are unenergetically pursued.) The precinct committeepersons are the key foot soldiers of any party, and their efforts are supplemented by party committees above them in the wards, cities, counties, towns, villages, and congressional districts.

The state governing body supervising this welter of local party organizations is usually called the state central (or executive) committee, and it comprises representatives from all major geographic units, as determined by and selected under state law. Generally, state parties are free to act within the limits set by their state legislatures without interference from the national party except in the selection and seating of presidential convention delegates. National Democrats have been particularly inclined to regulate this aspect of party life.[51]

The formal structure of party organization is supplemented by numerous official, semiofficial, and unaffiliated groups that combine and clash with the parties in countless ways. Both the DNC and RNC have affiliated organizations of state and local party women (the National Federation of Democratic Women and the National Federation of Republican Women), and there are youth divisions as well (the Young Democrats of America and the Young Republicans National Federation), which have a generous definition of "young"—up to and including age 35 for the Young Democrats of America. The state governors in each party have their own party associations, too. Just outside the party orbit are the supportive interest groups and associations that often provide money, manpower, or other forms of assistance to the parties. Labor unions, progressive political action committees, teachers, African American and liberal women's groups, and the Americans for Democratic Action comprise some of the Democratic party's organizational cohorts, while business groups, the U.S. Chamber of Commerce, fundamentalist Christian organizations, and some antiabortion groups work closely with the Republicans.[52]

Each party also has several institutionalized sources of policy ideas. Though unconnected to the parties in any official sense, these so-called think tanks are quite influential. President Bill Clinton and numerous Democratic candidates have drawn on the Progressive Policy Institute—a centrist group affiliated with the Democratic Leadership Council—for policy ideas.[53] The reliance on think tanks for policy ideas is not new, of course. Nor is it limited to Democrats. During the Reagan administration, for instance, the right-wing, well-funded Heritage Foundation placed many dozens of its conservatives in important governmental positions, and its policy studies on a range of issues carried considerable weight with policymakers.[54] The more moderate and bipartisan American Enterprise Institute also supplied the Reagan team with people and ideas.

There also exist extra-party organizations that form for a wide variety of purposes, including "reforming" a party or moving it ideologically to the right or left. There is a long history of these groups; among the better-known efforts are some in Wisconsin, California, and New York.[55] In the latter case, for example, Democratic reform clubs were originally established to fight the Tammany Hall machine, and some of these clubs still prosper by attracting well-educated activists committed to various liberal causes.

More recently, both national parties have been favored (or bedeviled) by the formation of extra-party outfits. The Democratic Leadership Council (DLC) has been by far the most prominent of these extra-party organizations. The DLC was launched in 1985 by moderate-to-conservative Democrats concerned about what they perceived as the leftward drift of their party and its image as the captive of liberal special interest groups.[56] Initially, the DLC was not popular with the national party leadership, which viewed it as a redundant rival and a potentially divisive and money-draining forum.[57] But gradually, the national party has come to accept the DLC's policy formation role. In 1991, DNC chair Ron Brown even attended the DLC's annual convention and went so far as to praise the group's policy development efforts.[58] By the early 1990s, the DLC had a staff of fifteen, an annual budget of nearly $2 million, and an office across the street from the DNC in Washington.[59] Today, the DLC's membership includes hundreds of elected officials nationwide—including many Democratic U.S. Senators, House members, governors, and state and local officials. The organization disseminates its policy ideas through a bimonthly magazine (*The New Democrat*) and a policy journal (*Blueprint: Ideas for a New Century*). Democrats associated with the DLC have been extraordinarily influential within the Democratic Party. President Clinton chaired the DLC from 1990–1991, and his chairmanship helped serve as a springboard for his 1992 presidential campaign.[60] Several other Democratic heavyweights—including Vice President Al Gore, Senator (and vice presidential candidate) Joe Lieberman, and House Democratic Leader Richard Gephardt—have also played prominent roles in the DLC at once time or another, and rising star Senator Evan Bayh of Indiana took the DLC reigns in 2001.[61] Although other extra-party organizations exist on both sides of the partisan aisle, it is fair to say that none has been as effective or as influential as the DLC—at least during the last decade.

THE PARTY IN GOVERNMENT

The Congressional Party

The structure of political parties we have reviewed so far has been electoral, self-contained, and apart from governing institutions. Another dimension of party exists—and, to a great degree, thrives—within government, as a critical, essential mechanism of all its branches and layers.

In no segment of American government is the party more visible or vital than in the Congress. In this century, the political parties have dramatically increased the sophistication and impact of their internal congressional organizations. Prior to the beginning of every session, each party in both houses of Congress caucuses separately to select party leaders (House Speaker or minority leader, Senate majority and minority leaders, whips, and so on) and to arrange for the appointment of members to each chamber's committees. In effect, then, the parties organize and operate the Congress. Their management systems have grown quite elaborate; the web of whips for both House parties now includes a significant portion of each party's entire membership.[62] Although not invulnerable to pressure from the minority, the majority party in each house generally holds sway, even fixing the size of its majority on all committees—a proportion frequently in excess of the percentage of seats it holds in the house as a whole.

Party leaders have some substantial tools at their disposal to enforce a degree of discipline in their troops. While many factors are relevant in allocating committee assignments, members who occupy (or desire to occupy) plum committee slots are expected to be party loyalists on issues that are important to the party.[63] A member's bills can be lovingly caressed through the legislative process or summarily dismissed without so much as a hearing. Pork barrel—government projects yielding rich patronage benefits that are the sustenance of many a legislator's electoral survival—may be included or deleted in the appropriations process. Small favors and perquisites (such as the allocation of desirable office space or the scheduling of floor votes for the convenience of a member) can also be useful levers. Then, too, there are the campaign aids at the command of the leadership: money from party sources or the leader's personal political action committee (see Chapter Three), endorsements, appearances in the district or at fundraising events, and so on.[64] On rare occasions, in extreme cases, the leaders and their allies in the party caucus may even impose sanctions of various sorts (such as the stripping of seniority rights or prized committee berths) to punish recalcitrant lawmakers.[65] But in general, rank-and-file members—who elect party leaders—have limited tolerance for such tactics.[66]

In spite of all these weapons in the leadership's arsenal, the congressional parties lack the cohesion that characterizes parliamentary legislatures. This is not surprising, since the costs of bolting the party are far less in the United States than in, say, Great Britain. A disloyal English parliamentarian might very well be replaced as a party candidate at the next election; in America, it is more likely that the independent-minded member of Congress would be electorally rewarded—hailed as a free spirit, an individual of the people who can stand up to the party bosses. Moreover, defections from the ruling party in a parliamentary system bring a threat of the government's collapse and, with it, early elections under possibly unfavorable conditions; fixed unchangeable election dates in the United States mean the consequences of defection are much less dire. Also, a centralized, unicameral parliament, with executive and legislative branches effectively fused, permits relatively easy hierarchical, programmatic control by party leaders. The separate executive, the bicameral power-sharing, and the extraordinary decentralization of Congress's work are all institutional obstacles that limit the effectiveness of coordinated party action. Finally, party discipline is hurt by the individualistic nature of American politics: campaigns that are candidate-centered rather than party-oriented; the diversity of electoral constituencies to which members of Congress must understandably be responsive; the largely private system of election financing that obligates legislators to wealthy individuals and nonparty interest groups as much as to their parties; and the importance to lawmakers of attracting the news media's attention, often more easily done by showmanship than by quiet, effective labor within the party system.

These are formidable barriers indeed to the operation of responsible, potent legislative parties. Therefore, it is impressive to discover that party labels consistently have been the most powerful predictor of congressional roll call voting, and in the last two decades an unprecedented number of votes have closely followed the partisan divide. While not invariably predictive, as in strong parliamentary systems, the average representative or senator now votes with his or her party on about 85 percent of the votes that divide a majority of Democrats from a majority of Republicans. (See Table 2.1 and Figure 2.1.) In recent years, more than half of the roll call votes in the House and Senate have typically found majorities of Democrats and Republicans on opposite sides; in 1995, opposing Democratic and Republican majorities were present on a record high 71 percent of recorded roll call votes. (See Table 2.2 and Figure 2.2.) High levels of party cohesion are especially likely when a party's basic interests are at stake. The votes that organize the legislative chambers (such as the election of a Speaker), for instance, command nearly unanimous support among party members. Party platform issues that directly and manifestly affect the party's image or its key constituencies also typically produce substantial party voting.[67]

TABLE 2.1. PARTY UNITY SCORES IN THE HOUSE AND SENATE (AVERAGE INDIVIDUAL SUPPORT FOR PARTY ON VOTES DIVIDING PARTY MAJORITIES), 1959–1998.

YEAR	CONGRESS	HOUSE D (%)	HOUSE R (%)	SENATE D (%)	SENATE R (%)	ALL CONGRESS AVERAGE D (%)	ALL CONGRESS AVERAGE R (%)
1998	105	82	86	87	86	84.5	86.0
1997	105	82	88	85	87	83.5	87.5
1996	104	80	87	84	89	82.0	88.0
1995	104	80	91	81	89	80.5	90.0
1994	103	83	84	84	79	83.5	81.5
1993	103	85	84	85	84	85.0	84.0
1992	102	79	79	77	79	78.0	79.0
1991	102	81	77	80	81	80.5	79.0
1990	101	81	74	80	75	80.5	74.5
1989	101	81	72	78	78	79.5	75.0
1988	100	80	74	78	68	79.0	71.0
1987	100	81	74	81	75	81.0	74.5
1986	99	79	70	72	76	75.5	73.0
1985	99	80	75	75	76	77.5	75.5
1984	98	74	73	70	76	72.0	74.5
1983	98	76	74	71	74	73.5	74.0
1982	97	72	69	72	76	72.0	72.5
1981	97	69	74	71	81	70.0	77.5
1980	96	69	71	64	65	66.5	68.0
1979	96	69	73	68	66	68.5	69.5
1978	95	63	69	66	59	64.5	64.0
1977	95	68	71	63	66	65.5	68.5
1976	94	66	67	62	61	64.0	64.0
1975	94	69	72	68	64	68.5	68.0
1974	93	62	63	63	59	62.5	61.0
1973	93	68	68	69	64	68.5	66.0
1972	92	58	66	57	61	57.5	63.5
1971	92	61	67	64	63	62.5	65.0
1970	91	58	60	55	56	56.5	58.0
1969	91	61	62	63	63	62.0	62.5
1968	90	59	64	51	60	55.0	62.0
1967	90	67	74	61	60	64.0	67.0
1966	89	62	68	57	63	59.5	65.5
1965	89	70	71	63	68	66.5	69.5
1964	88	69	71	61	65	65.0	68.0
1963	88	73	74	66	67	69.5	70.5
1962	87	70	70	65	64	67.5	67.0
1961	87	77	73	74	68	75.5	70.5
1960	86	65	65	60	66	62.5	65.5
1959	86	79	79	67	72	73.0	75.5

Source: Congressional Quarterly Almanacs (Washington, D.C.: Congressional Quarterly, Inc.).
D = Democrats   R = Republicans

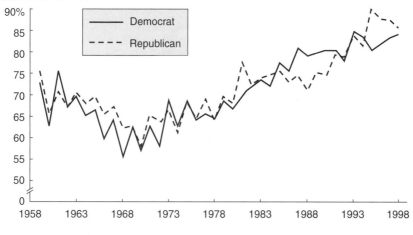

FIGURE 2.1 Party Unity Scores, 1959–1998
Source: See Table 2.1

Until the decade of the 1980s, there had been a substantial decline in party voting in Congress. At the turn of the last century, almost three-quarters of all the recorded votes saw a majority of one party voting against a majority of the other party, and, astoundingly, a third or more of a session's roll calls would pit at least 90 percent of one party against 90 percent or more of the other party. This was at a time when two Speakers of the House (Republicans Thomas B. Reed and Joseph G. Cannon) possessed almost dictatorial authority and therefore could enforce strict voting discipline.[68] But the Speaker's powers were curtailed drastically between 1909 and 1911, a development that combined with the internal GOP strains and splits produced by Progressivism to reduce party harmony and unity in congressional voting. The Democrats of the New Deal coalition also had their own fractures and contradictions (African Americans versus whites, northern liberals versus southern conservatives, urban areas versus rural locales, and so forth). The effect of these tensions and the other antiparty trends discussed in Chapter One was to leave party majorities opposing each other on only about 40 percent of recorded votes through the latter 1960s and the 1970s. In the past two decades, however, party voting has surged dramatically. (See again Tables 2.1 and 2.2 and Figures 2.1 and 2.2.) The first session of the 104th Congress (1995)—which followed the GOP takeover of both the House and Senate—produced the greatest partisan divide in more than four decades.[69] A majority of Democrats opposed a majority of Republicans on 71 percent of all recorded votes. (No other year, save for 1993, has come close to this percentage since

TABLE 2.2. PARTY VOTING IN THE HOUSE AND SENATE (PERCENT OF VOTES FINDING MAJORITIES OF DEMOCRATS AND REPUBLICANS ON OPPOSITE SIDES), 1954–1998.

YEAR	CONGRESS	HOUSE (%)	SENATE (%)	ALL CONGRESS AVERAGE
1998	105	56	56	56.0
1997	105	50	50	50.0
1996	104	56	62	59.0
1995	104	73	69	71.0
1994	103	62	52	57.0
1993	103	65	67	66.0
1992	102	64	53	58.5
1991	102	55	49	52.0
1990	101	49	54	51.5
1989	101	55	35	45.0
1988	100	47	42	44.5
1987	100	64	41	52.5
1986	99	57	52	54.5
1985	99	61	50	55.5
1984	98	47	40	43.5
1983	98	56	44	50.0
1982	97	36	43	39.5
1981	97	37	48	42.5
1980	96	38	46	42.0
1979	96	47	47	47.0
1978	95	33	45	39.0
1977	95	42	42	42.0
1976	94	36	37	36.5
1975	94	48	48	48.0
1974	93	29	44	36.5
1973	93	42	40	41.0
1972	92	27	36	31.5
1971	92	38	42	40.0
1970	91	27	35	31.0
1969	91	31	36	33.5
1968	90	35	32	33.5
1967	90	36	35	35.5
1966	89	41	50	45.5
1965	89	52	42	47.0
1964	88	55	36	45.5
1963	88	49	47	48.0
1962	87	46	41	43.5
1961	87	50	62	56.0
1960	86	53	37	45.0
1959	86	55	48	51.5
1958	85	40	44	42.0
1957	85	59	36	41.5

(continued)

TABLE 2.2. CONTINUED

YEAR	CONGRESS	HOUSE (%)	SENATE (%)	ALL CONGRESS AVERAGE
1956	84	44	53	48.5
1955	84	41	30	35.5
1954	83	38	47	42.5

Source: Congressional Quarterly Almanacs (Washington, D.C.: Congressional Quarterly, Inc.).

these figures were first compiled by the *Congressional Quarterly* in 1954.) In 1995, the average Democratic member voted with his or her party about 80 percent of the time on party votes, while the average Republican did so on 90 percent of such votes.

There are many reasons for the recent growth of party unity and cohesion. Some are the result of long-term political factors. Both congressional parties, for instance, have gradually become more ideologically homogeneous and internally consistent. Southern Democrats today are more moderate and far closer philosophically to their northern counterparts than the South's legislative barons of old ever were; similarly, there are few liberal Republicans left in either chamber of Congress, and GOP representatives from all regions of the country—with a few exceptions—are moderately to very conservative.[70] At the same time, strong two-party competition has come to almost all areas of the nation,[71] and the electoral insecurity produced by vigorous competition seems to encourage party unity and cooperation in a legislature (perhaps as a kind of "circling the wagons" effect).[72]

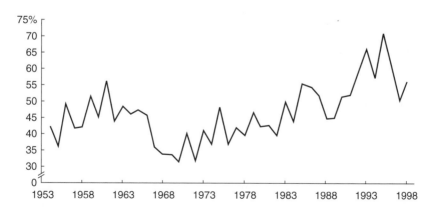

FIGURE 2.2   PARTY VOTING IN THE HOUSE AND SENATE, 1954–1998
Source: See Table 2.2

Institutional changes in both congressional parties—especially in the House—also helped to produce heightened party unity within each party. One of most enduring effects of the Watergate scandal was to stimulate the strengthening of the congressional parties long after Richard Nixon had departed the White House. The Watergate-spawned election of seventy-five reform-minded freshman House Democrats in 1974 led to a revolt against the seniority system in early 1975. Three senior, unresponsive chairmen were deposed, the power of the committee system was diminished, and a crucial barrier to the influence of party thus fell. When a rigid seniority system could be guaranteed to protect members who consistently bucked their party, committee chairs' support of party positions in recorded votes was quite low. After the 1975 display of party caucus muscle, though, chairpersons dramatically increased their solidarity with the party majority, scoring even higher than backbenchers on party unity scales.[73] The occasional rebellion, such as the one directed against House Armed Services Committee Chairman Les Aspin in early 1987, served to remind other committee leaders of the importance of staying within party norms.[74]

Around the same time, House Democrats began making other changes that empowered the party.[75] For one, the House Democratic Caucus (the group of all Democratic House members) began taking on life and new responsibilities beyond challenging chairpersons, and this development has assisted the furtherance of party cohesion.[76] Closed caucus meetings to discuss upcoming bills, to plan general strategy, to air complaints about the actions (or inaction) of party leaders and committees, and to direct that certain legislation be taken up or killed began to be held with some frequency. If nothing else, the meetings provided leaders and chairpersons with a clear sense of party opinion. In addition to the revitalization of the caucus, a number of other post-Watergate changes have strengthened the party role in Congress.[77] Party leaders were given greater control over the flow of House business in 1975 through the Speaker's power to nominate the chair and the majority party members of the Rules Committee; once obstructionist, the committee was transformed into a reliable ally of the leadership. Additionally, the assignment of members to committees and the nomination of committee chairs were placed more firmly in the control of party leaders (though their choices were still occasionally rejected by the party caucus). Increasing centralization of the budget process also gave the Democratic leadership more influence,[78] and their reach was extended still further by a substantial increase in staffing and support services for the Speaker, majority leader, and party whips.[79] Not all of the

1970s' changes built up party power; some, such as the proliferation of subcommittees, made Congress more difficult to manage and mobilize. But on the whole, the reforms facilitated a much more purposive party leadership than at any time since the early 1900s, and rank-and-file party members expected leaders to deploy their newly conferred powers to pass legislation on which there was consensus within the party.[80]

Party power reached its zenith when the GOP captured control of the House in 1994 and Newt Gingrich rose to the speakership. One way Gingrich further empowered the party leadership was by implementing rules (with the full support of the GOP conference) that weakened the power of committees and committee chairs.[81] Perhaps most importantly, Gingrich assumed the power to appoint all committee chairs. And although the Speaker generally deferred to seniority in making his selections, for three committees, he passed over the most senior members in favor of more aggressive and ideologically committed allies. House Republicans also passed a Gingrich-backed rule limiting committee chairs to three two-year terms, which guaranteed that chairs would be unable to compete with party leaders by developing their own power centers. Under the GOP majority, committee chairs would also now be prohibited from chairing subcommittees—a move designed to disperse power as widely as possible on each committee. Finally, the GOP conference gave Speaker Gingrich the power to appoint all of the Republican members of the House Oversight Committee—the panel that deals with the House's administrative tasks and has jurisdiction over issues such as campaign finance reform. With its members appointed by the Speaker, the House Oversight Panel joined the Rules Committee as an ally of the party leadership. Although Gingrich ultimately stepped down after the GOP's poor showing at the polls in the 1998 midterm elections, the power-centralizing changes he pushed through live on. Indeed, as many GOP committee chairs were term-limited out of their posts for the 107th Congress, members who aspired to chairs were forced to interview with a steering committee headed by Speaker Hastert[82]—a process that would have been unimaginable to vaunted Democratic committee chairs such as John Dingell (D-Mich.) less than a decade ago.

It should be noted that the increasingly powerful party campaign committees have probably played a role in the renewed party cohesiveness within Congress. As we will discuss at length in the next chapter, each party's campaign committee has been recruiting and training House and Senate candidates as never before and devising common themes for all nominees in election seasons—work that may help to produce a consensual legislative agenda for each party. The carrot and stick of party money and campaign services, such as media advertising production and polling, is also being used to convert independent candidates into party team players. Clearly, the more important the party organization can be to a legislator's election and reelection, the more attention a legislator is likely to pay to his or her party.

Finally, the role of aggressive leaders willing to pull out all of the stops should not be underestimated in contributing to increased partisanship. Democratic Speaker Jim Wright unapologetically employed his powers to relegate House Republicans to the sidelines on important policy debates.[83] In turn, growing dissatisfaction on the Republican side of the House aisle with their seemingly semi-permanent minority status produced increasingly militant GOP leaders who were more interested in winning control of the House than in attempting to forge compromises with Democrats.[84] This period witnessed the beginning of a shrill, new partisanship in the House that would damage the political careers of more than a few members. In 1989, for example, Representative Newt Gingrich (R-Ga.)—who engineered the GOP takeover of the House in 1994—played a leading role in forcing Speaker Jim Wright to step down due to serious ethics charges. Democratic whip David Bonior returned the favor in 1995 by filing numerous ethics charges against Gingrich (who by this time had risen to Speaker) that, along with other missteps, would damage his standing in the House Republican Conference and help inspire a coup attempt to remove him as Speaker.[85] While other incidents continued to poison the atmosphere in Congress,[86] partisanship reached new heights with President Clinton's impeachment in the House and subsequent acquittal in the Senate—both of which occurred on nearly party-line votes.[87] Since then, partisan vitriol in Congress has shown no signs of abating. Indeed, the Democratic Congressional Campaign Committee (DCCC), led by Patrick Kennedy (D-R.I.), filed a racketeering suit against GOP Majority Whip Tom Delay (R-Texas) in 2000 over his fundraising practices.[88] By November 2000, Speaker Dennis Hastert (R-Ill.) and Democratic Leader Richard Gephardt (D-Mo.) had not spoken to one another formally for months,[89] and Hastert actually visited Gephardt's district to campaign for his opponent.[90] Moreover, the bitter struggle over Florida's electoral votes in 2000 presidential election, combined with a House and Senate almost evenly divided between the parties, suggests that shrill partisanship on the Hill may not end anytime soon.

The Presidential Party

Political parties may well be more integral to the operation of the legislative branch than the executive branch, but it is the presidential party that captures the public imagination and shapes the electorate's opinion of the two parties. In our very personalized politics, voters' perceptions of the incumbent president and the presidential candidates determine to a great degree how citizens perceive the parties.

A chief executive's successes are his or her party's successes; the president's failures are borne by the party as much as the individual. The image projected by a losing presidential candidate is incorporated into the party's contemporary portrait, whether wanted or not. As the only independently elected candidate of the national party, the president today naturally assumes the role of party leader (as does the White House nominee of the other party), though this was not the intention of the nation's founders. They had hoped for a nonpartisan presidency, a great unifier and elected monarch. George Washington fit the preconceived notion perfectly, but his was a brief tradition. From 1800 onwards (with the lone exception provided by James Monroe's White House tenure), presidents were identified with party groupings, and beginning with Andrew Jackson, were formally the nominees of full-fledged national parties.

The juggling of contradictory roles is not always easy for a president. Expected not only to bring the country together as ceremonial chief of state and to forge a ruling consensus as head of government, the president must also be an effective commander of a sometimes divisive partisan subgroup. Along with the inevitable headaches party leadership brings, though, there are clear and compelling advantages that accompany it (as suggested in Chapter One). Foremost among them is a party's ability to mobilize support among voters for a president's program, especially among its own partisans. Also, the executive's legislative agenda might be derailed more quickly without the common tie of party label between the chief executive and many members of Congress; all presidents appeal for some congressional support on the basis of shared party affiliation, and they generally receive it. In the most recent decades, as Table 2.3 and Figure 2.3 indicate, the average legislator of the president's party has backed the chief executive roughly two-thirds to four-fifths of the time, whereas the average member of the opposition has done so at much lower rates. There is considerable variance among presidents, of course, since circumstances, agendas, and executive skill differ. Bill Clinton's support among House Democrats was exceptionally high, for example, as was (to a lesser extent) George H.W. Bush and Ronald Reagan's support among House Republicans. In contrast, Jimmy Carter and Dwight Eisenhower (in his second term) had more than the usual degree of trouble with their House partisans. Finally, in this listing of presidential party assets, it is worth noting that a president's own

TABLE 2.3. AVERAGE SUPPORT SCORES FOR MEMBERS OF CONGRESS ON VOTES RELATED TO THE PRESIDENT'S PROGRAM, 1953-1998.

YEAR	PARTY OF PRESIDENT	SENATE D (%)	SENATE R (%)	HOUSE D (%)	HOUSE R (%)	ALL CONGRESS AVERAGE D (%)	ALL CONGRESS AVERAGE R (%)
1998	Democrat	82	41	74	26	78.0	33.5
1997	Democrat	85	60	71	30	78.0	45.0
1996	Democrat	83	37	74	38	78.5	37.5
1995	Democrat	81	29	75	22	78.0	25.5
1994	Democrat	86	42	75	47	80.5	44.5
1993	Democrat	87	29	77	39	82.0	34.0
1992	Republican	32	73	25	71	28.5	72.0
1991	Republican	41	83	34	72	37.5	77.5
1990	Republican	38	70	25	63	31.5	66.5
1989	Republican	55	82	36	69	45.5	75.5
1988	Republican	47	68	25	57	36.0	62.5
1987	Republican	36	64	24	62	30.0	63.0
1986	Republican	38	79	25	66	31.5	72.5
1985	Republican	35	75	30	67	32.5	71.0
1984	Republican	41	76	34	60	37.5	68.0
1983	Republican	42	73	28	70	35.0	71.5
1982	Republican	43	74	39	64	41.0	69.0
1981	Republican	49	80	42	68	45.5	74.0
1980	Democrat	62	45	63	40	62.5	42.5
1979	Democrat	68	47	64	34	66.0	40.5
1978	Democrat	66	41	60	36	63.0	38.5
1977	Democrat	70	52	63	42	66.5	47.0
1976	Republican	39	62	32	63	35.5	62.5
1975	Republican	47	68	38	63	42.5	65.5
1974	Republican	39	56	44	58	41.5	57.0
1973	Republican	37	61	35	62	36.0	61.5
1972	Republican	44	66	47	64	45.5	65.0
1971	Republican	40	64	47	72	43.5	68.0
1970	Republican	45	60	53	66	49.0	63.0
1969	Republican	47	66	48	57	47.5	61.5
1968	Democrat	48	47	64	51	56.0	49.0
1967	Democrat	61	53	69	46	65.0	49.5
1966	Democrat	57	43	63	37	60.0	40.0
1965	Democrat	64	48	74	41	69.0	44.5
1964	Democrat	61	45	74	38	67.5	41.5
1963	Democrat	63	44	72	32	67.5	38.0
1962	Democrat	63	39	72	42	67.5	40.5
1961	Democrat	65	36	73	37	69.0	36.5
1960	Republican	43	66	44	59	43.5	62.5
1959	Republican	38	72	40	68	39.0	70.0
1958	Republican	44	67	55	58	49.5	62.5

(continued)

TABLE 2.3. *CONTINUED*

YEAR	PARTY OF PRESIDENT	SENATE D (%)	SENATE R (%)	HOUSE D (%)	HOUSE R (%)	ALL CONGRESS AVERAGE D (%)	ALL CONGRESS AVERAGE R (%)
1957	Republican	51	69	49	54	50.0	61.5
1956	Republican	39	72	52	72	45.5	72.0
1955	Republican	56	72	53	60	54.5	66.0
1954	Republican	38	73	44	71	41.0	72.0
1953	Republican	46	68	49	74	47.5	71.0

Source: Congressional Quarterly Almanacs (Washington, D.C.: Congressional Quarterly, Inc.).

D = Democrats　　　R = Republicans

Note: Scores represent the percentage of recorded votes on which members voted in agreement with the president's announced position.

election to office would be nearly impossible without the volunteer work and organizational aid provided to the nominee by the party.

These party gifts to the president are reciprocated in numerous ways. In addition to compiling a record for the party and giving substance to its image, presidents appoint many activists to office, recruit candidates, raise heaping amounts of soft and hard money for the party treasury, campaign extensively for party nominees during election seasons, and occasionally provide some "coattail" help to fellow office-seekers who are on the ballot in presidential election years.

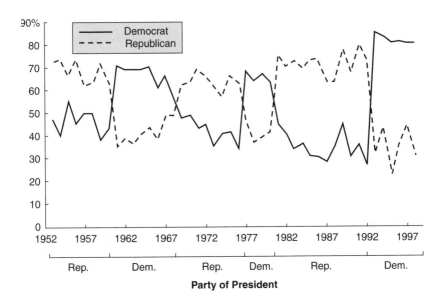

FIGURE 2.3 AVERAGE SUPPORT SCORES FOR MEMBERS OF CONGRESS ON VOTES RELATED TO THE PRESIDENT'S PROGRAM, 1953–1998

Some presidents take their party responsibilities more seriously than others. In this century, Democrats Woodrow Wilson and Franklin Roosevelt were exceptionally party-oriented and dedicated to building their party electorally and governmentally.[91] In his first term, Wilson worked closely with Democratic congressional leaders to fashion a progressive and successful party program, and Roosevelt was responsible for constructing the enduring New Deal coalition for his party and breathing life into a previously moribund Democratic National Committee. Republican Gerald Ford, during his brief tenure in the 1970s, also achieved a reputation as a party builder, and he was willing to undertake campaign and organizational chores for the GOP (especially in fundraising and barnstorming for nominees) that most other presidents minimized or shunned.

Sadly, some modern chief executives have been in an entirely different mold. Dwight Eisenhower elevated nonpartisanship to an art form, and while it may have preserved his personal popularity,[92] it proved a disaster for his party. Despite a full two-term occupancy of the White House, the Republican party remained mired in minority status. Eisenhower never really attempted to transfer his high ratings to the party, and in 1958 even implied that he would not mind if some of his GOP critics were defeated for reelection.[93] And his impolitic vetoing of an important bill sponsored by Maine's Republican Senator Frederick G. Payne just two days before the 1958 election contributed to Payne's loss.[94] Lyndon Johnson kept the DNC busy with such important tasks as answering wedding invitations sent to the First Family,[95] and, when many of the Democratic senators and representatives elected on his presidential coattails were endangered in the 1966 midterm election, LBJ canceled a major campaign trip on their behalf lest his policies get tied too closely to their possible defeats. Democrats lost forty-seven House seats, three Senate seats, and eight governorships in a 1966 debacle Johnson did little to prevent. Probably no other president's attitude toward his party was ever as contemptuous as Richard Nixon's. He discouraged the GOP from nominating candidates against conservative southern Democrats in order to improve his own electoral and congressional position and subordinated the party's agenda almost wholly to his own reelection in 1972. Shunting aside the Republican National Committee, Nixon formed the infamous Committee to Re-elect the President, known by the most appropriate acronym of our time: CREEP. So ignorant of CREEP's abuses were party leaders that the Republican party organization itself was essentially exonerated during the Watergate investigations. (Unfortunately for GOP candidates in 1974, the public failed to make this fine distinction.) Jimmy Carter showed little interest in his national party either. Elected as an outsider in 1976, Carter and his top aides at first viewed the party as another extension of the Washington establishment they had pledged to ignore. Carter and his DNC chairmen failed to develop the Democratic party organizationally and financially to keep it competitive during a critical period when the Republicans were undergoing a dramatic revitalization. Later, during his fateful 1980 reelection campaign, Carter was properly criticized for diverting DNC personnel and resources to his presidential needs rather than permitting them to pursue essential partywide electoral tasks.

Yet modern chief executives were provided with an alternative model in President Ronald Reagan—one of the most party-oriented presidents of recent times. "As one who often has been critical of other aspects of Reagan's stewardship," wrote the journalist David Broder, "I want to salute the man who, more than any other president I have ever covered, pays his dues and unselfishly aids the growth of his political party."[96] In 1983 and 1984 during his own reelection effort, Reagan made more than two dozen campaign and fundraising appearances for all branches of the party organization and candidates at every level. More than 300 television advertisement endorsements were taped as well, including one for an obscure Honolulu city council contest.[97] Reagan even exhibited a willingness to get involved in the nitty-gritty of candidate recruitment, frequently calling in strong potential candidates to urge them to run.[98] During the pitched and ultimately losing battle to retain control of the Senate for the Republicans in 1986, Reagan played the good soldier, visiting twenty-two key states repeatedly and raising $33 million for the party and its candidates.[99] Unlike Eisenhower, Reagan was willing to attempt a popularity transfer to his party and to campaign for Republicans whether they were strongly loyal to him personally or not;[100] unlike Johnson, Reagan was willing to put his prestige and policies to the test on the hustings; unlike Nixon, Reagan spent time and effort helping underdogs and longshot candidates, not just likely winners;[101] and unlike Carter, Reagan signed more than seventy fundraising appeals for party committees and took a personal interest in the further strengthening of the GOP's organizational capacity.

By and large, President Bush followed the example set by Reagan. Bush brought to the presidency years of extensive party experience—first as a county chairman in Texas and then as the chair of the Republican National Committee.[102] Not surprisingly, given those credentials,

Bush took his party building responsibilities seriously, raising large sums of campaign dollars for Republican candidates and for the party.[103] Bill Clinton, of course, raised enormous sums of money for the Democratic National Committee and for Democratic candidates nationwide—and he continued to do so even in 2000 when he was not on the ballot.[104] At the same time, much of the money Clinton raised for the DNC during his first term was used to finance activities designed largely to bolster his own 1996 campaign (rather than to shore up the Democratic party and its candidates more generally).[105] Clinton also waited until fairly late in the campaign before he started raising funds for Democratic congressional candidates, and reports of the Clinton-Gore campaign's questionable fundraising tactics—which came to light during the last few weeks of the 1996 campaign—may well have hurt Democratic candidates at the polls.[106] So, while Clinton surely took his party responsibilities more seriously than did Carter or Nixon, his party-building marks are not as high as those for Reagan or Bush.

Even the most party-oriented chief executives, it should be noted, have not been able to provide much coattail help to party nominees lower on the ballot. For example, while Reagan's initial victory in 1980 was one factor in the election of a Republican Senate, his landslide reelection in 1984 (like Nixon's in 1972) had almost no impact on his party's congressional representation.[107] Similarly, George H.W. Bush's victory in 1988 did little to help Republican congressional candidates,[108] and Democrats actually *lost* nine seats in the House when Democrat Bill Clinton won the presidency in 1992. There is little question that the coattail effect has diminished sharply compared to a generation ago, as a number of studies have shown.[109] Partly, the decreased competitiveness of congressional elections has been produced by artful redistricting and the growing value of incumbency.[110] But voters are also less willing to think and cast ballots in purely partisan terms—a worrisome development that limits presidential leadership and hurts party development. We will be returning to this subject in subsequent chapters.

The Parties and the Judiciary

Americans view the judiciary as "above politics" and certainly nonpartisan. Many judges are quick to agree. Yet, not only do justices follow the election returns and allow themselves to be influenced by popular opinion, they are also products of their party identification and possess the very same partisan perceptual screens as all other politically aware citizens.

While legislators are far more partisan than judges, it is wrong to assume that judges reach decisions wholly independent of partisan values. First of all, judges are creatures of the political process, and their posts are considered patronage plums. They are selected by presidents or governors for their abilities but also as members of the executive's party and sometimes as representatives of a certain philosophy or approach to government. In this century every president has appointed judges overwhelmingly from his own party;[111] Jimmy Carter, Ronald Reagan, and George H.W. Bush, for instance, each drew more than 90 percent of their federal court appointees from their respective parties.[112] Likewise, 89 percent of Bill Clinton's federal judge appointments during his first two years in office came from the ranks of the Democratic party.[113] Research has long indicated, moreover, that party affiliation is a moderately good predictor of judicial decisions, at least in some areas.[114] Indeed, judicial decisions in the protacted struggle for Florida's electoral votes during the 2000 presidential contest illustrate this point. Whereas the Florida State State Supreme Court—dominated by Democratic appointees—aided Democratic presidential candidate Al Gore by ordering a statewide recount of all "undervotes," the U.S. Supreme Court—controlled by Republican appointees—assisted GOP presidential candidate George W. Bush by halting the recount (which had the effect of handing the presidency to Bush). In other words, party matters in the judiciary, though it usually matters less on the bench than in the legislature and the executive.

It should not be surprising that judges are influenced by party. Many of the judges appointed to office have long careers in politics as loyal party workers or legislators.[115] Some jurists are even more overtly political, since they are elected to office. Indeed, thirteen states presently hold outright partisan elections, with both parties nominating opposing candidates and running hard hitting campaigns.[116] Appointment and nonpartisan election of judges, moreover, hardly produce jurists' without partisan stripes.[117] In some rural counties across America, local judges are not merely elected figures; they are the key public officials, controlling patronage jobs and the party machinery itself. Obviously, therefore, in many places in the United States, judges, by necessity and by tradition, are not above politics, but in the thick of it. While election of the judiciary is a questionable practice in light of its specially sanctioned role as impartial arbiter, partisan influence exerted both by jurists' party loyalties and by the appointment (or election) process is useful in retaining some degree of accountability in a branch often accused of being arrogant and aloof.

Party affiliation affects judges, then, but their decisions in cases involving political parties have had a profound effect on the health of party organizations as well. The judicial record on party has been very mixed. Few would argue with some Supreme Court decisions invalidating party rules and nomination procedures that violated basic constitutional rights, such as *Smith* v. *Allwright* in 1944,[118] when the Texas Democratic party was prohibited from permitting only whites to vote in its primary. But for advocates of a strong two-party system, the Court has been too insistent on the "right" of third-party and Independent candidates to easy access to the ballot, ignoring both the essential stability a two-party system brings and society's right to shore up that system.[119] And in the area of patronage, the Court has devastated the parties. In three separate decisions in 1976, 1980, and 1990,[120] the Court severely constrained the ability of elected officials to make appointments to government jobs on the basis of party affiliation—a time-honored practice that gives the parties vital rewards and incentives to use in building their organizations. While patronage will be the subject of further commentary in the concluding chapter, it suffices for now to cite Supreme Court Justice Lewis Powell's dissent in one of the Court's ill-considered patronage rulings: "Patronage—the right to select key personnel and to reward the party 'faithful'—serves the public interest by facilitating the implementation of policies endorsed by the electorate."[121]

In another legal sphere, however, the judicial news for parties has been better. Twice (in 1975 and 1981), the Supreme Court has held that when national party rules for presidential delegate selection conflict with state law, the party rules take precedence.[122] In both cases, the national Democratic party's specifications overrode conflicting state (Illinois and Wisconsin) statutes on the basis of a party's constitutionally protected "freedom of political association." This associational right was taken a giant step further in 1986 in *Tashjian* v. *Republican Party of Connecticut*,[123] when the Court ruled that a state could not require a political party to hold "closed" primary elections, where only registered party members may vote, if the party preferred another system. A party's First Amendment associational rights, said the Court, guaranteed the party, not the state, the choice of nominating conditions. In 1989, the Supreme Court further removed parties from the chokehold of government regulation with its decision in *Eu, Secretary of State of California* v. *San Francisco County Democratic Central Committee*, where the Court struck down burdensome California statutes limiting state party chairs to two-year terms, requiring state party chairmanships to be rotated between northern and southern Californians, and banning party endorsements in primaries.[124] More recently, the Supreme Court gave its imprimatur to states seeking to bolster the two-party system when it ruled that the Minnesota State Election Commission could prohibit fusion balloting—a practice helpful to minor parties by allowing them to nominate candidates already nominated by one of the major parties.[125] "The Constitution permits the Minnesota Legislature to decide that political stability is best served though a healthy two-party system," wrote Chief Justice William Rehnquist in his majority (6–3) opinion for the Court."[126] Finally, in a 7–2 decision issued in June 2000, the Supreme Court handed parties another victory by striking down California's blanket primary— a primary in which all candidates are listed by party label on a single ballot, all voters are eligible to participate (regardless of party affiliation), and the two candidates receiving the most votes face off in the general election. In it decision, the Court argued that California's statute mandating blanket primaries violated parties' freedom of association rights by undermining the ability of parties to control their nominating procedures.[127]

Recent federal court decisions in the area of campaign finance have also decidedly empowered the parties. In *Colorado Republican Federal Campaign Committee* v. *Federal Election Commission*, the Supreme Court ruled that political parties enjoy the same First Amendment protections as do individuals and PACs in making independent expenditures on behalf of or against federal political candidates. The Court's decision permits parties to spend unlimited sums of hard (regulated) money on campaign materials that expressly advocate the election or defeat of a specific federal candidate—as long as the spending is done independently of the benefited federal candidate's campaign.[128] Perhaps more importantly, a federal court in Colorado recently invalidated federal limits on party-coordinated expenditures (spending by parties in conjunction with their candidates); the ruling will no doubt make its way to the Supreme Court.[129] The broad implications of these court decisions for regulation of the parties will be discussed in Chapter Seven.

The Parties and State Governments

Most of the conclusions just reached about the party's relationship to the legislature, the executive, and the judiciary apply as well to the state level. The national parties, after all, are organized around state units, and the basic structural arrangement of party and government is much the same in Washington and the state capitals. Remarkably, too, the major national parties are the dominant political forces in all fifty states. This has been true consistently; unlike Great Britain or Canada, the United States has no regional or state parties that displace one or both of the national parties in local contests. Occasionally in American history, a third party has proven locally potent, as did Minnesota's Farmer-Labor party and Wisconsin's Progressives, both of which elected governors and state legislative majorities earlier in this century. But over time none have survived,[130] and every state's two-party system mirrors national party dualism, at least as far as labels are concerned.

There are some party-oriented differences at the state level, though. Governors in many states tend to possess even greater influence over their parties' organizations and legislators than do presidents.[131] Many governors, for example, have ample patronage positions at their command, and these material rewards and incentives give governors added clout with activists and officeholders.[132] Moreover, forty-three governors possess the line item veto denied the national executive.[133] The item veto permits the governor to veto single items (such as individual pork barrel projects) in appropriations bills. Whereas a president must often accept objectionable measures as part of a bill too urgent or important to be vetoed, a governor gains enormous leverage with legislators by means of the item veto. Gubernatorial influence over legislative party politics may be slightly less dominant as legislatures have become more professionalized.[134] For example, the governor's role in selecting legislative party leaders—for years a tradition in some states—has diminished somewhat over the past few decades, though some governors clearly remain influential in this area.[135] Overall, however, governors retain a powerful upper hand in the realm of state party politics.[136]

Sporadic data and significant variation across states make it difficult to compare party cohesiveness levels in state legislatures with that in Congress. Simply put, relatively high levels of party voting can be found in some state legislatures, while little partisan cohesion can be detected in others. In general, party voting has tended to be higher in urban and industrial states and lower in rural states.[137] Legislative partisanship also tends to be more pronounced in states where vigorous two-party electoral competition exists and where parties are strong organizationally.[138] Until fairly recently, the lack of two-party competition in the South essentially produced one-party legislatures split into factions, regional groupings, or personal cliques. But as two-party competition reaches the legislative level in southern states, party cohesion in southern state legislatures is beginning to emerge.[139]

One other party distinction is notable in many state legislatures. Compared to Congress, many state legislative leaders have much more authority and power.[140] The seniority system for allocating committee assignments is less influential in many state legislatures than in Congress, and legislative leaders often have considerable discretion in appointing committee chairs and members.[141] The party caucuses, too, are typically more active and influential in state legislatures than in their Washington counterparts. In some legislatures, the caucuses meet weekly or even daily to work out strategy and count votes,[142] and some caucuses occasionally bind party members to support the group's decisions on procedural votes or key issues (such as budget measures).[143] Many legislative parties have also created sophisticated new legislative party campaign committees to assist the campaigns of their legislative candidates.[144] We address this development in Chapter Three. For now, suffice it to say that the campaign assistance provided by these party campaign committees has the potential to strengthen party leaders (who typically control the resources) and bolster party cohesion among legislators.[145]

The party in government has changed in important ways in recent decades, as we have just reviewed. But its modifications have been evolutionary compared to the revolution in party organization that has taken place in the matter of a few years. This transformation in party machinery—its dimensions and implications—is the focus of the next chapter.

NOTES

1. E. E. Schattschneider, *Party Government* (New York: Rinehart, 1942), 6–8.
2. Ibid., 8.
3. George Washington, "Farewell Address," in *Writings* (Washington, D.C.: U.S. Government Printing Office, 1940), vol. 35, 223–228.
4. See, generally, John H. Aldrich, *Why Parties? The Origin and Transformation of Party Politics in America* (Chicago: University of Chicago Press, 1995). William Nisbet Chambers, *Political Parties in a New Nation: The American Experience, 1776–1809* (New York: Oxford University Press, 1963); Chambers and Walter Dean Burnham, eds., *The American Party Systems: Stages of Political Development* (New York: Oxford University Press, 1967); Richard Hofstadter, *The Idea of a Party System: The Rise of Legitimate Opposition in the United States, 1780–1840* (Berkeley: University of California Press, 1970); Richard P. McCormick, *The Second American Party System: Party Formation in the Jacksonian Era* (Chapel Hill: University of North Carolina Press, 1966); Roy F. Nichols, *The Invention of the American Political Parties* (New York: Macmillan, 1967); and Clifton McCleskey, "Democratic Representation and the Constitution: Where Do Political Parties Fit In?" *University of Virginia Newsletter* 60 (July 1984): 61–64, at 62–63.
5. The National Republicans (one forerunner of the Whig party) and the Anti-Masonic parties each had held more limited conventions in 1831.
6. Great Britain, by contrast, did not develop truly modern parties until the 1870s, once the electorate had been broadened by the Reform Acts of 1832 and 1867.
7. Voter turnout in presidential elections from 1876 to 1900 ranged from 75 to 82 percent of the potential (male) electorate, compared with about 50 percent in contemporary presidential elections. See *Historical Statistics of the United States: Colonial Times to 1970*, Part 2, Series Y 27–28 (Washington, D.C.: Government Printing Office, 1975), based on unpublished data prepared by Walter Dean Burnham.

8. Paul Allen Beck, *Party Politics in America*, 8th ed. (New York: Addison Wesley Longman), 24.
9. This topic will be discussed in Chapter Seven.
10. Schattschneider, *Party Government*, 48.
11. See V.O. Key, Jr., *American State Politics: An Introduction* (New York: Knopf, 1956).
12. See V. O. Key, Jr., *Southern Politics in State and Nation* (New York: Knopf, 1949).
13. See Malcolm E. Jewell and Sarah M. Morehouse, *Political Parties and Elections in American States* (Washington, D.C.: Congressional Quarterly Press, 2001), Chap. 2; John F. Bibby, Cornelius P. Cotter, James L. Gibson, and Robert J. Huckshorn, "Parties in State Politics," in Virginia Gray, Herbert Jacob, and Kenneth Vines, eds., *Politics in the American States*, 4th ed. (Boston: Little, Brown, 1983), 66, Table 3.3; Larry Sabato, *Goodbye to Good-Time Charlie: The American Governorship Transformed*, 2nd ed. (Washington, D.C.: Congressional Quarterly Press, 1983), 116–138.
14. Beck, *Party Politics in America*, 56.
15. Steven J. Rosenstone, Roy L. Behr, and Edward Lazarus, *Third Parties in America*, 2nd ed. (Princeton, N.J.: Princeton University Press, 1996).
16. The seven are: Anti-Masonic party (1832—7 electoral votes), American (Know-Nothing) party (1856—8 electoral votes), People's (Populist) party (1892—22 electoral votes), Progressive (Bull Moose) party (1912—88 electoral votes), Progressive party (1924—13 electoral votes), States Rights (Dixiecrat) party (1948—39 electoral votes), and American Independent party (1968—46 electoral votes).
17. Roosevelt's 1912 effort was the most successful; the Bull Moose party won 30 percent of the popular vote for president (though only 17 percent of the Electoral College votes). Roosevelt's is also the only third party to run ahead of one of the two major parties (the Republicans). We follow Rosenstone, Behr, and Lazarus in using the terms "third party," "minor party," and "independent" interchangeably. See Rosenstone, Behr, and Lazarus, *Third Parties in America*, 10.
18. Louis Jacobson, "Getting Beyond Charisma," *National Journal* (28 October 2000): 3430–3431.
19. Rosenstone, Behr, and Lazarus, *Third Parties in America*, 243.
20. Jack W. Germond and Jules Witcover, "Thanks for Nothing, Ralph," *National Journal* (11 November 2000): 3691. CNN exit poll data show that without Nader on the ballot, a third of Nader voters nationwide would have stayed home on election day, 2 percent would have voted for Gore, and one percent would have supported Bush (http://www.cnn.com/ELECTION/2000/results/).
21. Christian Collet and Martin P. Wattenberg, "Strategically Unambitious: Minor Party and Independent Candidates in the 1996 Congressional Elections," in Daniel M. Shea and John C. Green, eds., *The State of the Parties: The Changing Role of Contemporary American Parties*, 3rd ed. (Lanham, Md.: Rowman & Littlefield, 1999), 229–248.
22. Paul S. Herrnson, *Congressional Elections: Campaigning at Home and in Washington* 3rd ed. (Washington, D.C.: Congressional Quarterly Press), 202.
23. Collet and Wattenberg, "Strategically Unambitious: Minor Party and Independent Candidates in the 1996 Congressional Elections."

24. Anderson only received 7 percent of the vote in the end, though at points in the contest polls had shown him well above 20 percent.

25. Paul Abramson, John Aldrich, Philip Paolino, and David W. Rohde, "Challenges to the American Two-Party System: Evidence From the 1968, 1980, 1992, and 1996 Elections," *Political Research Quarterly* 53 (September 2000): 495–522.

26. Rosenstone et al., *Third Parties in America*, 257.

27. Adam Clymer, "For Third Parties, a Chance to Play Spoiler or Also-Ran," *New York Times* (12 August 2000), A1.

28. David Barstow, "Nader Assails His Exclusion From Debates," *New York Times* (2 October 2000): A24; Michael Janofsky, "The Road Less Traveled," *New York Times* (6 August 2000): 5; Clymer, "For Third Parties, a Chance To Play Spoiler or Also-Ran."

29. In a postelection survey conducted by John McLaughlin and Associates, 41.7 percent of Nader voters reported supporting him because they "didn't like [the] other candidates." See Appendix.

30. Richard Winger, "Institutional Obstacles to a Multiparty System," in Paul S. Herrnson and John C. Green, eds., *Multiparty Politics in America* (Lanham Md.: Rowman & Littlefield, 1997), 159–171.

31. Collet and Wattenberg, "Strategically Unambitious: Minor Party and Independent Candidates in the 1996 Congressional Elections, " 238–239.

32. Winger, "Institutional Obstacles to a Multiparty System." The major parties continue to make life difficult for minor party candidates. For example, in 1997, the Pennsylvania State Legislature passed legislation making it even more difficult for minor party and independent candidates to get on the state ballot. Katherine Q. Seelye, "Parties Team Up to Protect Their Turf," *New York Times* (24 June 1997): A12.

33. Leon Epstein, *Political Parties in the American Mold* (Madison, Wisc.: University of Wisconsin Press, 1986), 131.

34. August 2000 survey conducted by John McLaughlin and Associates for this book. See Appendix.

35. Beck, *Party Politics in America*, 38–42.

36. Rosenstone et al., *Third Parties in America*, 267–268.

37. New York election law makes the Conservatives and Liberals (and, more recently, the Right to Life antiabortion party) potential power brokers since, as an alternative to placing their own adherents on the ballot, they can nominate the candidates of a major party to run under their labels instead, thus encouraging the major parties and their nominees to court them assiduously.

38. David E. Price, *Bringing Back the Parties* (Washington, D.C.: Congressional Quarterly Press, 1984), 36–38.

39. The precise current party committee names are: the Democratic Congressional Campaign Committee, the National Republican Congressional Committee, the Democratic Senatorial Campaign Committee, and the National Republican Senatorial Committee.

40. John F. Bibby, *Politics, Parties, and Elections*, 4th ed. (Belmont, Calif.: Wadsworth Publishing, 2000), 111.

41. Philip A. Klinkner, *The Losing Parties: Out Party National Committees, 1956–1993* (New Haven, Conn.: Yale University Press, 1994).

42. Bob Woodward and Ruth Marcus, "Agendas Detail Use of DNC Ads To Help Clinton," *Washington Post* (18 September 1997), A1, A9; John F. Bibby, *Politics, Parties, and Elections*, 4th ed. (Belmont, Calif.: Wadsworth Publishing, 2000), 114.

43. Clinton actually appointed DNC co-chairs in 1994: Fowler, the national chair, who managed the day-to-day party activities, and Senator Christopher Dodd (D-Conn.), the general chair, who served as the party's public spokesperson. Clinton appointed co-chairs again in 1996, naming Colorado governor Roy Roemer as DNC general chair and Massachusetts Democratic Party leader Steve Grossman as national chair.

44. Richard L. Berke, "Democrats See a Party Adrift As Presidential Loss Sinks In," *New York Times* (February 16, 2001), A1, A16.

45. Barbra Murray, "The Torch Is Passed," *Congressional Quarterly's Guide to the 2000 Democratic National Convention* (12 August 2000): 75–77.

46. Price, *Bringing Back the Parties*, 275–279.

47. Ibid., 264–290.

48. Democratic Policy Commission, "New Choices in a Changing America" (Washington, D.C.: Democratic National Committee, September 1986).

49. Klinkner, *The Losing Parties*, 191.

50. Ibid., 194–195.

51. Price, *Bringing Back the Parties*, 38–40; Elaine Ciulla Kamarck and Kenneth M. Goldstein, "The Rules Do Matter: Post-Reform Presidential Nominating Politics," in L. Sandy Maisel, ed., *The Parties Respond: Changes in American Parties and Campaigns*, 2nd ed. (Boulder, Colo.: Westview Press, 1994). Andrew E. Busch, *Outsiders and Openness in the Presidential Nominating System* (Pittsburgh: University of Pittsburgh Press, 1997).

52. For an excellent discussion of groups in each party's network, see John F. Bibby, "Party Networks: National-State Integration, Allied Groups, and Issue Activists," in Daniel M. Shea and John C. Green, eds., *The State of the Parties: The Changing Role of Contemporary American Parties*, 3rd ed. (Lanham, Md.: Rowman & Littlefield, 1999).

53. Bibby, *Politics, Parties, and Elections in America*, 130–131.

54. Sidney Blumenthal, "Outside Foundation Recruited the Inside Troops," *Washington Post*, September 24, 1985, A1, A10.

55. Kenneth Finegold, *Experts and Politicians: Reform Challenges to Machine Politics in New York, Cleveland, and Chicago* (Princeton, N.J.: Princeton University Press, 1995); James Q. Wilson, *The Amateur Democrat: Club Politics in Three Cities* (Chicago: University of Chicago Press, 1962).

56. Richard E. Cohen, "Democratic Leadership Council sees Party void and is ready to fill it," *National Journal* 18 (1 February 1986): 267. Jon F. Hale, "The Democratic Leadership Council: Institutionalizing a Party Faction," in Daniel M. Shea and John C. Green, eds., *The State of the Parties: The Changing Role of Contemporary American Parties*, 1st ed. (Lanham, Md.: Rowman & Littlefield, 1994).

57. Dom Bonafede, "Kirk at the DNC's Helm," *National Journal* 18 (22 March 1986): 703–707.

58. Jon F. Hale, "The Democratic Leadership Council: Institutionalizing a Party Faction," in Daniel M. Shea and John C. Green, eds., *The State of the Parties: The Changing Role of Contemporary American Parties*, 1st ed. (Lanham, Md.: Rowman & Littlefield, 1994), 255.

59. Ibid.

60. Hale, "Democratic Leadership Council."

61. Gore and Gephardt were founding members of the DLC, and Lieberman chaired the DLC from 1995–2000.

62. David W. Rohde, *Parties and Leaders in the Postreform House* (Chicago: University of Chicago Press; 1991); Barbara Sinclair, *Legislators, Leaders, and Lawmaking: The U.S. House of Representatives in the Postreform Era* (Baltimore: Johns Hopkins University Press, 1995). John H. Aldrich and David W. Rohde, "The Transition to Republican Rule in the House: Implications for Theories of Congressional Politics," *Political Science Quarterly* 112 (1997–1998): 541–67. Barbara Sinclair, "Evolution or Revolution? Policy-oriented Congressional Parties in the 1990s," in L. Sandy Maisel, ed., *The Parties Respond: Changes in Parties and Campaigns*, 3rd ed. (Boulder, Colo.: Westview Press, 1998).

63. Rohde, *Parties and Leaders in the Postreform House;* Sinclair, *Legislators, Leaders, and Lawmaking.*

64. Larry J. Sabato, *PAC Power: Inside the World of Political Action Committees* (New York: Norton, 1985), 116; Barbara Salmore and Steve Salmore, *Candidates, Parties, and Elections*, 2nd ed. (Washington, D.C.: Congressional Quarterly Press, 1989), 268–269; Bruce A. Larson, "Ambition and Money in the U.S. House of Representatives: Analyzing Campaign Contributions from Incumbents' Leadership PACs and Reelection Committees" (Ph.D. diss., University of Virginia, 1998); Paul S. Herrnson, "Money and Motives: Spending in House Elections," in *Congress Reconsidered,* edited by Lawrence C. Dodd and Bruce I. Oppenheimer, 6th ed. (Washington, D.C.: Congressional Quarterly Press, 1997); Clyde Wilcox, "Share the Wealth: Contributions by Congressional Incumbents to the Campaigns of Other Candidates." *American Politics Quarterly* 17 (October 1989): 386–408. Ross K. Baker, *The New Fat Cats: Members of Congress as Political Benefactors* (New York: Priority Press Publications, 1989). Chuck Alston, "Members with Cash-on-Hand Reach Out to Help Others." *Congressional Quarterly Weekly Report* (28 September 1991): 2763.

65. Such cases are few, but a deterrent nonetheless. Several United States senators were expelled from the Republican caucus in 1925 for having supported the Progressive candidate for president the previous year. In 1965, two southern House Democrats lost all their committee seniority because of their 1964 endorsement of GOP presidential nominee Barry Goldwater, as did another southerner in 1968 for his backing of George Wallace's third-party candidacy. In early 1983, the House Democratic caucus removed Texas Congressman Phil Gramm from his Budget Committee seat because of his disloyalty in working more closely with Republican Committee members than his own party leaders. (Gramm resigned his seat, was reelected to it as a Republican, and used the controversy to propel himself into the United States Senate in 1984.) In 1995, Wisconsin Republican Mark Neumann, a constant thorn in the side of the GOP House leadership, was demoted by the GOP leadership to a considerably less influential subcommittee on the Appropriations Committee than the one he had previously occupied. See Philip D. Duncan and Christine C. Lawrence, *Politics in America, 1998: The 105th Congress* (Washington, D.C.: Congressional Quarterly Press, 1997), 1571–1572.

66. Indeed, Neumann's class of 1994 colleagues complained loudly when he was demoted by the GOP leadership, and Neumann was subsequently awarded a plum slot on the Budget Committee. Duncan and Lawrence, *Politics in America*, 1571–1572.

67. See Julius Turner (with Edward V. Schneier, Jr.), *Party and Constituency: Pressures on Congress* (Baltimore: Johns Hopkins Press, 1970), 33–39.

68. Price, *Bringing Back the Parties*, 51–53.

69. See *Congressional Quarterly Weekly Report* 54 (27 January 1996): 199–201.

70. Rohde, *Parties and Leaders in the Postreform House*, Chapters 3 and 6.

71. Jewell and Morehouse, *Political Parties and Elections in American States*.

72. Joseph A. Schlesinger, "The New American Political Party," *American Political Science Review* 79 (1985): 1168.

73. Sara Brandes Crook and John R. Hibbing, "Congressional Reform and Party Discipline: The Effects of Changes in the Seniority System on Party Loyalty in the House of Representatives." *British Journal of Political Science* 15 (1985): 207–226.

74. Aspin survived the challenge to his power, but only after a bitter struggle in the Democratic Caucus. Rohde, *Parties and Leaders in the Postreform House*, 72–75.

75. See Ibid., Chapters 2, 3, and 4 for an excellent in-depth discussion of these reforms.

76. Timothy E. Cook, "The Electoral Connection in the 99th Congress," *PS: Political Science*, 19 (Winter 1986): 19–20.

77. Price, *Bringing Back the Parties*, 64–69.

78. Elizabeth Garret, "The Congressional Budget Process: Strengthening the Party-in-Government," *Columbia Law Review* 100 (April 2000): 702–730; Allen Schick, *Reconciliation and the Congressional Budget Process* (Washington, D.C.: American Enterprise Institute for Public Policy Research, 1981). Sinclair, *Legislators, Leaders, and Lawmaking*, 183–188.

79. Price, *Bringing Back the Parties*, 67. Sinclair, *Legislators, Leaders, and Lawmaking*, 72–73.

80. Rohde, *Parties and Leaders in the Postreform House*.

81. This discussion draws heavily from Lawrence C. Evans and Walter J. Oleszek, "Congressional Tsunami? The Politics of Committee Reform," in Lawrence C. Dodd and Bruce I. Oppenheimer, eds., *Congress Reconsidered*, 6th ed., (Washington, D.C.: Congressional Quarterly Press, 1997).

82. Julie Hirschfield, "Power Plays and Term Limits," *Congressional Quarterly Weekly Report* (11 November 2000): 2656; Karen Foerstel, "Choosing Chairmen: Tradition's Role Fades," *Congressional Quarterly Weekly Report* (9 December 2000): 2796–2801.

83. Rohde, *Parties and Leaders in the Postreform House*.

84. William F. Connolly and John J. Pitney, Jr., *Congress' Permanent Minority? Republicans in the U.S. House* (Lanham, Md.: Littlefield Adams, 1994).

85. Jackie Koszczuk, "Effort to Cut Deal In Gingrich Case Leaves Ethics Process in Turmoil," *Congressional Quarterly Weekly Report* (11 January 1997): 111–116; Jackie Koszczuk, "Coup Attempt Throws GOP Off Legislative Track," *Congressional Quarterly Weekly Report* (19 July 1997): 1671–1674.

86. In 1997, for example, GOP conference chair John Boehner (R-Ohio) sued Democratic Jim McDermott (D-Wash.) for releasing to the media a taped

cellular phone conversation between numerous House GOP leaders. Philip D. Duncan and Christine C. Lawrence, *Politics in America, 1998: The 105th Congress* (Washington, D.C.: Congressional Quarterly Press, 1997), 1132.

87. *Congressional Quarterly Weekly Report* (22 December 1998): 3372.
88. Damon Chappie, "Majority Whip Opens Legal Defense Fund," *Roll Call* (24 July 2000): 3; John Bresnahan, "Delay Files Motion to Dismiss DCCC's Racketeering Suit," *Roll Call* (18 September 2000): 30.
89. Karen Foerstel, "The Limits of Outreach," *Congressional Quarterly Weekly Report* (11 November 2000): 2649.
90. Karen Foerstel, "Gephardt's Charge," *Congressional Quarterly Weekly Report* (4 November 2000): 2581.
91. But see Sidney Milkis's argument that Roosevelt purposely weakened the role of parties by institutionalizing programs in the executive branch. Sidney Milkis, *The President and the Parties: The Transformation of the American Party System Since the New Deal* (New York: Oxford, 1993).
92. See Fred I. Greenstein, *The Hidden-Hand Presidency* (New York: Basic Books, 1982).
93. *National Journal* 18 (11 October 1986): 2397.
94. Ibid.
95. Rhodes Cook, "Reagan Nurtures His Adopted Party to Strength," *Congressional Quarterly Weekly Report* 43 (28 September 1985): 1927–1930.
96. David S. Broder, "A Party's Soldier," *Washington Post*, 20 October 1985, C7.
97. Ibid.
98. Cook, "Reagan Nurtures His Adopted Party," 1927–1928.
99. *Washington Post*, November 3, 1986, A10, and November 5, 1986, A21.
100. Broder, "A Party's Soldier." Broder cites the case of Oregon Senator Robert Packwood, often a caustic critic of Reagan's, who asked for and received the first presidential media reelection endorsement of the 1986 campaign season.
101. Cook, "Reagan Nurtures His Adopted Party," 1930.
102. Norman C. Thomas and Joseph A. Pika, *The Politics of the Presidency*, 4th ed. (Washington, D.C.: Congressional Quarterly Press, 1997), 132.
103. Ibid.
104. Marc Lacey, "Noncandidate Clinton's Steady Refrain: I Believe in Fund-Raising," *New York Times* (25 September 2000): A22.
105. Sidney M. Milkis, "The Presidents and the Parties," in Michael Nelson, ed., *The Presidency and the Political System*, 5th ed. (Washington, D.C.: Congressional Quarterly Press, 1998), 399.
106. Milkis, "The Presidents and the Parties," 399; Brooks Jackson, "Financing the 1996 Campaign: The Law of the Jungle," in Larry J. Sabato, *Toward the Millennium: The Elections of 1996* (Boston: Allyn and Bacon, 1997), 247.
107. The GOP picked up just fifteen House seats and lost two Senate seats in 1984; in 1972 the tally was similar, with a gain of twelve House seats and a loss of two Senate berths.
108. Gary C. Jacobson, *The Politics of Congressional Elections*, 4th ed. (New York: Longman, 1997), 149.
109. Jacobson, *The Politics of Congressional Elections*, 128–134. George C. Edwards III, *Presidential Influence in Congress* (San Francisco: Freeman, 1980); Herbert M. Kritzer and Robert B. Eubank, "Presidential Coattails Revisited:

Partisanship and Incumbency Effects," *American Journal of Political Science* 23 (1979): 615–626.

110. Lyn Ragsdale, "The Fiction of Congressional Elections as Presidential Events," *American Politics Quarterly* 8 (1980): 375–398; Thomas E. Mann and Raymond E. Wolfinger, "Candidates and Parties in Congressional Elections," *American Political Science Review* 74 (1980): 617–632.

111. Beck, *Party Politics in America*, 350.

112. Ibid.

113. Ibid.

114. See Sidney Ulmer, "The Political Party Variable on the Michigan Supreme Court,"*Journal of Public Law* 11 (1962): 352–362; Stuart Nagel, "Political Party Affiliation and Judges' Decisions, *American Political Science Review* 55 (1961): 843–850; David W. Adamany, "The Party Variable in Judges' Voting: Conceptual Notes and a Case Study," *American Political Science Review* 63 (1969): 57–73; Sheldon Goldman, "Voting Behavior on the United States Courts of Appeals, 1961–1964," *American Political Science Review* 60 (1966): 374–383; Robert A. Carp and C. K. Rowland, *Policymaking and Politics in the Federal District Courts* (Knoxville: University of Tennessee Press, 1983). Randall D. Lloyd, "Separating Partisanship from Party in Judicial Research: Reapportionment in the U.S. Courts," *American Political Science Review* 89 (1995), 413–420.

115. Thomas and Pika, *The Politics of the Presidency*, 4th ed., 297.

116. Herbert Jacob, "Courts: The Least Visible Branch," in Virginia Gray and Herbert Jacob, eds., *Politics in the American States*, 6th ed. (Washington, D.C.: Congressional Quarterly Press, 1996); The figures for judicial elections include Ohio, where state judge candidates must compete in and win a partisan primary election in order to gain access to the nonpartisan general election ballot.

117. Beck, *Party Politics in America*, 351.

118. 321 U.S. 649 (1944).

119. See the Ohio cases involving George Wallace (*Williams* v. *Rhodes*, 393 U.S. 23 [1968]) and John Anderson (*Anderson* v. *Celebreeze*, 103 S. Ct. 1564 [1983]). The Court essentially ruled that Ohio and the other states could not discriminate against third-party and Independent presidential candidacies by placing burdensome restrictions on them (early deadlines, substantial signature-gathering requirements, and the like).

120. *Elrod* v. *Burns* 427 U.S. 347 (1976), *Branti* v. *Finkel* 445 U.S. 507 (1980), and *Rutan* v. *Republican Party of Illinois* (1990). See also Clifton McCleskey, "Parties at the Bar: Equal Protection, Freedom of Association, and the Rights of Political Organizations," *Journal of Politics* 46 (1984): 346–368.

121. *Branti* v. *Finkel*, ibid., at 526–529.

122. *Cousins* v. *Wigoda*, 419 U.S. 477 (1975) and *Democratic Party* v. *La Follette*, 450 U.S. 107 (1981). The former is the Illinois case; the latter is the Wisconsin case.

123. 107 S. Ct. 544 (1986). See Elder Witt and Jeremy Gaunt, "Closed Primary Laws Barred by 5–4 Supreme Court Ruling," *Congressional Quarterly Weekly Report* 16 (December 13, 1986): 3064–3065.

124. 109 S. Ct. 1013 (1989).

125. *Timmons* v. *Twin Cities New Party* (1997). In this case, the Minnesota state election commission prohibited Minnesota's New Party from nominating a state legislative already nominated by the state Democratic party.
126. Ibid.
127. *California Democratic Party* v. *Jones*, No. 99–401 (2000).
128. *Colorado Federal Campaign Committee* v. *Federal Election Commission*, 116 S. Ct. 2309 (1996). Interestingly, two Justices in the case—Scalia and Thomas—argued that federal limits on party coordinated expenditures are also unconstitutional, leaving the door open for a further deregulation of parties in the arena of campaign finance.
129. Susan B. Glassner, "Court's Ruling in Colorado Case May Reshape Campaign Finance," *Washington Post* (28 March 1999): A6. The FEC has already announced its intention to appeal the ruling.
130. The Farmer-Labor party did survive in a sense; having endured a series of defeats, it merged in 1944 with the Democrats, and Democratic candidates still officially bear the standard of the Democratic-Farmer-Labor (DFL) party. At about the same time, also having suffered severe electoral reversals, the Progressives stopped nominating candidates in Wisconsin. The party's members either returned to the Republican party, from which it had split off early in the century, or became Democrats.
131. Beck, *Party Politics in America*, 341; Alan Rosenthal, *The Decline of Representative Democracy: Process, Participation, and Power in State Legislatures* (Washington, D.C.: Congressional Quarterly Press, 1998), 299; Sarah McNally Morehouse, *The Governor as Party Leader* (Ann Arbor, Mich.: University of Michigan Press, 1998).
132. Thad Beyle, "Governors: The Middlemen and Women in Our Political System," in Virginia Gray and Herbert Jacob, eds., *Politics in the American States*, 6th ed. (Washington, D.C.: Congressional Quarterly Press, 1996), 241. Beck, *Party Politics in America*, 341; Alan Rosenthal, *The Decline of Representative Democracy: Process, Participation, and Power in State Legislatures* (Washington, D.C.: Congressional Quarterly Press, 1998), 298.
133. Thad Beyle, "Governors: The Middlemen and Women in Our Political System, "in Virginia Gray and Herbert Jacob, eds., *Politics in the American States*, 6th ed. (Washington, D.C.: Congressional Quarterly Press, 1996), 233. Larry Sabato, *Goodbye to Good-Time Charlie: The American Governorship Transformed*, 2nd ed. (Washington, D.C.: Congressional Quarterly, 1983), 76–77.
134. Malcolm E. Jewell and Marcia Lynn Whicker, *Legislative Leadership in the American States* (Ann Arbor: University of Michigan Press, 1994), 68.
135. Thad Beyle, "Governors: The Middlemen and Women in Our Political System,"in Virginia Gray and Herbert Jacob, eds., *Politics in the American States*, 6th ed. (Washington, D.C.: Congressional Quarterly Press, 1996), 187. Malcolm E. Jewell and Marcia Lynn Whicker, *Legislative Leadership in the American States* (Ann Arbor: University of Michigan Press, 1994), 69. Rosenthal, *The Decline of Representative Democracy*, 299.
136. Rosenthal, *The Decline of Representative Democracy*, 299–300.
137. Samuel C. Patterson, "Legislative Politics in the States," in Gray and Jacob, *Politics in the American States*, 193.
138. Ibid.

139. Malcolm E. Jewell and Sarah M. Morehouse, *Political Parties and Elections in American States*, 4th ed. (Washington, D.C.: Congressional Quarterly Press, 2001), 250.
140. Sarah McCally Morehouse, "Legislatures and Political Parties," *State Government* 59: 1 (1976): 19–24.
141. Jewell and Whicker, *Legislative Leadership in the American States*, 91.
142. Samuel C. Patterson, "Legislative Politics in the States," in Gray and Jacob, *Politics in the American States*, 188.
143. Jewell and Whicker, *Legislative Leadership in the American States*, 101.
144. Anthony Gierzynski, *Legislative Party Campaign Committees in the American States* (Lexington: University of Kentucky Press, 1992); Daniel M. Shea, *Transforming Democracy: Legislative Campaign Committees and Political Parties* (Albany, N.Y.: SUNY Press, 1995).
145. Jewell and Whicker, *Legislative Leadership in the American States*, 101.

The Rise of Service-Oriented Party Organizations

THE GREAT IRONY of modern American political parties is that as the party-in-the-electorate has ebbed and flowed (as we discuss in the next chapter), both party organizations have grown increasingly mightier. Not long ago, there was hope among strong-party advocates that strengthened party organizations would help restore the tie between voters and parties. Indeed, the very technologies that enable candidates to run independently of their parties have created immense opportunities for the parties to bring candidates and voters back to their moorings. Candidates are now supplied with party funds and election services unparalleled in sophistication and quality, and the parties' increasing use of "soft" money has allowed them to involve themselves even more heavily in their candidates' campaigns.[1] But reinvigorated party involvement in American political campaigns has not served to make campaigns party-centered. Rather, the parties have carved out a role for themselves in a system of candidate-centered campaigns, and the bulk of party activities are designed not to bolster the party label but rather to ensure that the party's candidates succeed in a candidate-centered system. Certainly, the new widespread use of soft money-financed "issue advocacy" campaigns by the parties has afforded them greater influence in shaping campaign issue agendas. But rare is the party-sponsored issue ad that even mentions party labels.[2] It should come as no surprise, therefore, that the growing strength of party organizations has been associated with smaller gains in party loyalty among voters than might be expected.

THE PARTIES AND CAMPAIGN FINANCE

A review of the existing campaign finance framework will set the stage for our dissection of the resurgence of party organization strength. For an understanding of how these laws have affected the parties is a necessary precondition to comprehending the changes in party activity that have occurred. A thorough discussion of the massive overhaul in campaign finance from 1971 to 1979 is beyond our scope here,[3] but it is worth noting that the reformers in and out of Congress who spearheaded the changes did not purposely set out to harm the parties—though neither was party building one of their goals. In the rush to correct the abuses apparent during the Watergate scandals, the political parties were often treated as part of the problem, and the parties have had to adapt as best they could to a system not of their own making.

Laws governing party campaign finance in federal elections are the combination of three realms of lawmaking: amendments to the Federal Election Campaign Act (FECA) passed by Congress in 1974, 1976, and 1979; advisory opinions issued by the Federal Election Commission (FEC); and several federal court rulings. The early FECA Amendments (1974 and 1976) restricted both contributions *to* political parties and contributions and expenditures made *by* the parties to help their candidates. Limits on contributions to the parties were strict. The new laws limited to $20,000 per year the amount that an individual could contribute to a national party committee and to $15,000 per year the amount that a political action committee (PAC) could contribute to a national party committee. Any funds given to or spent on behalf of a federal candidate by state political parties had to be raised within these guidelines. Unfortunately, none of these limits were indexed to inflation, leaving the parties—forced to keep up with the ever-increasing costs of campaigns—in the precarious position of having to raise greater and greater sums of money under static contribution limits. On the bright side, the new legislation exempted donations to party "building funds"—accounts to pay for the construction of new party offices—from contribution limits.[4]

The new laws were equally burdensome in restricting the aid that parties could give *to* their candidates. The 1974 FECA amendments permitted each national, congressional, and state political party to contribute $5,000 per candidate per election to federal candidates. The 1976

FECA amendments raised to $17,500 per election the combined total that the national party committees and senatorial campaign committees may give to Senate candidates. (State party committees could add another $10,000, for a total of $27,500 in direct party gifts to Senate candidates.) Fortunately for the parties, the FECA amendments permitted direct contributions to be significantly augmented with *coordinated expenditures*—party-paid general election campaign expenditures (for television advertising, polling, etc.) made in consultation and coordination with the candidate. The coordinated expenditure limits were set surprisingly high. In the case of presidential candidates, the national party committees can spend up to two cents times the nation's voting age population (plus an adjustment for inflation); in 1996, this amounted to about $12 million.[5] For House candidates, the national and state parties may each spend $10,000 plus an inflation adjustment;[6] for 2000, the inflation-indexed limit reached $33,780.[7] Senate candidates are the beneficiaries of even higher limits on coordinated expenditures. The national and state parties can each spend $20,000 (plus an inflation factor) or two cents times the state's voting age population (plus inflation), whichever is greater. In 2000, the party expenditure limits ranged from $135,120 in Delaware to $3,272,876 in California.[8] Importantly, a national party committee is permitted to act as the state party committee's spending agent; that is, with the state party's agreement, the national committee can assume the state party's permitted portion of coordinated expenditures. By the mid-1990s, both national parties were assuming approximately 70 percent of the spending power of their state party affiliates.[9] This privilege centralizes power in the national committees and unburdens weaker state party committees that otherwise might not be able to contribute the maximum. Besides being indexed for inflation, party coordinated expenditures differ from direct contributions in that they can only be made for the general election.[10] The parties have taken on an informal division of labor. Congressional contests are the primary responsibility of the four congressional campaign (or "Hill") committees—the Democratic Congressional Campaign Committee (DCCC), the National Republican Congressional Committee (NRCC), the Democratic Senatorial Campaign Committee (DSCC), and the National Republican Senatorial Committee (NRSC)—whereas the Democratic and Republican National Committees have focused largely on presidential contests, state and local party building, and, to a lesser extent, specific gubernatorial and state legislative contests.[11] Although this division of responsibilities makes perfect sense, it has sometimes led to competition for funds between a party's national and congressional committees.[12]

Recent federal court decisions have given parties additional leeway in how they may spend money on their candidates. In *Colorado Republican Federal Campaign Committee* v. *Federal Election Commission* (1996), the Supreme Court ruled that parties enjoy the same First Amendment protections as do individuals and PACs in making independent expenditures on behalf of or against political candidates.[13] The effect of the Court's decision is to allow parties to spend unlimited sums of hard (regulated) money on campaign materials that expressly advocate the election or defeat of a specific federal candidate—so long as the spending is done independently of any federal candidate's campaign.[14] Critics of the Court's decision wondered aloud how parties could ever make expenditures that are truly independent of the candidates they spend countless hours working with. The NRSC responded to the Court's decision by immediately setting up an independent spending committee across town from its main headquarters in Washington, D.C. More recently, and perhaps more importantly, a federal court in Colorado held that federal limits on party-coordinated expenditures are also unconstitutional—a ruling that promises to end up before the Supreme Court.[15] If the Supreme Court ultimately upholds the lower federal court's ruling on party coordinated expenditures, the campaign financing role of political parties in the United States will be enhanced considerably.

With campaign costs far outpacing inflation, the contribution limits set by Congress in the 1974 and 1976 FECA amendments were not generous. The new campaign finance laws, moreover, were particularly destructive of political party roles in presidential contests. Party organizations in the United States typically involved themselves in presidential campaigns by footing the bill for grassroots activities and campaign paraphernalia—campaign buttons, yard signs, bumper stickers, get-out-the-vote drives, generic party advertisements, and the like. However, because these party-building expenditures indirectly benefited federal candidates, they were now subject to the FECA's tough new restrictions. The result, which party leaders rightly complained about, was a greatly reduced role for state and local political parties in presidential elections. Congress responded in 1979 by passing an amendment to the FECA that exempted party grassroots activities from the FECA's expenditure limits. Any portion of such expenditures that indirectly benefited federal candidates would still have to paid for with "hard" money (that is, money raised under the FECA guidelines).[16] But exempting grassroots activities from federal expenditure limits would at least help to restore the role of state and local parties in national elections.

The federal campaign finance laws passed during the 1970s applied only to political party activities in federal elections. But parties, of course,

play a role in nonfederal elections as well, and many party activities—
such as get-out-the-vote drives—are designed to bolster the entire party
ticket (federal *and* nonfederal candidates). The federalist nature of American parties, combined with state campaign finance laws that tend to be
more lenient than those at the federal level, thus presented a vexing problem for federal regulators. Can party activities that benefit the entire ticket
be paid for with money raised under typically lenient state regulations,
or must they be paid for using money raised under restrictive federal
guidelines? From the Federal Election Commission's answer to this question was born the distinction between "hard" and "soft" money—that is,
between money raised under "hard" federal guidelines and money raised
under "soft" state regulations.[17] In a series of advisory opinions, the Federal Election Commission ruled that state parties could pay for activity
and overhead expenses using a combination of hard and soft dollars, with
hard dollars paying for the federal share of party expenses and soft money
paying for the nonfederal share.[18] (Parties had the option of several different formulas in determining what the federal and nonfederal share of
their expenses were.) Not surprisingly, the national parties argued that
they too should be able to use unregulated money to pay for their nonfederal expenditures.[19] By the 1980 election cycle, the national committees
began raising significant sums of soft money, which they used to pay for
the nonfederal portions of their administrative, overhead, and grassroots
party activities. In 1991, the FEC issued new regulations dealing with the
flow of party soft money. Besides providing a complicated set of instruc-
tions on how parties must determine their federal and nonfederal
expenses,[20] the 1991 regulations required the national parties to report all
soft money contributions to the Federal Election Commission, resulting
in the first official data on how much soft money the national parties were
raising and who was donating it. Today, soft money plays an integral role
in the financing of party activities, with state party committees increasingly conducting their grassroots party efforts with soft money transferred
to them by the national party committees.[21] This development has
changed the balance of power in the party system from one in which state
and local parties held much of the power to one in which the national
committees are the dominant power brokers. It has also become common
for national and state party committees to engage in "money swaps,"
whereby the national committee reimburses a state party committee in
soft money for hard money expenditures made by the state party in a specific congressional contest.[22] To the dismay of campaign finance reform
advocates, new uses of soft money seem to emerge in each new election.
Taking advantage of a narrow, judicially constructed definition of election
advocacy, the parties have increasingly used soft money to finance party

activities that are quite transparently designed to influence the elections of specific federal candidates. We address this issue more thoroughly later in the chapter.

Table 3.1 shows that, for both hard and soft dollars, the national, congressional, and senatorial campaign committees continue to shatter fundraising records. As we would expect, given the division of labor among the parties, national party committee fundraising clearly ebbs and flows depending on whether there is a presidential contest. While large (in some cases six-figure) contributions make up the bulk of the national parties' soft money accounts, it's worth noting that considerable sums of hard money collected by the national committees are solicited through direct mail and given in increments of $100 or less.[23] For the Hill committees, the story is one of almost constant growth, with the committees raising greater amounts of both hard and soft dollars in every election cycle. Importantly, the table shows that soft money—raised in record amounts in 2000—continues to make up greater and greater percentages of each party committee's overall receipts. The explanation for parties' increased reliance on unregulated money is straightforward: campaigns have become more and more expensive, partisan competition remains intense, and the parties are forced to raise hard dollars under contribution limits set during the 1970s and never indexed for inflation. Finally, Table 3.1 also illustrates that, almost without exception, GOP committees continue to outraise their Democratic party counterparts in both hard and soft dollars. (At the time this book went to press, Congress was considering reform legislation that would prohibit the national parties from raising soft money.)

SERVICE-ORIENTED NATIONAL PARTIES: ONE-STOP SHOPPING FOR PARTY CANDIDATES

As we would expect, the national parties, especially the Hill committees, spend considerable sums of money on their candidates. Before the 1996 election, such expenditures typically came in one of two forms: direct contributions and coordinated expenditures. Not surprisingly, the parties decidedly favor coordinated expenditures over direct contributions. Coordinated expenditure limits are higher than are direct contribution limits, and coordinated expenditures allow the party greater involvement in a candidate's campaign than do direct contributions. Coordinated expenditures also allow the national parties to take advantage of agency agreements with state committees.[24]

Additional expenditure options have become available to the parties in recent years. As noted above, the Supreme Court ruled in 1996

TABLE 3.1. NATIONAL POLITICAL PARTY HARD AND SOFT MONEY RECEIPTS, 1989–2000 (IN MILLIONS).

| | *National Committees* | | | | *National Congressional Campaign Committees* | | | | *National Senatorial Campaign Committees* | | | |
| | *DNC* | | *RNC* | | *DCCC* | | *NRCC* | | *DSCC* | | *NRSC* | |
	Hard	Soft	Hard	Soft	Hard	Soft	Hard	Soft	Hard	Soft	Hard	Soft
89-90[a]	14.4	***	68.7	***	9.1	***	33.2	***	17.5	***	65.0	***
91-92	65.8	31.3	85.4	35.9	12.8	4.3	35.2	6.1	25.4	0.6	73.8	9.1
93-94	41.8	43.9	87.3	44.8	19.4	5.1	26.7	7.4	26.4	0.4	65.3	5.6
95-96	108.3	101.9	193.0	113.1	26.6	12.3	74.2	18.5	30.8	14.2	64.5	29.4
97-98	64.8	57.0	104.0	74.8	25.2	16.8	72.7	26.9	35.6	25.9	53.4	37.8
99-00[b]	103.9	106.2	177.3	138.9	35.1	49.2	84.8	41.1	34.1	52.3	43.2	37.6

Source: Federal Election Commission

[a]Federal regulations did not require the national party committees to disclose soft money receipts until the 1991–92 election cycle.
[b]Figures for 1999-2000 are through October 18, 2000.

that political parties enjoy the same First Amendment protections as do individuals and PACs to make independent expenditures (financed with hard money) on behalf of or against political candidates. Thus far, however, the national parties have taken little advantage of this opportunity.[25] Rather, the parties' medium of choice has more and more become "issue-advocacy" expenditures—typically in the form of television advertisements.[26] Unambiguously designed to promote the election or defeat of specific federal candidates, issue advocacy ads fall just short of the Supreme Court's narrow test of election ("express") advocacy by carefully avoiding specific terms (such as "vote for" or "vote against") that expressly urge viewers to support or oppose a candidate at the polls. A 1998 issue ad run by the Democratic Senatorial Campaign Committee against GOP Senate candidate John Ensign is illustrative:

> Ad Narrator: In Nevada, John Ensign says he cares about seniors, but his record in Washington shows he couldn't care less. Tell John Ensign, 'Stop trying to fool Nevada voters.'

Since such ads do not (according to the Court's standard) technically advocate the election or defeat of a federal candidate, they may be financed in part with soft money raised outside of federal contribution limits. (In reality, the national parties and Hill committees typically transfer soft money to state party committees, which conduct the issue advocacy campaigns according to the dictates of the national committee that transferred the funds.)[27] The parties' discovery of the issue advocacy loophole has spurred them to raise ever-increasing sums of soft money—much of it in five- and six-figure donations—from interest groups, corporations, and wealthy individuals. Following the lead of the national parties, interest groups—and more recently several congressional party leaders—have also begun spending large sums of unregulated soft money on issue-advocacy ads.[28] For the parties, the choice of issue-advocacy expenditures over independent (express-advocacy) expenditures is straightforward. Whereas independent expenditures must be paid for with hard money raised under restrictive federal guidelines, issue-advocacy ads may be financed, at least partially, with soft money raised by the parties in unlimited sums.

The widespread use of party issue-advocacy ads designed to help the parties' respective presidential candidates occurred for the first time during the 1996 presidential elections.[29] The DNC spent millions of dollars on ads relentlessly attacking the "Dole-Gingrich" team. (That Gingrich was not actually on the presidential ticket was probably lost on most viewers!) The RNC countered by spending millions on commercials explicitly attacking Clinton's record. In the 2000 presidential elections, the two national parties spent record amounts of soft money on issue-advocacy ads designed to help their respective presidential candidates. Indeed, a study by the Brennan Center for Justice at New York University Law School reported that, between June 1 and September 20 of the election year, the two national committees had spent at least $52 million on issue-advocacy ads—more than twice as much as the Bush and Gore campaigns had spent on their own TV commercials during that period.[30] Among the Hill committees, one of the most prominent issue advocacy campaigns was the NRCC's 1998 "Operation Breakout."[31] Attempting to defend its House majority in the 1998 congressional elections, the NRCC conducted a soft money financed issue advocacy assault in thirty-two states—ultimately saturating at least fifty congressional districts with issue ads touting both the achievements of the GOP and the accomplishments of the district's Republican House candidate.[32] Unfortunately for Republicans, however, the ad campaign did little to improve the House GOP's overall electoral fortunes. Indeed, House Democrats actually gained five seats in the House in 1998—the first time in sixty years that the president's party gained House seats in a midterm election. Some observers argue that the soft money used to finance the GOP's anti-Clinton issue advocacy campaign might have been more fruitfully spent on campaign activities, such as direct mail or phone contact, that more effectively target supporters and don't run the risk of energizing opponents.[33] Still, the NRCC's Operation Breakout illustrates the extent to which the Hill committees are willing to employ soft money in modern campaigns. It goes without saying that the new use of party issue advocacy ads has allowed the parties to shape the issue agendas of candidate races to an unprecedented extent.

Parties at all levels remain highly efficient in doling out their resources. Whether making direct contributions, coordinated expenditures, or issue advocacy expenditures, the parties allocate the bulk of their resources in competitive contests, where they are most likely to influence the election outcome. Sure winners and certain losers are the beneficiaries of very little party support.

Besides direct contributions and the various types of candidate-specific expenditures outlined above, party funds are also spent on a dazzling variety of party personnel, activities, and campaign services:[34]

Party Staff. The institutionalization of the national party committees is well illustrated by considerable growth in party staff members during the past three decades. The DNC and RNC, for example, employed well over two hundred people in 1996; the Hill committees typically employ fewer people, though 150 individuals collected paychecks from the NRSC in 1996. Republican party committees in Washington, D.C., have substantially pared down

from their bloated size in the 1980s, when the number of personnel reached wasteful levels.[35] All of the D.C. party committees
have specialized staff divisions for activities such as fundraising,
research, communications, and the like.

Recruiting Candidates. In American politics, most candidates don't
wait for a party to ask them to run for elective office. Rather, individuals who run for public office—especially federal and prominent state offices—are ambitious self-starters who create their own
personal campaign organizations to win nomination and then
general election contests. Moreover, while a few congressional
leaders have taken sides in some select primary contests during
the past few years,[36] the national parties tend to stay out of nomination contests.[37] Still, for offices below the presidency, the
national committees identify and recruit strong candidates who
are a good fit for a particular seat. Much national party recruitment activity takes place in competitive districts or states,
where—with the right candidate—either party has a decent shot
at winning. Good candidates are lured with promises of party
support, support of groups allied with the party, and the possibilities of a victory. The GOP's recruitment efforts—along with
those of GOPAC, a committee run by then-minority leader Newt
Gingrich (R-Ga.)—paid off handsomely in 1994, allowing the
party to run record high numbers of challengers and open-seat
candidates.[38] Parties also sometimes recruit candidates as political sacrificial lambs—that is, not to win an election but merely to
fill the party slot on the ballot, lest the seat go uncontested. Finally,
the national parties and Hill committee sometimes attempt to dis-
suade a candidate from running for the party's nomination, usually in order to pave the way for a candidate the party views as
having a better chance to win the general election. This has even
happened at the presidential level, when the RNC in 1992 actively
sought to discourage insurgent Pat Buchanan from challenging
incumbent George H.W. Bush for the GOP nomination.[39]

Managing Campaigns The national parties and Hill committees provide essential campaign services for their candidates. For example, candidates, campaign managers, and campaign staff can
attend an array of campaign training seminars run by the Hill
committees. Congressional incumbents surely appreciate Hill
committee seminars that focus on staying in touch with the district, using the congressional frank, and explaining votes to constituents back home.[40] During the 2000 election cycle, the NRCC,
in an attempt to polish the media skills of Republican candidates,

organized media training programs in several states.[41] The national committees also involve themselves in campaign training. As political scientist Paul S. Herrnson points out, during the 1998 election cycle, the RNC created campaign management schools in thirty-five states and provided assistance to more than 5,000 Republican activists.[42] The RNC also has its training manuals available for downloading on its web site (www.rnc.org/2000/trainingcatolog. html). Both Hill committees also provide the services of experienced field staff—operatives stationed in key districts and states who maintain close communication between local and national party offices. In addition, the parties aid candidates by hooking them up with political consultants who have long-standing relationships with the parties.[43] No less importantly, the parties also assist candidates with relatively mundane tasks, such as completing forms and disclosure reports required by the Federal Election Commission. At the presidential level, the national parties provide presidential candidates with strategic advice, legal counsel, and public relations aid.[44] Indeed, the DNC and RNC had a large hand in coordinating the Florida recount battles following the extraordinary 2000 presidential election.[45]

Monitoring, Analyzing, and Shaping Voter Opinion: Not surprisingly, the national party and Hill committees are heavily involved in analyzing public opinion and using it in a way that helps their respective partisans. The national party committees commission polls and focus groups to help them form strategic game plans in presidential elections. The national committees also commission polls during the general election and share the results with their presidential candidates, state party committees, and party activists.[46] The congressional and senatorial campaign committees have surveys conducted for congressional candidates involved in tight races. Since the parties buy polls at "wholesale" rates from firms they do business with, they can usually provide them to candidates at a cheaper rate than the candidates could purchase them for themselves.[47] The Hill committees also manage and analyze voluminous spreadsheets of precinct-level voting data for individual congressional districts; the data are used to help candidates construct voter targeting strategies.[48]

Conducting Research. The national parties and Hill committees all spend considerable resources on issue and opposition research. Research conducted by the national committees tends to be general, focusing on the parties' issue stances and the policy positions of presidential candidates.[49] Both national committees distribute party newsletters—packed with helpful information about voter attitudes on important issues—to party leaders, activists, and candidates. Both national committees, moreover, are involved in state party issue development.[50] The Hill committees are heavily involved in conducting issue and opposition research at the individual level for congressional candidates in competitive elections. The committees prepare detailed research reports on their candidates' opponents, analyzing their public statements, votes, and attendance records. Competitive candidates receive "issue packets" from the Hill committees; these packets advise candidates on how to exploit issues to their own advantage.[51] The national parties also develop campaign issue agendas. Most notable among these was the GOP's "Contract with America," a manifesto of ten campaign promises developed by national Republican leaders and signed by 367 GOP House candidates on the Capitol steps a month before the 1994 midterm elections. Although evidence suggests that most voters were unaware of the Contract per se, the document provided GOP challengers with issue positions that effectively exploited public frustration with the Clinton administration.[52] Similar state GOP electoral contracts, developed by the RNC in conjunction with state Republican parties, apparently contributed to GOP state legislative gains in 1994.[53]

Campaign Communications. All of the national parties spend considerable resources on communication efforts. The DCCC and NRCC both operate sophisticated in-house media studios that specialize in the design and production of TV and radio advertisements for their candidates. These services are especially important for non-incumbents, who have difficulty footing the bill for their own media consultants. Satellite technology in each committee's studio allows candidates to beam ads to television stations located in their districts.[54] The senatorial campaign committees provide less help in the areas of advertising design and production, though the Senate committees do advise their candidates on advertising strategy.[55]

Party communications can also come in the form of party institutional advertisements. Since 1978, the Republicans have aired spots designed to the party label rather than any specific candidate. Beginning with the 1980 election, the GOP used institutional advertising to establish basic election themes. "Vote Republican— for a Change" spots attacked the Democratic Congress in 1980. Then-House Speaker Tip O'Neill was lampooned by an actor who ignored all warning signs and drove a car until it ran out of fuel.

("The Democrats are out of gas," surmised the narrator as "Tip" futilely kicked the automobile's tire.) Another ad starred a "real-life" unemployed factory worker from Baltimore, a lifelong Democrat who plaintively asked, "If the Democrats are so good for working people, then how come so many people aren't working?"[56] The Democrats soon realized the benefits of party institutional advertising and greatly stepped up the money devoted to such advertising during the 1992 presidential election.[57] The RNC put a policy twist on party institutional advertising in 1993, when it spent a significant sum of money on radio advertisements criticizing President Clinton's 1993 budget blueprint.[58] Similarly, under chair David Wilhelm, the DNC ran ads to build public support for President Clinton's health care initiative, though the expenditure didn't sit well with congressional Democrats who believed the money would have been better spent supporting Democratic congressional candidates.[59] Since 1996, advertising designed to benefit the party ticket has increasingly taken the form of issue advocacy attack ads, with pure party advertising gradually giving way to ads that contain both generic and candidate-specific components. (See the discussion of party issue-advocacy advertising earlier in this chapter.)

Not surprisingly as we move into the twenty-first century, the national parties and Hill committees each have their own sophisticated web sites. The web sites are packed with information. For example, the RNC web site contains a short history of the committee, a description of its organizational structure, links to the web sites of allied groups and party organizations, party platforms and issue positions, contribution and membership invitations, a chatroom, absentee ballot applications, and attacks on the Democratic party and its candidates. The RNC's web site also allows visitors to view television ads run by the party and to download training manuals on topics such as precinct organization and candidate recruitment.

Fundraising Help. The parties, especially the Hill committees, provide considerable fundraising assistance to their candidates.[60] In addition to helping organize fundraisers, the Hill committees conduct sessions where candidates can meet PAC directors. The candidates also provide candidates with "PAC kits" designed to help candidates negotiate the PAC universe. Especially competitive candidates can sometimes get the Hill committees to loan them their contributor lists. Hill committee leaders also try to steer individual and PAC contributions to candidates in tight contests

by providing contributors with objective information on the status of the races. (The Hill committees also distribute information
on their candidates to the editors of influential newsletters such
as the *Cook Political Report*—a political newsletter devoted to
handicapping congressional contests.) For many important contributors, the Hill committees serve as a cue: backing from a
party's Hill committee signifies that a candidate has a good shot
at success and is worth supporting. Recently, Hill committee leaders have stepped up their efforts to get safe incumbents to contribute to the party's needy candidates and to the Hill committees
themselves. (We address this development further below.) Finally,
the national party committees attempt to steer large contributions
to state party committees,[61] and they also transfer considerable
sums of money directly to state committees (including to state legislative committees). Such funds are often spent by state parties
on activities that benefit federal candidates.[62]

Grass-Roots Activities. Each of the national and Hill committees is
involved in financing and conducting grass-roots activities that
help the entire ticket. For example, both national parties, working
in conjunction with state parties, conduct extensive voter identification and mobilization operations. Since such activities benefit
a party's federal and nonfederal candidates, they may be paid for
with a combination of hard and soft money. In the 1992 election,
the DNC sent roughly $9.5 million to 47 state parties, which used
the money to identify and mobilize Democratic voters. These
efforts were critical to Democrats' success in 1992.[63] In 1996, the
GOP voter mobilization program included 84 million pieces of
direct mail and 14.5 million phone calls designed to boost voter
turnout among Republican voters.[64] Both parties spent record
amounts on grass-roots activities during the 2000 elections.[65]

Party Building. Party-building activities conducted by the national
committees are designed largely to help state and local committees and to produce coordination between the different levels of
parties. For example, the two committees provide field staff to
assist party leaders with strategy. They offer seminars and written materials about an array of political activities to help train
state and local party leaders. In addition, the two national committees have helped to strengthen state and local party fundraising abilities, and they have increasingly provided campaign
assistance to state legislative candidates. Indeed, in 1993, the DNC
opened a new unit, the Democratic Legislative Campaign Com-
mittee(DLCC), "charged with providing strategic services and

financial assistance to Democratic leaders and candidates at the state level."[66] The DLCC has helped to strengthen Democratic legislative campaign committees at the state level. (We discuss the increasing importance of state legislative campaign committees below.) In addition to these services, the national committees assist state and local committees in the areas of redistricting, staff development, computer use, polling and survey data analysis, issue research, and candidate recruitment.

In the 1970s and early 1980s, the Republican party thoroughly outclassed its Democratic rivals in conducting these party-building activities. Much of the initial credit goes to RNC chair Bill Brock, who from 1976–1980 presided over a thorough overhaul of RNC finances and organization. Fueling the RNC's strength under Brock was a hugely successful direct mail program. From a base of just 24,000 names in 1975, for example, the RNC expanded its direct mail list of donors to well over a million in 1980. Besides producing significant sums of money for the GOP, the direct mail program helped build the party's base of grassroots volunteers and dispel the image of the GOP as the party of the wealthy.[67] Under Brock, moreover, the RNC developed an extensive computer network that gave state party committees access to the national committee's extensive computer files—files that included survey, electoral, and issue information of all types. The computer hookups were provided to state parties for small fees; subscribers gained entry to a sophisticated data processing network called "Repnet," which contained programs for financial accounting and reporting, political targeting and survey processing, mailing list maintenance, donor preservation and information, and correspondence and word processing. Finally, Brock made huge strides in shoring up Republican candidate recruitment, and he initiated an expansive new party institutional advertising program. Brock's successor, Frank Fahrenkopf (1981–1988), maintained and expanded many of the programs developed by Brock and initiated some new ones.[68]

The DNC began its efforts to catch up with the GOP under the regime of DNC chair Charles Manatt (1981–1985). Manatt—who after the 1980 election rightly lamented that the DNC had been "out-conceptualized, out-organized, out-televised, out-coordinated, out-financed, and out-worked" by the RNC—immediately set out to create a major direct mail fundraising operation, develop the national committee's computer capabilities, and shore up cooperation with state and local Democratic committees.[69] By all accounts, Manatt's work provided a strong start. The DNC's small contributor base grew, albeit slowly at first;[70] but by the close of 1984, the DNC's direct mail list included more than 600,000 names and had brought in about 13.5 million dollars.[71] Paul Kirk, DNC chair from 1985–1989, built on Manatt's fundraising successes with some extraordinary fundraising successes of his own.[72] With the DNC's expanded coffers, Kirk created a task force of political consultants to assist Democratic state and local committees in many of the same ways that the RNC was aiding GOP state and local parties.[73] Indeed, Kirk's task forces have received accolades from many party faithful for having greatly modernized state and local Democratic parties.[74]

More recent national chairs of both parties—DNC Chair Ron Brown (1989–1992) and RNC Chair Haley Barbour (1993–1996), for example— have continued to expand and develop the party building efforts of their respective committees. As political scientist Philip Klinkner illustrates, though, it's no surprise that the most innovative party chairs are those who have headed up their party following a presidential loss.[75] Indeed, there's nothing like a good electoral drubbing to galvanize innovation at the top of the party structure. National committee party-building activities have helped to upgrade and professionalize many state and local party committees. The increasing coordination between national, state, and local party committees, moreover, has produced a coordinated party "network" that is more integrated than at any time in United States history.[76] For state and local parties, though, the cost of national party assistance has been a considerable loss in autonomy. As the national parties supply ever-increasing sums of money to the state parties, their control over state party strategies and decision making continues to increase. Unfortunately, however, the aid afforded state and local parties by the national committees too often ebbs and flows with the exigencies of the party's presidential campaign. As long-time party scholar John F. Bibby writes, "State parties run the risk of quite literally being taken over by national party operatives in presidential years as staff are brought in to run campaigns in crucial states. These campaign operatives and their supporting resources are normally pulled out as soon as the election is over."[77]

MONEY AND THE PARTY OF OFFICEHOLDERS: LEADERSHIP PACS AND MEMBER-TO-CANDIDATE CONTRIBUTIONS IN CONGRESS

The Hill committees are not the only source of campaign funds for congressional candidates. Incumbents themselves have become an integral part of the party fundraising machinery. In both the House and Senate, well-funded, electorally secure incumbents now often contribute considerable sums of campaign money to their party's needy incumbent and nonincumbent legislative candidates.[78] Although this activity has long occurred in some state legislatures (notably California), it has recently become increasingly important at the congressional level.[79] Generally, members contribute to other candidates in one of two ways. First, some members establish their own PACs—informally dubbed "leadership" PACs—through which they distribute campaign support to candidates. Republican Majority Leader Dick Armey's (R-Tex.) PAC—The Majority Leader's Fund—contributed $879,892 to 122 Republican (mostly House) candidates during the 1997–1998 election cycle. On the Democratic side, Nancy Pelosi's (D-Calif.) leadership PAC—PAC to the Future—doled out at least $600,000 to Democratic candidates during the 1999–2000 election cycle. Second, members also make contributions to other candidates directly from their own reelection accounts. Veteran House Democrat Charlie Rangel (D-N.Y.), for instance, contributed at least $172,500 from his reelection committee to fellow Democratic candidates during the 1999–2000 election cycle.[80] Members are limited in the amount of hard money that they may contribute to other federal candidates: $1,000 per candidate per election from their reelection committees and $5,000 per candidate per election through a leadership PAC.

The late 1990s witnessed an astounding increase in this activity. The growth in the number of leadership PACs has been particularly remarkable. While forty-two leadership PACs existed in the 1991–1992 election cycle, 130 of these committees were active in 1999–2000. Part of the growth can be accounted for by the increasing popularity of leadership PACs among newer members. Although these committees were initially created largely by senior members, it's not uncommon now for first and second term members to form their own PACs.[81] In the 104th Congress, for example, freshmen members David McIntosh (R-Ind.), Jerry Weller (R-Ill.), Patrick Kennedy (D-R.I.), and Earl Blumenauer (D-Ore.) all had their own leadership PACs. During the 105th Congress, sophomore Republicans Mark Foley (R-Fla.), J.C. Watts (R-Okla.), and Deborah Pryce (R-Ohio) added to this trend by forming their own leadership committees. There have also been some particularly innovative twists on leadership PAC sponsorship. Several leadership PACs are now raising and spending soft money.[82] For example, Republican majority whip Tom Delay's (R-Tex.) leadership PAC, Americans for a Republican Majority (ARMPAC), has both federal and nonfederal accounts; Delay is also associated with a committee set up explicitly to raise soft money to finance issue advocacy ads (the Republican Majority Issues Committee).[83] The broad scope of Delay's PAC activity was observed by former NRCC chair

Bill Paxon (R-N.Y.), who explained that "Tom [Delay] really has his own political operation.... It's probably the most aggressive political operation besides the Speaker's operation, then and now, around town."[84] By 1999, at least eighteen other congressional leadership PACs, both Democratic and Republican, were trafficking in soft money.[85] In another twist on this activity, Senator Evan Bayh's (D-Ind.) PAC, Americans for Responsible Leadership, took a page from the Emily's List playbook and developed a significant "bundling" operation, whereby the PAC served as a conduit for individual contributions to several competitive Democratic candidates during the 1999–2000 election cycle.[86] Representative John Boehner's (R-Ohio) PAC, The Freedom Project, attempted to influence the flow of interest group PAC money during the 1999–2000 election cycle by using his committee's web site to rate the generosity of PACs toward GOP candidates.[87] Many leadership PAC sponsors use their committees to foot the bill for travel expenses incurred while making campaign appearances on behalf of other candidates; the travel expenses are then reported as in-kind contributions to the benefited candidates.[88] Delay's ARMPAC has provided in-kind contributions to competitive candidates in the form of political consulting assistance.[89]

Collectively, member contributions can add up to a substantial boost for needy candidates. For example, in 1996, fifty-four House Republicans contributed a total of $111,242 to the campaign of Randy Tate (R-Wash.), an electorally vulnerable Republican House incumbent running for reelection in Washington State's Ninth Congressional District. Remarkably, the amount contributed to Tate by his colleagues was $41,167 greater than that contributed in cash and coordinated expenditures by the National Republican Congressional Committee, the primary fundraising arm of the House Republican conference. More recently, Republican Heather Wilson (R-N.M.) received $250,000 from dozens of House Republican incumbents in her special election campaign to replace Representative Steve Schiff (R-N.M.), and large numbers of House Democrats contributed to Wilson's opponent.[90] By October 18 of the 1999–2000 election cycle, more than twenty congressional candidates had already received well over $100,000 from incumbent partisans— with Michigan open-seat candidate Michael Rogers raking in a whopping $202,000 from GOP congressional incumbents.

Members generally dole out the bulk of their contributions to the same candidates who receive congressional campaign committee resources. In fact, the Hill committees are often involved in mobilizing the money. As one House Democrat noted, "The DCCC is very helpful. They publish their lists and we have briefings by the DCCC chair, who says 'these guys are on the watch list, these guys are in trouble.'" Another noted that "sometimes the DCCC will come to us directly, and ask if you could give to, say, any of these eight seats.... That's usually on behalf of nonincumbents."[91] On the GOP side, efforts to get incumbents to contribute to competitive candidates have been highly aggressive, with House GOP leaders actually setting quotas for how much safe incumbents must contribute to other candidates.[92] "There will be some serious fall-out if members don't reach the targets assigned to them," noted NRCC chair Tom Davis (R-Va.) about the NRCC's efforts to collect money from incumbents during the 1999–2000 cycle.[93]

Besides contributing to other candidates, members of Congress also dole out significant sums to the congressional campaign committees.[94] The DCCC formally initiated the practice of soliciting contributions from incumbents during the 1991–1992 electoral cycle, when campaign committee chair Vic Fazio (D-Calif.) levied a "suggested" dues of $5,000 for all Democratic incumbents.[95] Following the DCCC's lead, the NRCC launched its own program to encourage incumbent financial support during the 1993–1994 election cycle.[96] The party committees' efforts—especially those of the NRCC—have paid off. Indeed, the NRCC collected nearly $7 million in hard dollars from House GOP incumbents during the 1997–1998 cycle, and the Committee was pushing to raise twice that during the 1999–2000 election cycle.[97] Although the totals have been slightly lower for Democrats, the DCCC and DSCC have nevertheless raked in record amounts from Democratic incumbents during the past few election cycles.[98]

In persuading incumbents to share their wealth, the national parties have some favorable regulations on their side. In particular, Federal Election Commission regulations permit a federal candidate's reelection committee to transfer unlimited amounts of unobligated hard money to any national party committee.[99] During the 1995–1996, 1997–1998, and 1999–2000 election cycles, multiple House members and senators took advantage of this rule and transferred six-figure sums to their respective Hill committees.[100] Indeed, no fewer than eighteen House incumbents contributed $100,000 or more to the Hill committees during the 1997–1998 cycle—with GOP Majority Leader Dick Armey providing a handsome $515,000 donation to the NRCC.[101] The 1999–2000 election cycle witnessed further increases in member-to-party transfers, with party leaders once again leading the way. By October 20 of the election year, for instance, GOP Senate Majority Leader Trent Lott (R-Miss.) had transferred $300,000 from his reelection account to the NRSC.[102]

Members don't raise money for the party and other candidates just to be nice, of course; they do it out of self-interest. The most generous member contributors, not surprisingly, are party leaders, whose careers are linked to the party's collective electoral fortunes and who are expected to provide aid to candidates and the Hill committees. The party leader who shirks her fundraising responsibilities is unlikely to be reelected to her leadership position. Members who *aspire* to win leadership posts are also especially generous to other candidates and to the Hill committees. Spirited intraparty leadership contests bring enormous benefits to many congressional candidates. During the heated contest for party whip in 1994 between Representatives Delay, Bill McCollum (R-Fla.), and Bob Walker (R-Pa.), the three contestants contributed campaign funds and services to hundreds of Republican candidates, with each whip aspirant hoping to translate a candidate's victory into an additional vote for himself in the leadership election. (Delay won.) Besides greatly aiding the individual candidates, the money surely helped the GOP collectively, as the party gained control of the House that year for the first time in forty years. In the 1999–2000 election cycle, many candidates, as well as the NRCC, have no doubt benefited from the financial generosity of Representatives Billy Tauzin (R-La.) and Mike Oxley (R-Oh.), who were locked in a heated contest for the chair of the influential Commerce Committee for the 107th Congress.[103] The increasing amounts of campaign funds doled out by leadership aspirants illustrates how incumbents' individual self-interest can coincide with—and help advance—the party's collective well-being.

Member contributors in Congress have emerged as an important component of the party funding network. As a practical matter, the increasing willingness of House incumbents to support the congressional campaign committees has important implications for party politics. First, in a campaign finance system that greatly favors incumbents, member contributions to nonincumbents and to the party campaign committees—which devote a substantial portion of their campaign resources to competitive challengers—have the potential to play an important redistributive role. Second, with electorally secure incumbents typically more willing to transfer funds than incumbents anticipating stiff electoral competition, it is increasingly important for each party to recruit quality challengers in as many congressional districts as possible. Indeed, for each district a party fails to contest, it risks facilitating the enrichment of opposition party and candidate coffers.

THE TRANSFUSED REVIVAL OF STATE PARTY ORGANIZATIONS

The transformation that has occurred in state party organizations is best illustrated by irony. The national parties were once creatures of the state affiliates and financed by them; today, the state parties are chartered chapters of Washington-based groups, and they owe much of their health and wealth to the national party committees. A relationship that V.O. Key once described as independent and confederated[104] has become integrated and centralized. Stimulated by new campaign finance laws that encourage collaborative efforts under national party direction, and in fourteen states aided by public financing provisions that funnel money through the state parties (a subject discussed in Chapter Seven), most state parties are organizationally stronger now than at any time in their history. Much like the national parties, they have begun to offer a wide array of candidate services while recruiting candidates and providing direct financial assistance to nominees and some local parties.

Increases in state party organizational strength have been detailed in studies by James Gibson et al. and, more recently, John Aldrich.[105] Just four decades ago most state parties subsisted without paid staff or headquarters and had paltry budgets of $50,000 or less. By 1980, the average (election year) state party budget was $340,000, and by 1999, this figure had grown to $2.8 million.[106] State party staffing also points to growing organizational strength. Gibson et al. report that 90 percent of the state parties had either a full-time chair or executive director by 1980, up from 63 percent in the early 1960s.[107] In addition, the average number of state party full-time staffers has grown steadily since the 1960s, with parties employing an average of nine full-time and seven part-time staffers by the late 1990s.[108] Also important are the increases in state party activities during the past four decades. Between 1960 and 1980, the percentage of state parties engaged in a wide range of institutional support and candidate-specific activities grew considerably.[109] Aldrich's 1999 survey of state party chairs illustrates that further increases in these important state party activities have occurred since 1980. Indeed, as Table 3.2 illustrates, the percentage of state parties that contribute to elected officials, hold fundraising events, and conduct public opinion surveys has increased dramatically since 1980. In addition, the late 1990s saw increases in the already high percentage of state committees that were offering campaign seminars, running voter identification programs, and publishing party newspapers in 1980. On the

TABLE 3.2. STATE PARTY ACTIVITY, 1983 AND 1999.

	1983	1999
Contributed to governor	47%	89%
Contributed to other statewide constitutional offices	44%	81%
Contributed to congressional candidates	48%	85%
Contributed to state legislative candidates	47%	92%
Held fundraising event	19%	98%
Conducted campaign seminars	89%	95%
Published newspaper	80%	91%
Operated voter ID programs	70%	94%
Conducted public opinion research	32%	78%
Recruited gubernatorial candidates	11%	28%
Recruited state legislative candidates	65%	22%
Issued preprimary endorsements	28%	19%

Source: John H. Aldrich, "Southern Parties in State and Nation," *Journal of Politics* 62 (August 2000): 663. Used by permission.

other hand, fewer state parties appear to be making preprimary endorsements these days. The ability to influence nominations was of course one of the most important—if not *the* most important—tools that state party leaders had in the past; that few state parties now make preprimary endorsements is a powerful commentary on the changing nature of state parties. (We address the issue of preprimary endorsements further in Chapter Seven.) Notwithstanding the decline in preprimary endorsements, the growth in state party organizational strength in the last four decades has been nothing short of remarkable.

There is, of course, variation in state party activity by region and by party, but on the whole, state parties have gradually become more organizationally uniform. Across regions, the most exciting story is surely in the South. Although southern state parties tended to be the least developed organizationally—a product of their relative lack of two-party competition—they have gradually transformed themselves into organizational powerhouses. Across a multitude of organizational indicators, southern state party organizations are now better developed organizationally than are their northern counterparts. Indeed, by 1999, the mean southern state party election-year budget exceeded by $1 million the mean for all state parties.[110] Particularly impressive are the southern state GOP parties, which have strengthened more dramatically than their Democratic counterparts and are now among the strongest state party organization units in the nation. Not surprisingly, gains in southern state party organizational strength have paralleled increases in party competition in the South.

There are also differences between the two parties. In many categories of campaign organization, Republican state parties have a significant edge over their Democratic counterparts. Whereas almost all GOP state organizations conduct public opinion polling, for example, only about two-thirds of state Democratic parties do so.[111] And, while almost all Republican state parties make financial contributions to candidates at every level, a considerably smaller percentage of state Democratic parties are able to do this.[112] Not surprisingly, Republican state organizations have an average election-year budget that is $1.4 million dollars higher than that of Democratic state parties.[113] On the other hand, state Democratic parties now rival Republican organizations in the areas of candidate recruitment, county party assistance, voter identification, and direct mail operations.[114] Still, the age-old financial advantage enjoyed by state GOP organizations persists, and their superior financial prowess clearly translates into greater organizational strength.

Another noteworthy development at the state level is the involvement of political parties in statewide ballot initiative campaigns. Although political parties have historically remained on the sidelines during initiative campaigns, state and national parties now endorse ballot initiatives and contribute significant sums of money and in-kind support to select ballot campaigns.[115] Three related factors evidently motivate party involvement in ballot campaigns. First, support for select ballot initiatives can help parties mobilize their bases of support on election day. Second, ballot initiatives can serve as useful wedge issues against the opposition party. Third, party support for ballot initiatives may increase the party's success in soliciting campaign contributions.[116] Party involvement in ballot campaigns is a healthy development. By providing a partisan cue in campaigns that lack one, the involvement of political parties in ballot initiative campaigns can help voters make more informed voting decisions.

NEW PLAYERS AT THE STATE LEVEL: STATE LEGISLATIVE CAMPAIGN COMMITTEES

No discussion of modern party organization can ignore the emergence of powerful state legislative campaign committees (LCCs).[117] Like the congressional campaign committees at the national level, LCCs are run by a party's legislative incumbents and exist primarily to help maximize the number of legislative seats held by the party of which they are part. The Democratic Assembly Campaign Committee (DACC) in New

York state, for instance, is organized by New York State Assembly Democratic members and seeks primarily to maximize the number of Democrats elected to the Assembly. Several states have had LCCs for some time now, but the number of these committees increased dramatically during the 1980s. Not surprisingly, LCCs tend to emerge in states with more professionalized legislatures and high levels of legislative party competition.[118] Legislative leaders raise much of the money for state LCCs, and in some states, leaders have established PACs that serve as de facto LCCs. Today, thirty-six states have at least one LCC or leadership committee fund.[119]

LCCs are playing an increasingly important role in the financing of state legislative elections.[120] Although many state legislative candidates still tend to receive the bulk of their party funds from the state party committees, LCC funds constitute an increasingly important resource for state legislative candidates.[121] Indeed, political scientist Anthony Gierzynski identified instances in which LCC funds constituted as much as 60 percent of a candidate's total campaign resources.[122] Moreover, as with the Hill committees at the national level, the LCCs provide not only dollars to state legislative candidates but also a wide variety of valuable campaign services—everything from campaign workers to media assistance to opposition research to fundraising help.[123] The provision of such services, of course, allows LCCs to play an influential role in the campaigns of some candidates, particularly those in close races. In part, LCCs have been effective because, as with the Hill committees at the national level, they concentrate their efforts on competitive contests, where their assistance is most likely to affect the election outcome.[124]

LCCs no doubt aid many competitive state legislative candidates. Yet it is important to understand that, unlike the state central party committees, LCCs do relatively little to help the party ticket as a whole. Rather, most of the services they provide are candidate-specific, and the candidates supported are typically only those running for seats in the specific legislative chamber where the LCC is housed.[125] As political scientist Dan Shea writes, "few [LCC] resources are spent on nonlegislative candidates or general party-building activities."[126] In addition, LCCs work in coordination with state and county party organizational units far less than one might expect. And, indeed, the committees have been known to distance their candidates from unpopular candidates on the party ticket—a far cry from the role of traditional party organizations.[127] Not surprisingly, given LCC tactics, there is sometimes a hostile relationship between LCC officials and those of other party units.[128] The relative absence of concern for unified party efforts has prompted Shea to ask whether LCCs resemble independent political consulting firms more than they do traditional party organizations.[129]

PARTY ORGANIZATIONS AT THE LOCAL LEVEL

When Americans think of local political parties, most quickly cite New York's Tammany Hall or Chicago's Daley machine. But Tammany died before midcentury, and the Daley organization gradually faded after Mayor Richard J. Daley's death in 1977, decimated by fratricide, by court rulings striking at the heart of the patronage system, and by opponents that one long-time machine alderman characterized as "intellectuals, troublemakers, and know-hows." ("When you give them a $10 bill, they can't even get a dog out of the dog pound for you!" he noted.)[130]

Yet several studies during the last two decades have revealed that many local parties—Democratic as well as Republican—are surprisingly active. Although party organizational atrophy is unmistakable in some cities and counties, the percentage of local parties with the essential ingredients for effective organization—headquaters, staff, telephone listings—has increased markedly, and these parties are involved in a range of campaign activities.[131] Some local parties are aided by substantial help from the state and national committees. But some also find strength in a well-nourished grassroots organization.

Even some traditional, machine-like local party organizations still exist in the United States. Until very recently, one potent local organization could be found in the Republican party of Nassau County, New York. No doubt Mayor Daley would have found much to like about this rigid and hierarchical machine that controlled more than 20,000 jobs and featured an elaborate superstructure of ward chairpersons, precinct committee members, and block captains to turn out the vote on election day.[132] Originally built on New York City's out-migration of blue-collar Irish and Italian ethnics who wanted to disassociate themselves from the city's liberal politics, the machine took great care to recruit young people, in part by distributing plum summer jobs. Many of these youths went on to base their whole careers on service to the party. In the best tradition of machine politics, aspiring officeholders were expected to work their way up the ladder slowly, toiling for years in the backrooms and the neighborhoods, delivering votes for the party candidates and dollars for the party war chest. Party chiefs encouraged competition among committee members to see who could attract the most new registrants or sell the most tickets to a fundraiser. The machine was not without its problems, of course. Corruption charges against its leaders were not uncommon, for instance, and its command of so many patronage positions often came under attack. Yet, electoral success kept the organization humming, and until 1999, it regularly won a large majority of the area's county, state legislative, and congressional posts. The machine even produced one of New York's United States senators, Alfonse D'Amato, first elected in 1980. D'Amato had been a supervisor of Nassau's Hempstead township and a top leader of the party organization prior to his Senate bid. The conservative Republican learned constituency service politics well in the county machine, and he attended assiduously to the state's interests just as he had done for his township—even earning an endorsement from the liberal *New York Times* in 1986.

In 1999, however, Nassau County Republicans were humiliated by a county fiscal crisis and went down to demoralizing defeat, with county voters ousting five GOP incumbents from the nineteen-seat county legislature and giving Democrats a slim one-seat majority.[133] The GOP machine's 100-year reign over the County's government ended. (To make matters worse, Senator D'Amato had been defeated a year earlier by Democratic House member Chuck Schumer.) Yet it seems likely that we haven't seen the last of Nassau County's vaunted GOP organization. Ousted GOP county legislators were replaced with largely inexperienced Democratic candidates, whose skills are sure to be sorely tested by the County's mounting fiscal crisis.

The Nassau County machine was not the only traditional party machine to survive into the late twentieth century. Old-style machine parties persisted in cities such as Albany and Philadelphia, and several other local machines are still scattered across the nation.[134] Yet, by and large, the patronage-driven machines of the past have given way to modern local parties. Under new leadership, for instance, even the once powerful Mahoning County Democratic Party in Youngstown, Ohio, has been transformed from an old-style party machine to a modern, service-oriented organization.[135] Moreover, as political scientist Paul Allen Beck points out, all-powerful local party machines never were the norm in American politics, and many localities had little more than ineffective, skeletal party units—even during the so-called strong party era. In that sense, the new service-oriented county parties of the 1990s may well represent an increase rather than a decrease in local party strength.[136]

REVITALIZED PARTY ORGANIZATIONS: THE IMPLICATIONS FOR POLITICS AND GOVERNMENT

If this extended discussion of the strengthening of party organizations has proven anything, it is that the new technologies of politics, which have so often been used to weaken the parties by liberating individual candidates from party influence, are now being employed to build more vital political parties. No technology, after all, is inherently good or evil; the uses to which it is put determine its morality. Party advocates can only be delighted that these techniques are enabling parties to rebuild and fortify themselves at a time when either an antiparty mood prevails or people simply do not care very much about the parties' fate.

The consequences of reinvigorated party organization and financing are many. First of all, an obvious result is that parties are in a much better position to help their nominees win elections—a fact that does not escape the notice of candidates and officeholders. More importantly, the parties' new recruitment efforts, financial contributions, and provision of campaign services are bearing fruit in another way. The evolving ties between the parties and their elected decision makers may be helping to enact the party agenda and to increase cohesion among the party's officeholders. During the 1990s, both congressional parties displayed record high levels of party cohesion on floor votes, as Chapter Two noted. There are many reasons for this, of course, including the dwindling of the ranks of both southern conservative Democrats and northern liberal Republicans, which has made each party more ideologically and internally consistent. But party organizational influence may be playing a role as well. Although the evidence is mixed on whether party committee campaign resources induce greater levels of party loyalty among members of Congress, it is difficult to believe that party resources have *no* effect.[137] Indeed, research has yet to consider the impact of party issue-advocacy spending on member party loyalty, and no research has assessed the impact of leadership PAC assistance on loyalty to the party (at least at the national level).[138] Moreover, in estimating the impact of party resources on party loyalty, it is surely difficult to construct a measure of party fundraising aid that captures the valuable "brokering" role that parties play on behalf of their candidates.[139] So, while it may be difficult to exhibit empirically, it seems likely that the parties are now able to counteract—at least to some small degree—the individualistic, atomizing forces that favor personalized, candidate-centered, interest–group-responsive politics and legislative voting.

Nonetheless, there are considerable limitations on the influence American parties can exert on legislators under even the most favorable of conditions. Parties are certainly a more substantial source of cash and campaign technology than ever before, but they are not the only source by any means. While a legislator will not wish to offend any major benefactor, he or she will do so when necessary so long as other alternative support is available. Then, too, parties are hardly inclined at election time to discipline even the most uncooperative of incumbents. Since the overriding objective is victory, the parties will normally choose the pragmatic course and aid any party candidate, rather than reward only some while punishing others and risking their defeat. After all, a candidate completely deprived of party assistance will be less pliable and even more hostile in the future. That said, it would be difficult to believe that the parties' legislative influence has not been at least marginally enhanced by the vastly expanded electoral services they are providing their candidates.

There is another consequence of strengthened party organization that deserves mention. To this point, at least, party development has extended from the top down, from national to state party organizations. All politics may be local, but more and more, the key political decisions and allocations are being made nationally. Economies of scale and campaign finance rules have encouraged the centralization of electoral services and technology in the national party committees. While the national organizations were at one time financed by the state parties, the opposite pattern is closer to the truth today. This reversal of the flow of party power disturbs some federalists. Yet the health of federalism is also dependent on the vitality of the parties as a whole. The fact that the national party organizations have been revivified can only help the parties perform their linkage role in the federal configuration. If nothing else, the centralization of party resources permits the national parties to target weak state and local parties for special remedial help, freeing them from the demoralizing cycle of inbred defeat. By infusing money and services to anemic parties that otherwise might not have been competitive, vigorous two-party competition is spread in sometimes unlikely places. Surely, the federal division of power is fortified under such an arrangement. Beyond that, we must remember that the national parties have slowly but surely transferred the means and methods of new campaign technologies to the state and local parties themselves. Indisputably, centralization is probably a permanent feature of the new party system, but the dependency of state parties on their national counterparts will likely lessen somewhat as they develop quasi-independent capabilities. This process ought to be accelerated as much as possible, and the two concluding chapters will suggest some ways to build parties from the ground up, a goal that will serve the purposes of both parties and federalism. Then, too, the degree of centralization in party activity that has actually taken place can be exaggerated. The parties remain firmly rooted in the states both because the vast majority of party leaders and officeholders are elected and reside there and because the states, far more than the national government, regulate and control the parties.

The mushrooming of party organizational strength has come at a crucial moment. All of the forces arrayed against the parties (discussed in Chapter One) have weakened them and would have continued to do so except for the parties' self-initiated innovations. Now instead of continuing a slide into oblivion, parties are battling those forces, using their expanded capacities to aid their candidates and to contact more voters. The big question, though, is whether the parties' revived organizational strength has led to reinvigorated party ties in the electorate—to a slowdown of the troubling partisan dealignment and antiparty trends that have characterized much of American politics in the late 20th century.[140] While public attitudes about the parties are examined in the next two chapters, one important point seems worth making here. The modern, service-oriented parties have become tremendously effective at helping candidates compete more effectively within a candidate-centered environment. But in terms of restoring ties between voters and parties, the technologically savvy, candidate-specific services that parties provide to candidates are no substitute for generic party-building activities that help to generate support for the party ticket as a whole. As political scientist Dan Shea writes, organizations "holding little affinity for broad-based or long-range activities may strain even the most inclusive view of 'party.'"[141] Indeed, even the many issue-advocacy ads now run by the parties in each election are unlikely to shore up party ties in the electorate, given that only a small portion of these party-sponsored ads even mention party labels.[142] It is, of course, understandable that the short-term goal of winning elections takes precedence for parties over the long-term goal of solidifying long-term party attachments in the electorate. After all, parties in the United States exist primarily to contest and win elections. But parties, especially the Hill and state legislative campaign committees, must strike a better balance between these short- and long-term goals.

At the very least, parties should halt the practice of downplaying party labels in their ads. And whether at the national or state level, legislative campaign committees should seek to distance their legislative candidates from other candidates on the party ticket only under the most extraordinary of circumstances. For while such strategies and tactics may benefit parties in the short term, they promote an increasing apartisan electorate, which in the long run guarantees only greater electoral volatility and reduced public support for the parties.

We return to these issues later in the book. After using the next two chapters to evaluate the parties' relationship with the public, the final two chapters will focus on how the parties—on their own and with the help of government—can translate money and organization into voter loyalty.

NOTES

1. This has been made clear by countless studies. See, for example, Paul Herrnson, "Do Parties Make a Difference? The Role of Party Organizations in Congressional Elections," *Journal of Politics* 48 (August 1986): 589–615; Paul S. Herrnson, *Party Campaigning in the 80s* (Cambridge, Mass.: Harvard, 1988); Frank J. Sorauf, "Political Parties and the New World of Campaign Finance," in L. Sandy Maisel, ed., *The Parties Respond: Changes in Parties and Campaigns*, 3rd ed. (Boulder, Colo.: Westview Press, 1998).

2. Jonathan Krasno and Daniel Seltz, *Buying Time: Television Advertising in the 1998 Congressional Elections* (New York: Brennan Center for Justice at New York University Law School, 2000). In their comprehensive study of television advertisements during the 1998 congressional elections, Krasno and Seltz found that only 15 percent of party-sponsored issue ads mentioned a party label.

3. For the reader who wants to know more about party campaign finance, there are several excellent sources: Anthony Corrado, "Party Soft Money," in Anthony Corrado, Thomas E. Mann, Daniel R. Ortiz, Trevor Potter, Frank J. Sorauf, eds., *Campaign Finance Reform: A Sourcebook* (Washington, D.C.: Brookings, 1997). Sorauf, "Political Parties and the New World of Campaign Finance." Herrnson, *Party Campaigning in the 80s*. Frank J. Sorauf, *Money In American Elections* (Glenview, Ill.: Scott, Foresman and Company, 1988). Frank J. Sorauf, *Inside Campaign Finance: Myths and Realities* (New Haven: Yale University Press, 1992). Frank J. Sorauf and Scott A. Wilson, "Political Parties and Campaign Finance: Adaptation and Accommodation Toward a Changing Role," L. Sandy Maisel, ed., *The Parties Respond: Changes in the Party System*, 2nd ed. (Boulder, Colo.: Westview Press, 1994).

4. Corrado, "Party Soft Money," 168.

5. Ibid., 169.

6. For states with only one House district, the coordinated expenditure limit was $20,000.

7. FEC, "FEC Announces 2000 Party Spending Limits," press release prepared by the Federal Election Commission, March 1, 2000. For states with only one House district, the party coordinated spending limit for 2000 was $67,560.

8. FEC, "FEC Announces 2000 Party Spending Limits."

9. Sorauf, "Political Parties and the New World of Campaign Finance," 227.

10. Corrado, "Party Soft Money," 169.

11. Paul S. Herrnson, *Congressional Elections: Campaigning at Home and In Washington*, 3rd ed. (Washington D.C.: Congressional Quarterly Press, 2000), 113.

12. Herrnson, *Party Campaigning in the 1980s*, 40–44.

13. 116 S. Ct. 2309 (1996).

14. Ibid. Interestingly, two Justices in the case—Scalia and Thomas—argued that federal limits on party-coordinated expenditures are also unconstitutional, leaving the door open for a further deregulation of parties in the arena of campaign finance.

15. Susan B. Glassner, "Court's Ruling in Colorado Case May Reshape Campaign Finance," *Washington Post* (28 March 1999): A6. The FEC has already announced its intention to appeal the ruling.

16. See Corrado, "Party Soft Money," for an excellent account of the 1979 FECA amendments. As Corrado rightly notes, the 1979 FECA Amendments did not create unregulated "soft" money, as is commonly believed. Rather, the 1979 amendments "simply exempted any federal monies ('hard dollars') a party committee might *spend* on certain political activities from being considered a contribution to a candidate under the law." Corrado, "Party Soft Money," 170 (italics in original). The reality, as Corrado points out, is that the FEC, in a series of advisory opinions, paved the way for use of soft money in elections that featured federal candidates. In 1976, for example, the Commission ruled that the Illinois Republican State Central Committee could use unregulated corporate and union funds to pay for the nonfederal share of its overhead and administrative expenses. Then, in 1978, the Commission issued an advisory opinion allowing the Republican State Committee of Kansas to pay for the nonfederal share of its voter drives with unregulated corporate and union money. "Party Soft Money," 171–172. We address the soft money development in more detail below.

17. Hard and soft money are also referred to as, respectively, federal and nonfederal money.

18. Corrado, "Party Soft Money," 171–172.

19. Ibid., 172.

20. The regulations treated national parties differently than state and local parties, and they differed depending on the type of party activity being funded. See Robert Biersack, "Hard Facts and Soft Money: State Party Finance in the 1992 Federal Elections," in Daniel M. Shea and John C. Green, eds., *The State of the Parties: The Changing Role of Contemporary American Parties* (Lanham, Md.: Rowman & Littlefield, 1994).

21. FEC, "Party Fundraising Escalates," prepared by the FEC Press Office, November 3, 2000; Biersack, "Hard Facts and Soft Money"; Corrado, "Party Soft Money," 172–173.; Corrado, "Party Soft Money," 174–175.

22. Herrnson, *Congressional Elections*, 3rd ed., 94.

23. Bibby, *Politics, Parties, and Elections*, 4th ed., 116.

24. Herrnson, *Congressional Elections*, 3rd ed., 94.

25. Ibid., 112.

26. Marianne Holt, "The Surge in Party Money in Competitive 1998 Congressional Elections," in David Magleby, ed., *Outside Money: Soft Money and Issue Advocacy in the 1998 Congressional Elections* (Lanham, Md.: Rowman & Littlefield, 2000). It's difficult to document precisely the amounts of soft money that the parties are spending on issue-advocacy ads, since, unlike hard money expenditures, party soft money expenditures need not be reported to the FEC on a line-item basis.

27. Herrnson, *Congressional Elections*, 3rd ed., 112.

28. House Majority Whip Tom Delay (R-Tex.), for example, heads up a soft money financed issue advocacy group called the Republican Majority Issues Committee. See Karen Foerstel, Peter Wallsten, and Derek Willis, "Campaign Overhaul Mired in Money and Loopholes," *Congressional Quarterly Weekly Report* (13 May 2000), 1084–1093.

29. Brooks Jackson, "Financing the 1996 Campaign: The Law of the Jungle," in Larry J. Sabato editor, *Toward the Millennium: The Elections of 1996* (Boston: Allyn and Bacon, 1997).

30. Peter Marks, "Parties Playing a Larger Role in Elections," *New York Times* (28 September 2000), A1, A23.

31. Holt, "The Surge in Party Money in Competitive 1998 Congressional Elections."

32. Ibid.

33. Ibid. David Magleby, "Conclusions and Implications," in Magleby, ed., *Outside Money*, 215.

34. This discussion relies heavily on Paul S. Herrnson, "The National Parties at Century's End," in L. Sandy Maisel, ed., *The Parties Respond: Changes in Parties and Campaigns*, 3rd ed. (Boulder, Colo.: Westview Press, 1998), and Herrnson, *Congressional Elections*, 3rd ed., 100-111.

35. Jennifer Babson and Beth Donovan, "GOP Fundraiser Raises Sights and Tightens Belt." *Congressional Quarterly Weekly Report* (2 April 1994): 809–11.

36. In the special election to replace Walter Capps (D-Calif.), several Republican congressional leaders split their support among two GOP candidates. Ultimately, Capps' widow won. In 1996, Republican House leaders also got involved in the nomination contest in New York's 19th congressional district in order to help protect incumbent Sue Kelly.

37. In 2000, the DCCC got involved in several primary contests. John Mercurio, "DCCC Endorsement in Arkansas Runoff Sparks New Controversy," *Roll Call* (12 June 2000): 15; Rachel Van Dongen, "Hoping to Keep Pennsylvania Seat, DCCC Taps DA," *Roll Call* (13 May 2000): 11.

38. Herrnson, *Congressional Elections*, 3rd ed., 66.

39. Anthony Corrado, "The Politics of Cohesion: The Role of the National Committees in the 1992 Election," in John C. Green and Daniel M. Shea, eds., *The State of the Parties: The Changing Role of American Parties* (Lanham, Md.: Rowman & Littlefield, 1996).

40. Herrnson, *Congressional Elections*, 3rd ed., 101.
41. Rachel Van Dongen, "Looking for Some Polish: GOP Candidates Head to N.Y. For Some Image Help," *Roll Call* (29 June 2000): 15.
42. Herrnson, *Congressional Elections*, 3rd ed.,, 101.
43. Herrnson, "National Party Organizations at Century's End," 74.
44. Ibid., 68.
45. James Dao, "GOP Warns That It, Too, May Seek Some Recounts," *New York Times* (11 November 2000): A15. Katherine Q. Seelye, "Gore Lives in the Eye of a Surreal Storm," *New York Times* (13 November 2000): A27.
46. Corrado, "The Politics of Cohesion."
47. Ibid, 103.
48. Herrnson, *Congressional Elections*, 3rd ed., 104.
49. Herrnson, "National Party Organizations at Century's End," 74.
50. John H. Aldrich, "Southern Parties in State and Nation," *Journal of Politics* 62 (August 2000), 643–670.
51. Herrnson, "National Party Organizations at Century's End," 74.
52. Gary C. Jacobson, *The Politics of Congressional Elections*, 4th ed. (New York: Addison Wesley Longman), 162–163.
53. Thomas H. Little, "On the Coattails of a Contract: RNC Activities and Republican Gains in the 1994 State Legislative Elections," *Political Research Quarterly* (March 1998): 173–190.
54. Herrnson, "National Party Organizations at Century's End," 75–76; Herrnson, *Congressional Elections*, 3rd ed., 105–106.
55. Ibid.
56. Paul S. Herrnson, *Party Campaigning in the 1980s* (Cambridge, Mass.: Harvard University Press, 1988), 60; Corrado, "The Politics of Cohesion," 81; Anthony Corrado, *Paying For Presidents: Public Financing in National Elections* (New York: Twentieth Century Fund Press, 1993), 75.
57. Corrado, "The Politics of Cohesion."
58. Philip A. Klinkner, *The Losing Parties: Out Party National Committees, 1956–1993* (New Haven: Yale University Press, 1994), 194.
59. David Broder, "The Road Back," *Washington Post* (20 January 1994): C7.
60. This section relies on Herrnson, *Congressional Campaigns*, 3rd ed., 106–109.
61. Bibby, *Politics, Parties, and Elections*, 4th ed., 123.
62. Herrnson, *Congressional Campaigns*, 3rd ed., 109. The national and Hill committees also transfer money to state parties to help with redistricting efforts. See John Bresnahan, "With Remap Ahead, GOP Seeks $5 million for Texas," *Roll Call* (3 April 2000): 16.
63. Corrado, "The Politics of Cohesion," 79–80.
64. Bibby, *Politics, Parties, and Elections*, 4th ed., 122.
65. James Dao, "Both Parties Plan to Empty Wallets to Draw Voters to the Polls," *New York Times* (8 August 2000): A23.
66. See www.democrats.org/dlcc/index.html
67. Klinkner, *The Losing Parties*, 139.
68. Herrnson, "National Party Organization at Century's End," 63.
69. Klinkner, *The Losing Parties*, 159.
70. Herrnson, *Party Campaigning in the 1980s*, 37; Klinkner, *The Losing Parties*, 165.

71. Klinkner, *The Losing Parties*, 165.

72. Ibid., 182.

73. Herrnson, "National Party Organizations at Century's End," 63; L. Sandy Maisel, *Parties and Elections in America: The Electoral Process* (Lanham, Md.: Rowman & Littlefield, 1999), 86.

74. Herrnson "National Party Organizations at Century's End," 63.

75. Klinkner, *The Losing Parties*.

76. John F. Bibby, "State Party Organizations: Coping and Adapting to Candidate-Centered Politics and Nationalization, " in L. Sandy Maisel, ed., *The Parties Respond: Changes in Parties and Campaigns*, 3rd ed. (Boulder, Colo.: Westview Press, 1998).

77. Bibby, "State Party Organizations" in Maisel, ed., *The Parties Respond: Changes in Parties and Campaigns*, 3rd ed., 43.

78. See, for example, Amy Keller, "Helping Each Other Out: Members Dip into Campaign Funds for Fellow Candidates," *Roll Call* (15 June 1998): 1.

79. On member contribution activity at the state level, see Jay K. Dow, "Campaign Contributions and Intercandidate Transfers in the California Assembly," *Social Science Quarterly* 75 (1994), 867–80. On member contribution activity at the congressional level, see Salmore and Salmore, *Candidates, Parties, and Elections*, 268–269; Bruce A. Larson, "Ambition and Money in the U.S. House of Representatives: Analyzing Campaign Contributions from Incumbents' Leadership PACs and Reelection Committees" (Ph.D. diss., University of Virginia, 1998); Paul S.Herrnson, "Money and Motives: Spending in House Elections," in *Congress Reconsidered*, edited by Lawrence C. Dodd and Bruce I. Oppenheimer, 6th ed. (Washington, D.C.: Congressional Quarterly Press, 1997); Clyde Wilcox, "Share the Wealth: Contributions by Congressional Incumbents to the Campaigns of Other Candidates," *American Politics Quarterly* 17 (October 1989): 386–408. Ross K. Baker, *The New Fat Cats: Members of Congress as Political Benefactors* (New York: Priority Press Publications, 1989). Chuck Alston, "Members with Cash-on-Hand Reach Out to Help Others," *Congressional Quarterly Weekly Report* (28 September 1991): 2763–6. Larry J. Sabato, *PAC Power: Inside the World of Political Action Committees* (New York: Norton, 1985), 114–117.

80. Data for Armey's PAC are from the Federal Election Commission. Data for Pelosi's PAC, as well as that for Rangel's campaign committee, are from the Center for Responsive Politics web site, www.opensecrets.org, and include contributions made through October 18, 2000.

81. Jackie Koszczuk, "Funds for Others—Or Maybe Themselves," *Congressional Quarterly Weekly Report* (18 April 1998): 965.

82. Susan B. Glasser and Julie Eilperin, "A New Conduit for Soft Money: Critics Decry Big, Largely Untraceable Donations to Lawmakers' 'Leadership PACs'," *Washington Post* (16 May 1999): A1.

83. Karen Foerstel, Peter Wallsten, and Derek Willis, "Campaign Overhaul Mired in Money and Loopholes," *Congressional Quarterly Weekly Report* (13 May 2000), 1084–1093.

84. Julie Eilperin and Jim VandeHei, "Contract High to Coup Low: How it Fell Apart," *Roll Call* (6 October 1997): 1, 21.

85. Susan B. Glasser and Julie Eilperin, "A New Conduit for 'Soft Money:' Critics Decry Big, Largely Untraceable Donations to Lawmakers' 'Leadership PACs,'" *Washington Post* (16 May 1999), A1, A8.

86. Paul Kane, "Senator's Rise Fueled by PACs," *Roll Call* (11 September 2000), 1, 41. Bundling is a process whereby political entrepreneurs gather checks written by others, present them in a "bundle" to a candidate, and earn political credit from the candidate for the entire package.

87. Derek Willis, "PAC Plays," *Campaigns and Elections* (19 April 1999): 26.

88. Larson, "Ambition and Money in the U.S. House of Representatives."

89. Ibid.

90. Amy Keller, "Helping Each Other Out: Members Dip Into Campaign Funds for Fellow Candidates," *Roll Call* (15 June 1998): 1, 24.

91. All quotes come from Larson, "Ambition and Money in the U.S. House of Representatives."

92. Timothy J. Burger, "Gingrich Hits Up Members for $3M To GOP," *Roll Call* (11 August 1994): 1,26; Jim VandeHei, "Hastert Launches ROMP II for House Members, *Roll Call* (13 September 1999): 1, 58; Jim VandeHei, "Armey Wants Millions for Ads," *Roll Call* (13 July 1998): 1, 32.

93. John Bresnahan, "Hastert Backs off Threats Over Committee Slots," *Roll Call* (15 June 2000): 3.

94. See Larson, "Ambition and Money in the U.S. House of Representatives." See also Bruce A. Larson, "Incumbent Contributions to the Congressional Campaign Committees, 1989–90 through 1997–98" (unpublished manuscript, 2000).

95. Tim Kenworthy, "Collaring Colleagues for Cash," *Washington Post* (14 May 1991): A17.

96. Jennifer Babson and Beth Donovan, "GOP Fundraiser Raises Sights and Tightens Belt," *Congressional Quarterly Weekly Report* (2 April 1994): 809–811; James G. Gimpel, *Legislating the Revolution: The Contract with America in Its First 100 Days*, (Boston: Allyn and Bacon, 1996).

97. For 1997–1998 see Larson, "Incumbent Contributions to the Congressional Campaign Committees, 1989–90 through 1997–98." On 1999–2000, see Rachel Van Dongen, "NRCC Expands Targets: House Republicans Kick in $16 Million for 'Battleground' Efforts," *Roll Call* (26 October 2000), 13, 16.

98. On the DCCC, see Larson, "Incumbent Contributions to the Congressional Campaign Committees, 1989–90 through 1997–98." On the DSCC, see Mark Preston, "Several Senators Still Have Not Paid Their DSCC Dues," *Roll Call* (11 September 2000): A3.

99. (11 CFR 113.2.) In contrast to regulations governing member contributions to other candidates, federal campaign finance regulations allow members to contribute more to the parties through a reelection account than through a leadership PAC. As noted in the text, members may transfer unlimited amounts to the national committees from their reelection accounts. As with all PACs participating in federal elections, leadership PACs may legally contribute only $15,000 per calendar year to any national party committee.

100. Larson, "Incumbent Contributions to the Congressional Campaign Committees, 1989–90 through 1997–98;" Preston, "Several Senators Still Have

Not Paid Their DSCC Dues;" Rachel Van Dongen, "NRCC Expands Targets: House Republicans Kick in $16 Million for 'Battleground' Efforts," *Roll Call* (26 October 2000), 13, 16.

101. Larson, "Incumbent Contributions to the Congressional Campaign Committees, 1989–90 through 1997–98."

102. Data on Lott are from the Federal Election Commission's web site, www.fec.gov, and include transfers made through October 18, 2000. See Preston, "Several Senators Still Have Not Paid Their DSCC Dues;" Rachel Van Dongen, "NRCC Expands Targets: House Republicans Kick in $16 Million for 'Battleground' Efforts," *Roll Call* (26 October 2000): 13, 16.

103. Karen Foerstel, "Chairmen's Term Limits Already Shaking up the House," *Congressional Quarterly Weekly Report* (25 March 2000): 628–634.

104. V. O. Key, Jr., *Politics, Parties, and Pressure Groups* (New York: Thomas Y. Crowell, 1964), 334.

105. John H. Aldrich, "Southern Parties in State and Nation," *Journal of Politics* 62 (August 2000): 643–670; James L. Gibson, Cornelius P. Cotter, John F. Bibby, and Robert J. Huckshorn, "Assessing Party Organizational Strength," *American Political Science Review* 27 (May 1983): 193–222; ACIR, "The Transformation in American Politics," 112–116. For additional reading on state party strength, see David R. Mayhew, *Placing Parties in American Politics* (Princeton: Princeton University Press, 1986).

106. Gibson et al., "Assessing Party Organizational Strength;" Aldrich, "Southern Parties in State and Nation."

107. Gibson et al., "Assessing Party Organizational Strength," 209.

108. Gibson et al., "Assessing Party Organizational Strength;" Aldrich, "Southern Parties in State and Nation."

109. Gibson et al., "Assessing Party Organizational Strength."

110. Aldrich, "Southern Parties in State and Nation."

111. Ibid., 656.

112. Ibid.

113. Ibid.

114. Ibid.

115. Daniel A. Smith, "The Initiative to Party: The Role of Political Parties in State Ballot Initiatives" (unpublished manuscript, 1999); Richard L. Hasen, "Parties Take the Initiative (and Vice Versa)," *Columbia Law Review* 100 (April 2000), 731–752.

116. Smith, "The Initiative to Party."

117. See Anthony Gierzynski, *Legislative Party Campaign Committees in the American States* (Lexington: University of Kentucky Press, 1992); Daniel M. Shea, *Transforming Democracy: Legislative Campaign Committees and Political Parties* (Albany, N.Y.: SUNY Press, 1995). Anthony Gierzynski and David A. Breaux, "The Financing Role of Parties," in Joel A. Thompson and Gary Moncrief, eds., *Campaign Finance in State Legislative Elections* (Washington, D.C.: Congressional Quarterly Press, 1998). Alan Rosenthal, *The Decline of Representative Democracy: Process, Participation, and Power in State Legislatures* (Washington, D.C.: Congressional Quarterly Press, 1998), 176–183. Malcolm E. Jewell and Marcia Lynn Whicker, *Legislative Leadership in the American States* (Ann Arbor: University of Michigan Press, 1994), 106–114. Tom Loftus, *The Art of Legislative Politics* (Washington, D.C.: Congressional

Quarterly Press, 1994), 36–41. Richard A. Clucas, "Legislative Leadership and Campaign Support in California," *Legislative Studies Quarterly* XVII (1992): 265–283.

118. Cindy Simon Rosenthal, "New Party of Campaign Bank Account? Explaining the Rise of State Legislative Campaign Committees," *Legislative Studies Quarterly* XX (May 1995), 249–268.

119. Jewell and Whicker, *Legislative Leadership in the American States*, 107.

120. Anthony Gierzynski and David A. Breaux, "The Financing Role of Parties," in Joel A. Thompson and Gary Moncrief, eds., *Campaign Finance in State Legislative Elections* (Washington, D.C.: Congressional Quarterly Press, 1998).

121. Gierzynski and Breaux, "The Financing Role of Parties," 192–193.

122. Gierzynski, *Legislative Party Campaign Committees in the American States*, 121.

123. Ibid., 50–58.

124. Ibid., Ch. 5.

125. Gierzynski, *Legislative Party Campaign Committees in the American States*, 53; Shea, *Transforming Democracy*.

126. Shea, *Transforming Democracy*, 171.

127. Ibid., 172. This criticism may also be leveled at the Hill committees—particularly the NRCC, which in 1990 advised House GOP candidates to run against President Bush's budget package and in 1996 sought to distance GOP candidates from Bob Dole's faltering presidential campaign.

128. Ibid., 1–5.

129. Ibid., 6.

130. Alderman Vito Marzullo as quoted in the *Washington Post* (2 November 1985): A3. Marzullo won 23 elections as a machine candidate and served for more than three decades on Chicago's city council before being forced to retire after unfavorable court-ordered redistricting in 1986. He spurned all offers of higher office over the years, explaining, "I just want to stay where I am … where I can help my friends and shaft my enemies." The weakening of Chicago's local Democratic organization was especially evident in 1998, when the organization-endorsed candidate failed to win the nomination contest to replace retiring House member Sidney Yates.

131. Cornelius P. Cotter, James L. Gibson, John F. Bibby, and Robert Huckshorn, *Party Organizations in American Politics* (Pittsburgh: University of Pittsburgh Press, 1989), ch. 3; Paul Allen Beck, Russell J. Dalton, Audrey Haynes, and Robert Huckfeldt, "Local Party Organizations in the 1992 Presidential Elections," paper presented at the annual meeting of the Southern Political Science Association. See also, Beck, *Party Politics in America*, 78–79; John Frendreis and Alan R. Giteson, "Local Parties in the 1990s: Spokes in a Candidate-Centered Wheel," in John G. Green and Daniel M. Shea, eds., *The State of the Parties: The Changing Role of Contemporary American Parties*, 3rd ed. (Lanham: Rowman & Littlefield, 1999).

132. See Tom Watson, "All-Powerful Machine of Yore Endures in New York's Nassau," *Congressional Quarterly Weekly Report* 43 (17 August 1985): 1623–1625.

133. David M. Halbfinger, "The 1999 Elections: Nassau County Halts a Century of GOP Rule," *New York Times* (3 November 1999): A1.

134. Bibby, *Politics, Parties, and Elections in America*, 143–144; A. James Reichley, *The Life of the Parties* (New York: Free Press, 1992), 401–404.

135. William C. Binning, Melanie J. Blumberg, and John C. Green, "Change Comes to Youngstown: Local Political Parties as Instruments of Power," in Green and Shea, *The State of the Parties*, 2nd ed.

136. Beck, *Party Politics in America*, 78.

137. A handful of studies have addressed this question. Kevin M. Leyden and Stephen A. Borrelli, "An Investment in Goodwill: Party Contributions and Party Unity Among U.S. House Members in the 1980s, "*American Politics Quarterly*" 22 (1994): 421–452; Richard Clucas, "Party Contributions and the Influence of Campaign Committee Chairs on Roll-Call Voting," *Legislative Studies Quarterly* XXII (1997): 179–194; David M. Cantor and Paul S. Herrnson, "Party Campaign Activity and Party Unity in the U.S. House of Representatives," *Legislative Studies Quarterly* XXII (August 1997): 393–415. Lyden and Borrelli found that the amount of campaign support that House members receive from party sources during a given election had a positive, if subtle, impact on their willingness to support the party position on the House floor during the session of Congress immediately following the election. Clucas found that congressional campaign committee contributions had a significant impact on a (freshman) member's loyalty to his or her party's congressional campaign committee chair but not on party loyalty more generally. Herrnson and Cantor find little evidence that party spending, recruitment efforts, or campaign assistance lead to greater party loyalty.

138. For an examination of this question at the state level, see Richard Clucas, "The Effect of Campaign Contributions on the Power of the California Assembly Speaker," *Legislative Studies Quarterly* XIX: (1994): 417–427. Clucas found that campaign contributions from the California Assembly Speaker had no statistically significant impact on the extent to which Assembly members sided with the Speaker on roll call votes associated with major legislation.

139. Cantor and Herrnson come closest, using data from two surveys of candidates asked to rate the importance of party fundraising assistance to their campaigns.

140. Martin P. Wattenberg, *The Decline of American Political Parties: 1952–1994* (Cambridge, Mass.: Harvard University Press, 1996).

141. Shea, *Transforming Democracy*, 170.

142. Krasno and Seltz, *Buying Time: Television Advertising in the 1998 Congressional Elections*.

4

The Parties and the People

A POLITICAL PARTY is far more than its organizational shell, however dazzling the technologies at its command, and its reach extends well beyond the relative handful of men and women who comprise the party-in-government. In any democracy, where power is derived directly from the people, the party's real importance and strength must come from the citizenry it attempts to mobilize. The party-in-the-electorate—the mass of potential voters who identify with the Democratic or Republican labels—is the third and most significant element in the party triad, providing the foundation for the organizational and governmental parties. But in some crucial respects it is the most troubled of the three special components of the American political parties. Although partisan loyalty in the electorate has rebounded somewhat in recent years, it has not returned to levels seen in the 1950s and early 1960s. Moreover, while partisan identification remains a powerful determinant of voter choice, voters of each partisan stripe regularly cast ballots for some candidates of the opposing party. The partisan affiliations, the voting practices, and the views about parties held by the American electorate will each be examined in turn in this chapter.

TRENDS IN PARTY IDENTIFICATION

Most American voters identify with a party but do not *belong* to it. There is no universal enrolled party membership, and there are no prescribed dues or enforceable obligations to the party assumed by the voter.[1] The party has no real control over or even an accurate accounting of its adherents, and the party's voters subscribe to few or none of the commonly accepted tenets of organizational membership, such as regular participation and some measure of responsibility for the group's welfare. Rather, party identification or affiliation is an informal and impressionistic exercise whereby a citizen acquires a party label and accepts its standard as a shorthand summary of his or her political views and preferences. Just because the acquisition is informal does not mean it is unimportant, however. As we discussed in Chapter One, the party label becomes a voter's central political reference symbol and perceptual screen, a prism or filter through which the world of politics and government flows and is interpreted. For many Americans, party identification is a significant aspect of self, the vital statistic of one's political personality and a way of defining and explaining oneself to others. The loyalty generated by the label can be as intense as any enjoyed by sports teams and alma maters; in a few areas of the country, "Democrat" and "Republican" are still fighting words.

On the whole, though, Americans regard their partisan affiliation with lesser degrees of enthusiasm, viewing it as a convenience rather than a necessity. Individual identifications are reinforced by the legal institutionalization of the major parties. Because of restrictive ballot laws, campaign finance rules, the powerful inertia of political tradition, and many other factors, voters for all practical purposes are limited to a choice between a Democrat and a Republican in virtually all elections—a situation that naturally encourages the pragmatic choosing up of sides. The party registration process that exists in many states, requiring a voter to state a party preference (or Independent status) when registering to vote and restricting participation in primaries to party registrants, also is an incentive for voters to affiliate.[2] Even the relentless drumbeat of public opinion surveys (to which this study, alas, has contributed) forces a choice of institutionalized party alternatives and may help to perpetuate the current alignment.

Whatever the societal and governmental forces undergirding party identification, the explanations of partisan loyalty at the individual's level are understandably more personal. Not surprisingly, parents are the single greatest influence in establishing a person's first party identification.[3] Politically active parents with the same party loyalty raise children who will be strong party identifiers, while parents without party affiliations or with mixed affiliations produce offspring more likely to be Independents.[4] Early socialization is hardly the last step in the acquisition and maintenance of a party identity; marriage and other facts of adult life can change one's loyalty.[5] So can charismatic political personalities, particularly at the national level (such as Franklin Roosevelt, Ronald Reagan, or Bill Clinton), cataclysmic events (the Civil War and the Great Depression are the best examples), and intense social issues (for instance, abortion). Interestingly, social class is not an especially strong indicator of likely partisan choice in the United States, at least by comparison to Western European democracies.[6] Not only are Americans less inclined than Europeans to perceive class distinctions—preferring instead to see themselves and most others as members of an exceedingly broad middle class—but other factors, including sectionalism and candidate-oriented politics, tend to blur class lines in voting.

Over the last several decades, many political scientists as well as other observers, journalists, and party activists have become increasingly anxious about a perceived decline in partisan identification and loyalty. Many public opinion surveys have shown a significant growth in Independents at the expense of the two major parties. The Center for Political Studies/Survey Research Center (CPS/SRC) of the University of Michigan, for instance, has charted the rise of self-described Independents from a low of 19 percent in 1958 to peaks of 38 percent in 1978 and 1992.[7] Before the 1950s, while the evidence is more circumstantial because of the scarcity of reliable survey research data, there are indications that Independents were many fewer in number, and party loyalties considerably firmer.[8]

Yet as Table 4.1 suggests, the recent decline of party identification can be, and often has been, exaggerated. The most lasting impression left by the table's data is one of remarkable stability (at least in the aggregate). Over more than forty years, during vast political, economic, and social upheavals that have changed the face of the nation, the Democratic party has nearly consistently drawn the support of a small majority (row A) and the Republican party has attracted a share of the electorate in the low-to-high 30 percent range (row B). Granted, there have been peaks and valleys for both parties. The Johnson landslide of 1964 helped Democrats top the 60 percent mark, while GOP electoral successes in 1984, 1988, and 1994 sent Democratic stock below the majority midpoint. The Goldwater debacle of 1964 and the Watergate disaster of 1974 left the Republicans with under a third of the populace. Reagan's reelection brought the GOP to the threshold of 40 percent; Bush's election in 1988 and the Republican tsunami of 1994 finally

TABLE 4.1. PARTY IDENTIFICATION, 1952–1998.

Percent, by Year

Partisan Category	'52	'54	'56	'58	'60	'62	'64	'66	'68	'70	'72	'74	'76	'78	'80	'82	'84	'86	'88	'90	'92	'94	'96	'98
A. Democrat	57	56	50	56	52	54	61	55	55	54	52	52	52	54	52	55	48	51	47	52	50	47	52	51
B. Republican	34	33	37	33	36	35	30	32	33	32	34	31	33	30	33	32	39	36	41	36	38	41	38	37
C. Independent[a]	6	7	9	7	10	8	8	12	11	13	13	15	15	14	13	11	11	12	11	10	12	11	9	11
D. Partisan total (D&R)[b]	91	89	87	89	88	89	91	87	88	86	86	83	85	84	85	87	87	87	88	88	88	88	90	88
E. Strong Democrats	22	22	21	27	20	23	27	18	20	20	15	17	15	15	18	20	17	18	17	20	18	15	18	19
F. Strong Republicans	14	13	15	11	16	12	11	10	10	9	10	8	9	8	9	10	12	10	14	10	11	15	12	10
G. All Independents (including leaners)[c]	23	22	23	19	23	21	23	28	30	31	34	37	37	38	34	30	34	33	36	34	38	36	35	36
H. Partisan total minus Independent leaners[d]	74	74	73	77	75	76	76	71	69	68	65	61	63	60	64	68	64	66	63	64	62	63	64	63

Source: National Election Studies Data, http://www.umich.edu/~nes/.

[a] Pure Independents only. Independent "leaners" have been added to the respective Democratic and Republican totals.

[b] That is, total percentages for Democrats and Republicans listed above have been added together in this row.

[c] That is, Independent Democrats + Independent Republicans + Pure Independents.

[d] That is, partisan total as listed above minus Democratic-leaning and Republican-leaning independents (not shown in table).

pushed the GOP over that threshold. Some slight average erosion over time in Democratic party strength is certainly apparent, as are Republican gains since the Reagan era. Yet, these sorts of gradations are more akin to rolling foothills than towering mountain ranges, or (to mix metaphors) gentle merry-go-rounds than turbulent roller coasters. The steady-state nature of modern partisanship goes beyond the fortunes of each party. Since we are concerned here with partisan loyalty as a whole, Row D—which adds Democratic and Republican strength together—is even more reassuring. Support for the two parties in modern times has never dipped below 83 percent of the American electorate (recorded during the disillusionment spawned by Watergate in 1974) and can usually be found in the mid-to-upper 80 percent range. A gradual downward drift from the 1952 and 1964 zeniths of 91 percent is obvious, but recent years have seen the partisanship proportion rise above its forty-year average of 87 percent. (See also Figure 4.1.)

Critics will properly point out that we have relied upon the strictest definition of "Independent" in the foregoing analysis. When pollsters ask for party identification information, they generally proceed in two stages. First they inquire whether the respondent considers himself or herself a Democrat, Republican, or Independent. Then the party identifiers are asked to categorize themselves as a "strong" or "not very strong" supporter, while the Independents are pushed to reveal their leanings with a question such as, "Well, which party do you normally

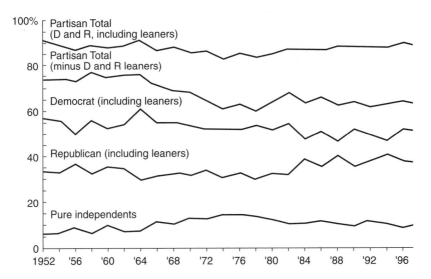

FIGURE 4.1 TRENDS IN PARTY IDENTIFICATION, 1952–1998

Source: See Table 4.1

support in elections—the Democrats or the Republicans?" It may be true that some Independent respondents are thereby prodded to pick a party under the pressure of the interview situation, regardless of their true feelings. But research demonstrates that independent "leaners" vote somewhat similarly to real partisans—in some elections more so than the "not very strong" party identifiers.[9] Thus, there is reason to count the Independent leaners as closet partisans, though voting behavior is not the equivalent of real partisan identification. If it were, we would not bother to ask poll respondents about their party affiliations, quizzing them only about how they normally vote.

In fact, the reluctance of "leaners" to admit their real party identities in itself is worrisome because it reveals a sea change in attitudes about political parties and their proper role in our nation. Being a socially acceptable, integrated, and contributing member of one's community once almost demanded partisan affiliation; it was a badge of good citizenship, motherhood, and apple pie, signifying that one was a patriot. Today the labels are shunned as an offense to a thinking person's individualism, and a vast majority of Americans insist they vote for "the man, not the party." These antiparty attitudes will be examined in more detail shortly, but the reasons for their prevalence are not hard to find. The growth of an issue-oriented politics that cuts across party lines for those voters who feel intensely about certain policy matters is partly to blame.[10] So too is the emphasis on personality politics by the mass media (especially television) and political consultants.[11] Others cite the broad-based higher educational levels achieved in recent decades, which supposedly enables voters to gain enough information to judge candidates on issues and character apart from party labels,[12] though this hypothesis has been seriously disputed by additional research.[13] Underlying all of these causes, though, is a far more disturbing and corrosive long-term phenomenon: the perceived loss of party credibility and the decline of the party's tangible connections to the lives of everyday citizens. This development—and possible mechanisms to reverse it—will be the focus of the concluding chapters, but for now it is enough to note that, while total real partisanship has not declined significantly since 1952 (as discussed earlier), voter-admitted partisanship has dropped considerably. Referring again to Table 4.1 (row H), about three-quarters or more of the electorate volunteered a party choice without prodding from 1952 to 1964, but, since 1970, an average of under two-thirds has been willing to do so. Self-professed Independents (including leaners)[14] have increased from around a fifth of the electorate in the 1950s to a third or more since the 1970s—reaching the record high of 38 percent in both 1978 and 1992 (row G). Also cause for concern is the marginal decline in strong Democrats (row E) and strong Republicans (row F). Although the 1990s saw some good years for both parties in terms of attracting strong partisans, the 90s also witnessed some worrisome lows. Indeed, only 10 percent of Americans considered themselves strong Republicans in both 1990 and 1998, and only 15 percent of Americans considered themselves strong Democrats in 1994. Strong partisans are a party's backbone, the source of its volunteer force, candidates, and dependable voters. Even slight shrinkage in these ranks can be troublesome. Finally, when we consider only *pure* Independents—the voter category least friendly to political parties—growth was apparent, especially during the 1970s (row C). Despite a partisan rebound in the 1980s and 90s, the proportion of pure Independents was nearly double in 1998 what it was in 1952.

THE SUBGROUP CONTINUUM OF PARTY LOYALTY

The national summary data on party identification are deceptive and simplistic, as all averages can be. There are enormous variations in the patterns of party loyalty from one region or demographic group to another, as Table 4.2 demonstrates:

- The Democratic party continues to hold a sizable advantage in partisan identifiers in the South (an affinity cultivated in the nineteenth century and stoked in the fires of the Civil War). Democrats also have a significant upper hand in the Midwest, enjoying a 12-percent lead in partisan identifiers over the GOP. In contrast, the West, Border states, and—especially—the Northeast, are relatively closely contested between the two parties. In all regions, party strengths vary by locality, with urban areas almost everywhere heavily Democratic, while suburbs, small towns, and rural areas are split fairly evenly between the two major parties.

- Over the course of the past few decades, a widening gap developed between the partisan identification of women and men, with women tending to identify with Democrats and men tending to favor Republicans. This so-called *gender gap* was largely the result of a gradual movement of men toward the Republican party without a commensurate movement among women.[15] Consistent with these trends, the first edition of this book in 1988 reported a 16-point gap between the partisan allegiances of men and women, with Democrats assuming a 10-point advantage over Republicans among women but a 6–point deficit to Republicans among men. In contrast, our 2000 survey results reveal only a 4-point gap between the

TABLE 4.2. Party Identification by Selected Subgroups, 2000 [a].

Selected subgroup	Republican	Democrat	Independent [b]	Democratic Advantage
National sample	37	45	12	+8
Geography				
Northeast	41	41	12	0
Midwest	34	46	13	+12
South	34	47	14	+13
West	43	46	8	+3
Border	41	49	8	+7
Demography				
Urban	33	52	10	+19
Suburban	41	43	10	+2
Small town	38	42	14	+4
Rural	41	40	13	−1
Gender				
Men	38	44	12	+6
Women	37	47	11	+10
Race				
African American	10	77	10	+67
White	42	41	12	−1
Hispanic	15	77	5	+62
Asian	43	43	7	0
Age				
18–24	25	54	16	+29
25–34	39	51	5	+12
35–44	36	46	13	+10
45–54	35	47	13	+12
55–64	42	35	16	−7
65 and over	44	40	9	−4
Occupation				
Executive/Professional/Mgt	40	44	11	+4
Blue collar	34	50	9	+16
Service/retail/clerical	40	42	11	+2
Govt (excluding military)	29	57	9	+28
Retired	42	39	12	−4
Homemaker	44	37	14	−7
Labor Union				
Union household	30	52	13	+22
Income				
Under $20,000	27	60	9	+33
$20,000–$40,000	35	47	13	+12
$40,001–$60,000	37	47	10	+10

(continued)

TABLE 4.2. CONTINUED

Selected subgroup	Republican	Democrat	Independent	Democratic Advantage
Income				
$60,001–$75,000	45	42	9	–3
More than $75,000	44	41	11	–2
Education				
Less than high school	24	57	9	+33
High school	35	46	14	+11
Some college	38	46	11	+8
College grad	45	37	13	–8
Grad or prof degree	33	53	10	+20
Internet Use				
Almost every day	39	43	12	+4
Few times a week	40	41	11	+1
Rarely or never	33	51	11	+18
Marital Status				
Married	41	40	12	–1
Single	30	56	11	+26
Widowed	35	42	15	+7
Divorced/separated	29	59	5	+30
Religion				
Mainstream Protestant	40	44	13	+4
Fund./Evan. Protestant	39	48	8	+9
Catholic	40	45	10	+5
Jewish	13	65	9	+52
Ideology				
Very liberal	17	68	11	+51
Somewhat liberal	18	69	10	+51
Moderate	34	47	13	+13
Somewhat conservative	50	34	12	–16
Very conservative	60	29	5	–31

Source: August 2000 survey conducted by John McLaughlin and Associates for this book. See Appendix. Sample subsets have higher sampling error and lower estimate reliability than the overall sample.

[a]The question wording and coding is as follows: "Generally speaking, do you usually think of yourself as a Republican, a Democrat, an Independent, or something else? Respondents who answered "Democrat" or "Republican were asked whether they are a strong or not very strong Democrat/Republican. Respondents who answered "Independent," "Other," or "No Preference" were asked which party do you normally support in elections, the Republican Party or the Democratic Party?" Respondents who answered "Independent," "Some Other Party," or "No Preference" in the initial question, but who in the follow-up question reported normally supporting either Republicans or Democrats in elections, were coded as partisan leaners of the party they normally support. Respondents who answered "Independent," "Some Other Party," or "No Preference" in the initial question, and who in the follow up question reported normally supporting both parties equally in elections, were coded as pure Independents. Respondents who answered "Independent," "Some Other Party," or "No Preference " in the initial question, and who in the follow up question reported normally supporting some other party in elections, were coded as "other party" "Don't know/refuse and "other party" responses are not included in the table; therefore, row percentages do not total 100 percent.

[b]Pure Independents only. Partisan leaners (those pushed to identify their partisan leanings after first categorizing themselves as "Independent") are included in Democrat and Republican totals.

partisan affiliation of men and women, with Democrats still holding a 10-point lead over the GOP among women but also now
enjoying a 6-point advantage over Republicans among men.[16] The
Democratic advantage in partisan identification among both
males and females vanishes when only whites are considered,
however. Among white males, the GOP has a 3 point advantage
over Democrats, whereas white females split evenly between
Democrats and Republicans.

- African Americans are the most dramatically different population
subgroup in party terms. The 67 percent advantage they offer the
Democrats dwarfs the edge given to either party by most other segments of the electorate—though the edge is considerably smaller
than the 82-percent advantage that African Americans provided
Democrats when the first edition of this book was published. Nevertheless, African Americans remain firmly in the Democratic camp.
Not only are they considerably more likely than whites to be
Democrats, within the Democratic party, African Americans are
more likely than whites to be strong Democrats. Perhaps as a reflec-
tion of the considerable party chasm separating whites and African
Americans, the two races differ greatly on many policy issues, with
African Americans more likely to be liberal than whites.[17] The much
smaller population group of Hispanics[18] supplements blacks as a
Democratic stalwart; by 77 percent to 15 percent, Hispanics prefer
the Democratic label.

- When the first edition of this book was published in 1988, young
people were clearly trending Republican. Table 4.2 indicates that
this has changed. Indeed, Democrats enjoy a 29-percent advantage
over the GOP in the 18–24 age group, and the Democratic advantage, while shrinking with age, evaporates completely only for
individuals 55 or older. The Democratic advantage among young
individuals harks back to the days of the early 1970s, when young
people, particularly students, were the only age cohort to support
Democratic presidential nominee George McGovern in 1972.[19]
Democratic President Bill Clinton's success in reaching out to
young people—appearing on youth-targeted programs such as
MTV, for example—may have helped the Democratic party
increase its share of identifiers among this group. For Democrats,
the task now is to boost voter turnout among young people, who
typically vote in relatively low numbers. Perhaps not surprisingly,
individuals in the 45–54 age group, whose political views were

shaped in part by the era of civil rights, Vietnam, and Watergate, identify with Democrats in significant numbers.

- Some traditional strengths and weaknesses persist for each party by occupation, income, and education. As one might expect, individuals who reside in labor union households—households in which at least one family member belongs to a labor union—are strongly Democratic, though the GOP's share of 30 percent suggests that Democratic support among individuals from labor union households is not monolithic. Republicans come close to Democrats among executives, professionals, and management employees, as well as among service, retail, and clerical workers. On the other hand, Democrats enjoy a significant lead over Republicans among blue-collar workers and non-military government employees. The more conservative retired population leans Republican, though not by a great measure, owing perhaps to Democratic skill in exploiting issues that concern seniors, such as Social Security, Medicare, and prescription drug benefits. Female homemakers, who tend to be less liberal than wage-earning women, favor Republicans over Democrats by about 7 percentage points—a reversal from this book's first edition.[20] Occupation, income, and education are closely related, of course, so many of the same partisan patterns can be detected in all three classifications. Democratic support drops steadily as one climbs the income scale. From a strong 33-percent lead among those whose families make under $20,000 a year, Democrats gradually move to a 2-percent deficit among those whose families earn more than $75,000 annually. Similarly, as years of education increase, identification with the Democratic party decreases—but only to a point. Although Republicans enjoy an 8-percent advantage in partisan identifiers among college graduates, individuals with graduate or professional degrees overwhelmingly favor Democrats.

- With the exception of the Jewish population—which identifies overwhelmingly with the Democratic Party—the two major parties are competitive in vying for identifiers within religious groups.[21] Although the GOP made inroads in the Jewish population in the past,[22] those inroads have vanished. Jews are predominantly Democratic in affiliation, providing the Democrats with a 52-percent advantage over Republicans in partisan identifiers. Other religions are more evenly split between the parties. While Catholics were a significant part of the Democratic New Deal coalition, Republicans can now claim 40 percent of the Catholic population. On the other hand, Democrats have a small edge among mainstream Protestants, who, during the 1960s, identified strongly with the Republican party. Perhaps more surprisingly, Republicans trail Democrats by nine percentage points among fundamentalist/evangelical Protestants—a group that has showed some signs of moving toward the GOP.[23] Certainly African Americans, who are slightly more likely than whites to be Protestant fundamentalists or evangelicals (and who are overwhelming Democratic), account for some of the Democratic advantage here. But Democrats hold a 5-percentage advantage even among white fundamentalist/evangelical Protestants.

- Even marital status reveals something about partisan affiliation. Those who are married, a traditionally more conservative group, and those who have never married, a segment weighted toward the premarriage young who are currently Democratic-leaning, are significantly divided in their party loyalties. Whereas Democrats have a 1-percent deficit among married individuals, they enjoy a striking 26-percent advantage over Republicans among the single population. While the widowed are also Democratic in nature, divorced and separated individuals are especially likely to identify with the Democrats—perhaps because they experience more economic hardship than do people in other circumstances.

- Ideologically, there are few surprises. Lending credence to the belief that both parties are now relatively distinct philosophically, liberals are overwhelmingly Democratic and conservatives staunchly Republican. One source of the overall Democratic edge in the general electorate is apparent from the ideological breakdowns. Democrats control the center, with a 13-percent advantage over the GOP among individuals who consider themselves moderate. Moreover, the Democratic defection rate among the party's natural philosophical constituency is much lower than the Republicans. Democrats lose just 17 percent of the "very liberal" to the GOP, but thanks mainly to continued Democratic strength in the South, the Republican party is deserted by a full 29 percent of the "very conservative" voters.

These subgroup partisan loyalties yield a kind of continuum of party identification in the American electorate, as Figure 4.2 depicts. Even a quick glance at the figure confirms some of the points made earlier. First, the Republicans have nothing comparable to the truly remarkable position of African Americans in the Democratic constellation. Second, Democrats maintain their edge partly by drawing disproportionately

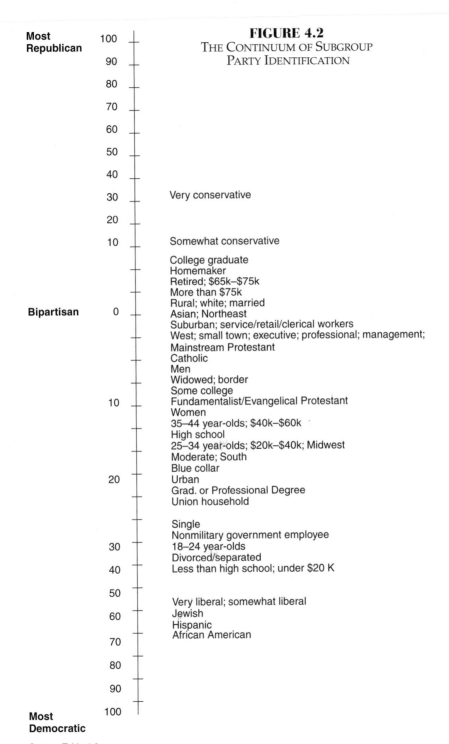

FIGURE 4.2
THE CONTINUUM OF SUBGROUP
PARTY IDENTIFICATION

Most Republican 100

90

80

70

60

50

40

30 — Very conservative

20

10 — Somewhat conservative

College graduate
Homemaker
Retired; $65k–$75k
More than $75k
Rural; white; married

Bipartisan 0 — Asian; Northeast
Suburban; service/retail/clerical workers
West; small town; executive; professional; management;
Mainstream Protestant
Catholic
Men
Widowed; border
Some college

10 — Fundamentalist/Evangelical Protestant
Women
35–44 year-olds; $40k–$60k
High school
25–34 year-olds; $20k–$40k; Midwest
Moderate; South
Blue collar

20 — Urban
Grad. or Professional Degree
Union household

Single
Nonmilitary government employee

30 — 18–24 year-olds
Divorced/separated

40 — Less than high school; under $20 K

50

Very liberal; somewhat liberal

60 — Jewish
Hispanic
African American

70

80

90

Most Democratic 100

Source: Table 4.2

from the GOP's base; the whole continuum seems to be shifted in the Democratic direction rather than being symmetrical. And third, while Democratic subgroup margins have shrunk vastly from Franklin Roosevelt's heyday, at least some vestiges of the New Deal coalition are still apparent. (This is a subject to which we will return in the next chapter.)

The subgroup continuum of Figure 4.2 is certainly not immutable. Events and personalities can affect individual segments of the population. For instance, an African American such as Secretary of State Colin Powell might well move some African Americans into the GOP column were he to run for president on the Republican ticket. But by and large, when the political drift pushes the electorate toward one or the other party, a marginal shift of just a few percent occurs in most or all of the subgroupings; save in special circumstances or during a full-scale party realignment, they tend to slide back and forth along the scale in roughly the same formation, flowing with the tidal currents of politics.

Perhaps as expected, many of the subgroups clustered toward the most partisan ends of the continuum have the greatest proportion of strong party identifiers, especially on the Democratic side. African Americans, Hispanics, those whose families make under $20,000 annually, individuals who have less than a high school education, Jews, and union members were all more likely to be strong Democrats than were others in the Democratic coalition. In the GOP more than the Democratic party, older voters rather than younger ones tended to exhibit firmer partisan identification. Still, the parties are strikingly similar to each other in the mix of strong, weak, and leaning identifiers that make up their respective bases.

Independents do not appear in the party subgroup continuum, of course, but like the partisans, they are differentiated. As Table 4.2 indicates, small town and rural dwellers, individuals in the 18–24 and 55–65 age groups, and the widowed are all more likely to be Independents than other groups. More importantly, political scientist Martin Wattenberg argues that there are really two types of political independents: those who consciously reject the two parties—for whom the parties are something to be independent *from*—and those for whom the parties have no meaning—who don't view the political world through the lens of parties.[24] While subtle, the distinction is meaningful. Individuals lacking a partisan perceptual filter tend to be apolitical, tuned-out nonvoters who care little for politics.[25] Independents who consciously reject the parties, in contrast, are more politically involved; they participate and vote in elections at rates not unlike weak partisans.

As we noted earlier, these national averages hide the richer and far more complex changes occurring simultaneously in individuals, population subgroups, and particular states. The diversity in the fifty states is not as dramatic as in subgroups and individuals, of course, but it is substantial. Table 4.3 presents party identification levels in the American states. Compared to the national partisan breakdown, there is wide variation. While states such as Arkansas and West Virginia have heavy Democratic advantages, states such Utah and Idaho favor the GOP by wide margins. In the middle of the partisan spectrum, however, exist a considerable number of states where partisan identification is virtually evenly split among the two parties. Some important changes are afoot in the states. Florida, long a Democratic haven, is clearly moving toward the GOP, as are Virginia and South Carolina—two southern states long dominated by the Democratic party. Indeed, southern states in general tend to be trending toward the GOP, a phenomenon we will address at length in the next chapter. Not incidentally, a state party identification can operate somewhat independently of a voter's national party affiliation; that is, voters may identify with one party at the state and/or local level and with the other party at the national level. This bifurcated, federalist pattern of party affiliation was especially common in the South from the mid-1960s through the 1980s (and indeed still persists at lower levels in the South today), when the national Democratic party was often viewed by southern Democrats as out of step with the traditional conservatism that characterized southern state Democratic parties.

TICKET-SPLITTING AND PARTY VOTING

Party identification is only one measure of party loyalty, of course. Just as important is the willingness of voters to support their party's nominees at election time. For those who hope for party-voter solidarity, there is at least some reason to be encouraged: the percentage of voters who engage in the practice of ticket-splitting—voting simultaneously for candidates of both parties—has gradually edged down. Since 1952, the NES survey has tracked Americans' voting behavior—including, importantly, their propensities for splitting their ballots between presidential and congressional candidates of different parties. The trends are instructive. While only 12 percent of survey respondents reported voting for presidential and House candidates of different parties in 1952, a record high of 30 percent reported casting split ballots for these offices in 1972.[26] Since 1972, however, the percentage of split-ticket voters has gradually decreased, declining to 17 percent in 1996, though the fragility of partisan identification by no means guarantees it will

TABLE 4.3. PARTY IDENTIFICATION IN THE STATES, 1989–1996.

State	Democratic	Independent	Republican	Party Margins
Arkansas	44	35	21	23 D
West Virginia	50	22	28	22 D
Hawaii	43	33	23	20 D
Louisiana	48	23	29	19 D
Maryland	47	24	29	18 D
Oklahoma	49	18	33	16 D
Kentucky	47	22	31	16 D
Massachusetts	31	52	17	14 D
Minnesota	37	36	27	10 D
Georgia	39	31	30	9 D
Delaware	37	35	28	9 D
Rhode Island	27	55	18	9 D
New York	38	31	31	7 D
North Carolina	40	26	34	6 D
Alaska	29	48	23	6 D
Mississippi	40	25	35	5 D
Pennsylvania	40	24	36	4 D
Tennessee	36	32	32	4 D
Missouri	33	38	29	4 D
Washington	31	41	28	3 D
Alabama	35	33	32	3 D
Illinois	34	35	31	3 D
Ohio	35	32	33	2 D
Wisconsin	32	38	30	2 D
Connecticut	30	42	28	2 D
California	38	25	37	1 D
Oregon	36	29	35	1 D
Texas	34	32	33	1 D
Florida	36	28	36	0
Michigan	32	37	32	0
Vermont	26	47	26	0
Montana	31	37	32	1 R
New Jersey	31	37	32	1 R
Iowa	30	39	31	1 R
Maine	28	43	30	2 R
New Mexico	35	28	37	2 R
Virginia	31	35	34	3 R
South Carolina	33	31	36	3 R
Colorado	28	39	33	5 R
Indiana	31	33	36	5 R
North Dakota	25	44	31	6 R
Arizona	31	29	39	8 R
New Hampshire	20	50	30	10 R
Kansas	29	32	39	10 R

(continued)

TABLE 4.3. CONTINUED

State	Democratic	Independent	Republican	Party Margins
South Dakota	34	21	45	11 R
Nevada	30	27	43	13 R
Nebraska	30	24	45	15 R
Wyoming	23	33	44	21 R
Idaho	21	36	43	22 R
Utah	21	30	49	28 R

Source: Data taken from Gerald C. Wright, unpublished data set, 1998, as reprinted in Malcolm E. Jewell and Sarah Morehouse, *Political Parties and Elections in the American States,* 4th ed. (Washington, D.C.: Congressional Quarterly Press, 2001), 40-41. Used by permission.

continue declining. Interestingly, survey research turns up more ticket-splitting when respondents are asked directly whether or not they usually split their tickets. (NES data on ticket-splitting are tabulated on the basis of respondents' reported vote choices, not a direct question about ticket splitting.) For example, in a 1996 Media Studies Center/Roper Center survey, a sizable majority of respondents reported typically splitting their tickets in elections.[27] Similarly, in a 2000 postelection survey conducted by John McLaughlin and Associates, 40 percent of respondents said they were usually "ticket-splitters" at the ballot box.[28] These high percentages (relative to NES data on ticket splitting) may reflect split-ticket voting below the national level. But they may also reflect a reluctance on the part of respondents to admit straight-ticket voting, lest they be thought of as nonthinking individuals blindly following a party's lead. As optimists who favor strong parties, we cling to the evidence of decreasing split-ticket voting revealed by NES data.

Not surprisingly, the intensity of party affiliation is a major determinant of a voter's propensity to ticket-split. According to NES data, strong party identifiers are the most likely to cast a straight party ticket; pure Independents are the least likely. Somewhat greater proportions of ticket-splitters are found among high-income and better-educated citizens, but there is little difference in the distribution by sex or by age. As expected, African Americans exhibit the lowest ticket-splitting rate of any population subgroup; in 1996 they were considerably less likely than the national average to cast ballots for presidential and House candidates of different partisan stripes.

There are a number of explanations for ticket-splitting, many of them similar to the perceived causes of the dip in party identification levels. The growth of issue-oriented politics, the mushrooming of single interest groups, the greater emphasis on candidate-centered personality politics, and broader-based education are all often cited. So too is the marked gain in the value of incumbency. Thanks in part to the enormous fattening of congressional constituency services, incumbent United States representatives and senators have been able to attract a steady share of the other party's identifiers.[29] Once again, though, the most powerful and telling explanation for yet another antiparty phenomenon may well be this: the parties simply do not matter as much as they once did to voters,[30] and they seem to have little relevance to the lives and daily needs of most Americans. The disconnection between the party and its voter may be more fundamental and pervasive than any of the other factors mentioned above, but at least it is a situation the parties can do something about, as we will argue in Chapter Six.

The problem with high levels of ticket-splitting, of course, is that it produces executive and legislative victors of different parties—which in turn produces divided government, an arrangement whereby different parties control the executive and legislative branches. Consistent with increases in split-ticket voting, the percentage of congressional districts with split election results for president and U.S. House increased markedly after the 1950s, though the percentage has ebbed somewhat during the 1990s. (See Figure 4.3.) In presidential elections from 1920 to 1944, an average of 13 percent of the congressional districts returned presidential and House candidates of different parties; in contrast, an average of 32 percent of congressional districts elected House members and presidents of different parties in the presidential elections from 1960 to 1996.[31] (The modern record was in 1972, when 44 percent of congressional districts chose presidential and House candidates of different parties.) The result has been a nearly permanent state of divided government at the national level. Republican presidential victories in 1956, 1972, 1980, 1984, and 1988 were accompanied by the election of substantial Democratic majorities in the House of Representatives. In 1996, the electoral situation reversed itself, with voters returning a Democrat to the White House but Republican majorities to both the House and Senate. The 2000 election brought unified control to Washington—but only temporarily. The historic election produced a GOP president, a slim GOP house majority, and an evenly split Senate (with GOP Vice President Dick Cheney casting tie-breaking votes). But five months into the 107th Congress, Republican Senator Jim Jeffords of Vermont quit the GOP, handing the party control of the Senate to Democrats and bringing back divided government. (Jeffords became an Independent who would caucus with Democrats on organizational matters.) With a razor thin partisan balance, control of the Senate could well undergo further shifts before the 2002 midterm elections. Divided government has increased markedly at the state level as well, with 25 states operating under divided government in the period from 1999–2000.[32] Divided government is troubling for advocates of strong parties, since split control of the government makes any sort of party-responsible government much more difficult to achieve.[33]

Another way to evaluate the parties' relevance to voters is by examining the extent to which a party's identifiers actually support the party's candidates on election day. Examining gubernatorial elections in 1986, 1990, and 1994, political scientists Malcolm E. Jewell and Sarah M. Morehouse point out that individuals vote for the candidate of the party with which they identify nearly 80 percent of the time.[34] At the presidential level, defections tend to be even fewer. In the 2000 presidential election, for instance, 87 percent of self-identified Republicans supported George Bush, while 85 percent of self-described Democrats voted for Al Gore.[35] Not surprisingly, a party's strongest identifiers typically support the party's presidential candidate at the highest rates.[36] In the 1996 presidential election, for example, 96 percent of the GOP's strongest identifiers supported Republican presidential candidate Bob Dole at the voting booth, and 94 percent of strong Democrats voted for Democratic presidential candidate Bill Clinton.[37] A party's weaker identifiers, in contrast, are more willing to abandon the party's presidential candidate on election day. Indeed, 17 percent of weak Democrats defected from

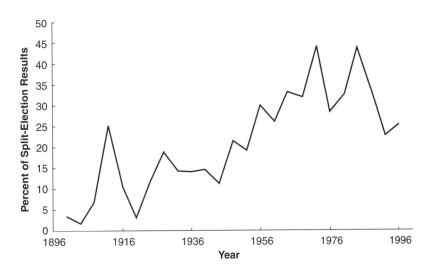

FIGURE 4.3 PERCENTAGE OF CONGRESSIONAL DISTRICTS WITH SPLIT ELECTION RESULTS FOR PRESIDENT AND U.S. HOUSE OF REPRESENTATIVES, 1900–1996

Source: Norman Ornstein et al. *Vital Statistics on Congress, 1997–1998* (Washington, D.C.: American Enterprise Institute, 1999). Also, Advisory Commission on Intergovernmental Relations, *The Transformation of American Politics* (Washington, D.C.: ACIR, 1986), 56.

Democrat Bill Clinton at the polls in 1996, as did 26 percent of Democratic leaners (the weakest category of partisans). Similarly, Dole's support was weaker among less-committed GOP partisans, with 29 percent of weak Republicans and 34 percent of Republican leaners supporting a presidential candidate other than Dole on election day.[38] Party defection rates tend to be even slightly higher in congressional contests. Remarkably, 13 percent of even the strongest Democratic identifiers failed to vote for Democratic congressional candidates in 1996.[39] Even more disturbing, as political scientist Gary Jacobson points out, party defections in congressional races typically come at the expense of challengers.[40] The good news in all of this is that a party's identifiers—weak, strong, and leaners—are more reliable supporters of the party's candidates than are independents. Also heartening is that each party has increased its corps of strong identifiers relative to the low point of the mid-1970s. (See Table 4.1).

PARTISAN IMAGES AND POPULAR ATTITUDES

In a country where politics is generally unappreciated and is viewed suspiciously as a source of duplicity, intrigue, and corruption, it should come as no surprise that Americans have skeptical if ambivalent opinions about partisan activity. On one hand, people recognize the civic virtue inherent in party work; on the other, they lack confidence in the parties, fail to appreciate their political centrality in our system, and resist ceding their individual political prerogatives to them. The political parties have experienced a measurable decline in their perceived legitimacy in the last quarter century. There has been a steady drop, for instance, in the proportion of people who believe that "political parties help to make the government pay attention to what the people think."[41] Political scientists differ about whether the public is more negative and openly hostile toward the parties or merely more indifferent and neutral about them,[42] but whichever description may be more accurate, it is indisputable that the political parties are not as highly respected and regarded as they once were.

Certainly the results of our survey offer little cheer to those concerned about the parties. As Table 4.4 shows, public attitudes on partisan subjects suggest that, while opinion is mixed and support for the parties has not collapsed by any means, there is no ringing endorsement for the parties. Americans say they vote for "the person, not the party" by as close to a unanimous margin as public opinion usually gets. Indeed, a full 90 percent of our survey respondents agreed with the statement "I usually vote for the candidate who I think is best for the

TABLE 4.4. CITIZEN ATTITUDES ABOUT
POLITICAL PARTIES (IN PERCENTAGES).

Statement	Agree	Disagree
A. I usually vote for the candidate who I think is best for the job, regardless of what party he or she belongs to.	90	7
B. If I don't know anything else about a candidate for public office, knowing the candidate's political party helps me decide whether or not to vote for him or her.	52	43
C. The two major political parties we have now in America are enough; we don't need any new ones.	37	57
D. It's wasting my vote to vote for a candidate that is not a Republican or Democrat, since Republicans and Democrats almost always win anyway.	38	57
E. There is little difference between the candidates and the policies of the Republican party and the candidates and policies of the Democratic party.	39	53
F. Overall, it really doesn't matter which political party holds the most seats in the U.S. House and Senate.	36	58

Source: August 2000 survey conducted by John McLaughlin and Associates for this book.
See Appendix.
Percentages do not add up to 100 since "don't know" and "refused" responses are not included.

job, regardless of what party he or she belongs to." Clearly, Americans
are quick to assert their independence from party labels. Moreover, as
statement C suggests, Americans have no special love for the two-party
system, with 57 percent of our survey respondents believing that the
United States needs more than the two parties it presently has. This is a
considerable shift from the sentiment reported in the first edition of this
book (1988)—when only 34 percent of survey respondents agreed that
America needed more than its two major parties.[43]

Other findings were more encouraging, if only slightly so. A small
majority (52 percent) acknowledged that "knowing the candidate's
political party helps me decide whether or not to vote for him or her" if
other information was lacking. This indicates that at least some people
still appreciate the useful voting cue provided by political parties. (See
Chapter One). The hopeful will also note that 53 percent of our respondents disagreed with the statement that there is little difference between
the candidates and policies of the two major parties. Also inspiring optimism is that 58 percent disagreed with the statement that "it really does-
n't matter which political party holds the most seats in the U.S. House
and Senate." On the other hand, of course, the pessimist will point out
that more than a third of our respondents *agreed* with these sentiments—
a remarkable view given the polarizing partisan politics of the past

decade. If individuals fail to see differences between the parties in this era of heightened partisanship, it's questionable whether they ever will.

At the same time the electorate as a whole does not seem to be hostile toward the parties. The institutions themselves are judged fairly highly. (See Table 4.5.) Not only do both major parties achieve favorability ratings well over 50 percent (very favorable and somewhat favorable), their percentage of "very favorable" ratings are quite similar to well-known partisan figures. Indeed, the Democratic Party's "very favorable" rating of 41 percent exceeds that of Democrats Bill Clinton and Al Gore. Naturally, each party is rated most highly by its own identifiers and primary constituency groups, but even Independents gave the two major parties fairly high ratings. For instance, 52 percent of Independents rated the Democratic Party favorably, and 57 percent of Independents bestowed a favorable rating on the GOP. Table 4.5 also indicates the extent to which the minor parties and their candidates play second fiddle to the major parties in the United States. Indeed, 38 percent of our respondents had no opinion about the Reform Party, and 10 percent had never even heard of it! Opinions about the Green and Libertarian Parties are even fewer, as is knowledge of these parties.

Respondents to our survey were also asked open-ended questions about the two major parties. (See Table 4.6.) As the table makes clear, well-worn images of the two major parties persist. "Liberal" was the most common badge given to the Democratic Party. In the tradition of the New Deal, moreover, Democrats are still viewed as the champions of the "working class." Yet they also remain tagged as the party of big spenders, high taxers, and proponents of wasteful government "giveaway" programs. The Republicans, on the other hand, retain the "party of the rich" label; indeed 10 percent of our respondents applied that appellation to the GOP. Not surprisingly, a considerable portion of respondents also labeled the GOP "conservative," though more than a few individuals spun that label negatively, calling the GOP "out of step," "old school," and "old white males." Interestingly, very few respondents associated the GOP with strong foreign policy, clearly a party strength when the GOP held the presidency during the final period of the Cold War. Relative to the major parties, only very small minorities had any comments at all about the minor parties, but when they did, the labels were as one might expect. "Environmentalists," "extremists," and "tree-huggers" topped the Green Party list of insignias, while labels such as "change" and "disorganized" were pinned on the Reform Party. Perhaps most troubling about our open-ended inquiries was that significant percentages of our respondents had *nothing* to say—good

TABLE 4.5. PARTY VS. PERSONALITY FAVORABILITY RATINGS.

Question: Please tell me if you have a favorable or unfavorable opinion of the following people/organizations. If you have no opinion or have never heard of each, just say so.

Name/Institution	Very favorable	Somewhat favorable	Somewhat unfavorable	Very unfavorable	No opinion	Never heard of
Bill Clinton	34	18	9	30	9	**
Al Gore	36	20	12	20	12	**
George W. Bush	39	20	12	19	8	1
Ralph Nader	15	16	13	15	29	11
Pat Buchanan	8	15	16	30	24	5
Republican Party	35	19	13	20	11	2
Democratic Party	41	19	12	16	10	2
Green Party	9	11	8	14	41	16
Reform Party	9	10	13	19	38	10
Libertarian Party	9	10	11	18	40	11

Source: August 2000 survey conducted by John McLaughlin and Associates for this book. See Appendix. Respondents who answered favorable/unfavorable were probed as to whether their opinions were very favorable/unfavorable or just somewhat favorable/unfavorable.

TABLE 4.6. SAMPLE COMMENTS OF CITIZENS' PARTY DESCRIPTIONS. [a]

Positive Comments

Democratic Party	Republican Party
"Fair/equality"	"Responsible/Realistic"
"For the working/middle class"	"Fair/Honest/Respectful"
"Down to earth"	"For the people"
"Problem solvers"	"Integrity of Candidates"
"Helping senior citizens"	"Party of Lincoln"
"Getting things done"	"Better for the Economy"

Negative Comments

Democratic Party	Republican Party
"Lack of Integrity/Morality"	"Party for the Rich"
"Wishy-washy"	"Greedy"
"Hypocritical"	"For Big Business"
"Jackasses"	"Selfish/Vengeful/Uncaring"
"Special interests"	"Out-of-Step/Old School"
"Unrealistic/out of touch"	"Old White Men"

Source: August 2000 survey conducted by John McLaughlin and Associates for this book.
See Appendix.

[a]The comments in this table are generally representative of the recorded comments.

or bad—about the parties. Remarkably, 39 percent provided no words to describe the Republican party, and 37 percent could think of nothing to say about the Democratic party. Needless to say, the percentages of "no answer" responses were even higher for the minor parties.[44] The significant portion of individuals with little to say about the parties makes clear the diminishing importance of the parties as perceptual screens through which people view the political world.

PARTY PERSONALITIES AND THE VOTERS

A party's image is also shaped to a great degree by the men and women who seek or secure its presidential and vice-presidential nominations, or become prominent in the national spotlight in other ways. Which candidates—from the past and present—do voters most identify with each political party? In the survey conducted for this study, respondents were asked, "Which person—either from the past or present—do you associate most with the Democratic/Republican party?" (Multiple responses were permitted.) Table 4.7 presents the five politicians most closely associated with the Democratic and Republican parties. For the Democrats, Bill Clinton surpassed John F. Kennedy as the brightest star in the firmament, with 31 percent of the total population naming him. Yet, who

TABLE 4.7. PARTY PERSONALITIES AND THE VOTERS (IN PERCENTAGES).

Question: "Which person—either from the past or present—do you associate most with the Democratic/Republican party?"

Democratic Party Figures	Total	By Rating of Democratic Party		By Age				
		Favorable	Unfavorable	18-24	25-39	40-54	55-64	65 and over
Bill Clinton	31	33	32	48	36	27	26	25
John F. Kennedy	25	28	17	10	21	35	28	15
Franklin D. Roosevelt	10	10	14	5	6	7	10	26
Jimmy Carter	8	7	9	2	11	8	9	2
Harry Truman	2	7	9	—	—	1	10	5
Other	5							
No answer	19							

Republican Party Figures	Total	By Rating of Republican Party		By Age				
		Favorable	Unfavorable	18-24	25-39	40-54	55-64	65 and over
Ronald Reagan	42	48	36	25	45	45	42	37
George H. W. Bush	12	11	14	13	18	13	11	11
Richard Nixon	12	11	14	9	11	12	14	13
Dwight D. Eisenhower	3	3	1	2	3	1	7	5
Gerald Ford	2	2	2	2	3	2	2	2
Other	6							
No answer	23							

Source: August 2000 survey conducted by John McLaughlin and Associates for this book. See Appendix.

one viewed as the top Democrat was very much a function of age. Clinton was the overwhelming pick of youngest adults, who have lived all of their adult lives (and much of their pre-adult lives as well) under the Clinton presidency. By contrast, only 10 percent of 18–24 year olds associated the Democratic party with President John F. Kennedy. Kennedy is still the most prominent Democrat among age groups 40–54 and 55–64, however, and Franklin D. Roosevelt remains the most notable Democrat for a plurality of seniors (65 and older).

For the Republicans, former president Ronald Reagan continues to dominate the field, though certainly less so than when the first edition of this book was published—which, granted, was at the tail end of Reagan's presidency.[45] In contrast to 1988, when 54 percent of Americans picked Reagan as the GOP's standard bearer, only 42 percent of the respondents in our 2000 survey named Reagan as the person they most associated with the GOP. Not surprisingly, although Reagan defines the GOP for a plurality (25 percent) of young adults (18–24 year olds), he comes nowhere close to Clinton in shaping his party's image for young people. Beyond the youngest age group, though, Reagan continues to be the dominating GOP presence for considerable pluralities of Americans. Placing a distant second to Reagan, Presidents George H.W. Bush and Richard Nixon were each named as the most notable Republican by 12 percent of our respondents. Surprisingly, given his high profile, not even 1 percent of our survey respondents identified former House Speaker Newt Gingrich as the figure they most closely associate with the GOP. Gingrich's minimal influence in shaping the GOP's partisan image illustrates that even the most visible members of Congress cannot compete with presidents in defining their party's image.

Of course, as Table 4.7 makes clear, prominence as a party figure does not necessarily translate into positive beliefs about the party among citizens. Bill Clinton, for example, was most closely associated with the Democratic party about equally among respondents who rated the Democratic party favorably and those who rated the party unfavorably. Reagan, on the other hand, can probably claim credit for more positive than negative opinion of the Republican Party: indeed, those who offered a favorable rating of the GOP were considerably more likely to associate Reagan with the party than were respondents who gave the GOP an unfavorable rating. Similarly, John F. Kennedy defines the Democratic party at higher levels among respondents who rated Democrats favorably than among those who rated Democrats unfavorably. Interestingly, people associate public figures with the parties somewhat similarly across different levels of ideology and partisan identification, though both liberals and conservatives link Reagan with the GOP at greater percentages than in the population as a whole.

THE PUBLIC, THE PARTIES, AND THE ISSUES

Despite the emphasis on personality in our politics, issues still matter a great deal, and a voter bases his or her overall evaluation of the parties on the substantive positions they take as well as on the individuals they nominate for office. As survey results presented earlier in this chapter showed (see Table 4.4), only a relatively small majority (53 percent) of Americans believe that there are important differences between the two parties' candidates and policy positions. Nevertheless, Table 4.8, which lists the public's views on which party would do a better job on a host of issues, suggests that the public does in fact see differences between the parties' policy stances. The contrast in party scores from item to item comprises a fascinating commentary on modern American politics. The public sees Democrats as able to do a better job than Republicans on education, the environment, managing the economy, and—surprisingly, given the GOP's traditional strength in this area—fighting crime and drugs. Republicans, on the other hand, are viewed as stronger than Democrats in the areas of foreign policy, cutting wasteful government spending, and restoring honesty and integrity to government and politics. Foreign policy execution and keeping the lid on government spending are traditional areas of GOP strength. Surely, though, eight years of the scandal-ridden Clinton administration has contributed to the Republicans' considerable upper hand in the issue area of cleaning up government and politics. Table 4.8 tells a few other noteworthy stories. For one, the public views Democrats and Republicans as equally able to hold the line on taxes. Second, 16 percent of our respondents chose the Green Party as able to do the best job on environmental issues—a decent showing for any minor party. As Democratic presidential candidate Al Gore discovered during the 2000 election, the Green Party's strength on the environmental issue has the potential to wreak havoc with the Democratic coalition in a close election. The other story in Table 4.8 is the relative absence of cynicism. On no issue did more than 11 percent of our respondents believe that neither party was up to the job—a welcome finding in this era of waning trust in government.

This chapter has identified some disturbing developments in the relationship between the American people and their political parties. Ticket-splitting, while not nearly as rampant as it was a few decades ago, remains a steady feature of American politics, and there has been a near doubling of the proportion of Independents in the electorate over the last several decades. Most worrisome and revealing of all is the reluctance of a growing number of partisans (the so-called Independent leaners) to readily acknowledge their party affiliations. The swelling ranks of leaners may act like partisans in their voting habits, but they do not necessarily think like partisans in their conception of the political world and their place in it.

Why have more citizens moved from categories of weak or strong partisan affiliations into the classification of Independent leaner? Partly, it is because the parties have been weakened generally by the forces described throughout this study, from the rise of primaries to the fall of patronage. Then, too, parties and partisanship are simply out of fashion, unchic in an era when individualism is celebrated. The television news media, in particular, have encouraged the departisanization of the electorate by focusing almost all attention on the personalities and issues of individual candidates and officeholders rather than the partisan super-

TABLE 4.8. PUBLIC VIEWS OF THE PARTIES
ON SPECIFIC ISSUES (BY PERCENTAGES).

Please tell me which political party you think would do a better job on the following issues—the Democratic Party, the Republican Party, the Reform Party, the Green Party, or the Libertarian Party.

Issue Area	Democrat	Republican	Reform	Green	Libertarian	All	None
Improving education	48	33	1	1	2	2	3
Managing the economy and creating jobs	47	36	1	1	1	2	2
Protecting the environment	39	24	2	16	1	2	3
Handling foreign policy crises	36	41	1	1	1	2	4
Restoring honesty and integrity to government and politics	29	38	2	1	1	2	11
Holding the line on taxes	38	38	2	0	1	2	6
Fighting crime and drugs	36	33	3	1	1	4	10
Cutting wasteful government spending	33	34	3	2	2	3	11

Source: August 2000 survey conducted by John McLaughlin and Associates for this book. See Appendix. Rows do not equal 100 percent since "don't know/refuse" responses are not included.

structure of politics and by persisting in the communication of outdated, negative stereotypes of the party role and operations. Yet, the prevailing media line probably could not have sold well if people had not been inclined to believe it in the first place. While the survey results presented in this chapter indicate that voters generally are not hostile to the parties, and in broad terms they judge the institutions favorably, neither does the public seem to care much about the parties' welfare or see the importance and centrality of parties in American political life. The steady deterioration in the perceived legitimacy of the political parties recorded in the last forty years underlines the modern difficulties they face.

Nonetheless, the prospects for party renewal in the electorate are brighter than this portrait might suggest. The absence of outright hostility and the presence of generalized favorability toward the parties offer some hope; after all, apathy and neutrality are much easier to counteract than open enmity and antagonism. The underlying partisanship of many supposed Independents, the reversal in the decline of partisan identification, and the voters' sharper differentiation of the parties also give cause for optimism. Finally, the ample cadre of strong party loyalists, who number in the millions, as well as the increasingly energetic party organizations on both sides, provide a firm foundation to build upon as the parties attempt to regenerate and intensify voter allegiance. What can be constructed on this base, and how, is proposed in the two concluding chapters. First, however, we turn to the final element in the modern party calculus: the condition of two-party competition at the national level and the state of party alignment and realignment.

NOTES

1. See E. E. Schattschneider, *Party Government* (New York: Rinehart, 1942), 55–56.
2. See Steven E. Finkel and Howard A. Scarrow, "Party Identification and Party Enrollment: The Difference and the Consequence," *Journal of Politics* 47 (May 1985): 620–642.
3. Angus Campbell et al., *The American Voter* (New York: John Wiley and Sons, 1964), 86–96. Paul A. Beck and M. Kent Jennings, "Parents as 'Middlepersons' in Political Socialization," *Journal of Politics* 37 (1975): 83–107.
4. Beck and Jennings, "Parents as 'Middlepersons' in Political Socialization."
5. Morris P. Fiorina, *Retrospective Voting in American National Elections* (New Haven: Yale University Press, 1981), 102.
6. See, for example, Angus Campbell and Henry Valen, "Party Identification in Norway and the United States," *Public Opinion Quarterly* 25 (1961): 514–515. More precisely, we refer here to socioeconomic status (SES), one's place in the pecking order of society.
7. Data are contained in Table 4.1 and discussed in the text that follows.

8. Leon D. Epstein, *Political Parties in the American Mold* (Madison, Wisc.: University of Wisconsin Press, 1986), 253–255. If nothing else, the much greater degree of straight-ticket voting earlier in the century would strongly suggest this.

9. See Bruce E. Keith, David B. Magleby, Candice 1. Nelson, Elizabeth Orr, Mark C. Westlye, and Raymond E. Wolfinger, "Further Evidence on the Partisan Affinities of Independent 'Leaners.'" Paper presented at the 1983 meeting of the American Political Science Association, Chicago, Ill., September 1–4, 1983.

10. Norman H. Nie, Sidney Verba, and John R. Petrocik, *The Changing American Voter* (Cambridge, Mass.: Harvard University Press, 1979), 374–375.

11. Larry Sabato, *The Rise of Political Consultants: New Ways of Winning Elections* (New York: Basic Books, 1981), 284–290.

12. Everett Carll Ladd, Jr. and Seymour Martin Lipset, *Academics, Politics, and the 1972 Election* (Washington, D.C.: American Enterprise Institute, 1973), 46.

13. Martin Wattenberg, *The Decline of American Political Parties, 1952–1994* (Cambridge, Mass.: Harvard University Press, 1996), 114–117.

14. This is often the way the public pollsters (Gallup, Harris, et al.) report Independent affiliation. See *Public Opinion* 9 (January/February 1987): 35.

15. Paul Allen Beck, "The Changing American Party Coalitions," in John G. Green and Daniel M. Shea, eds., *The State of the Parties: The Changing Role of Contemporary American Parties* (Lanham: Rowman & Littlefield, 1999).

16. These results are similar to partisan identification patterns found in the 1998 National Election Studies (NES) survey data. In that survey, Democrats held a 9-percent advantage over Republicans among men and a 19-percent advantage over the GOP among women.

17. In our survey, 19 percent of African American respondents classified themselves as "very liberal," whereas only 10 percent of whites did.

18. Hispanics comprised 4 percent of sample, compared to 10 percent for African Americans.

19. Even the 18–24 year olds were very closely split between McGovern and Nixon in most polls, but McGovern ran more than a dozen percentage points better among the very young than among the electorate as a whole.

20. In the survey conducted for the first edition of this book, homemakers favored the Democratic Party by about 5 percent over the Republican Party. See Sabato, *The Party's Just Begun*, 120.

21. The presidential election of 1960 may be an extreme case, but John Kennedy's massive support among Catholics and Nixon's less substantial but still impressive backing by Protestants demonstrates the polarization that religion could once produce. See Philip E. Converse, "Religion and Politics: The 1960 Election," in Angus Campbell et al., *Elections and the Political Order* (New York: John Wiley, 1966) 96–124.

22. In the survey conducted for the first edition of this book, 28 percent of Jewish respondents considered themselves Republicans.

23. Paul Allen Beck, "The Changing American Party Coalitions," in John G. Green and Daniel M. Shea, eds., *The State of the Parties: The Changing Role of Contemporary American Parties* (Lanham: Rowman & Littlefield, 1999).

24. Wattenberg, *The Decline of American Political Parties, 1952–1994.*

25. Key, *The Responsible Electorate*. Wattenberg, *The Decline of American Political Parties, 1952–1994*, 49.
26. The NES surveys also found reduced straight-ticket balloting in local elections as well.
27. The survey is reported in John Kenneth White and Daniel M. Shea, *New Party Politics: From Jefferson and Hamilton to the Information Age* (New York: St. Martin's Press, 2000), 159.
28. See Appendix.
29. See Gary C. Jacobson, *The Politics of Congressional Elections*, Fourth Edition (New York: Addison Wesley Longman, 1997), 91–92.
30. Wattenberg, *The Decline of American Political Parties, 1952–1994*.
31. Voters are also willing to split their ballots across the different levels of government. Of the 135 occasions between 1980 and 1996 when gubernatorial and U.S. Senate candidates were on the ballot together, 46 percent resulted in the election of a senator and governor from different parties. John F. Bibby, *Politics, Parties, and Elections*, 4th ed. (Belmont, Calif.: Wadsworth, 2000), 325. William J. Keefe, Parties, *Politics, and Public Policy in America*, 8th ed., (Washington, D.C.: Congressional Quarterly Press, 1998), 374.
32. Malcom E. Jewell and Sarah Morehouse, *Political Parties and Elections in the American States*, 4th ed. (Washington, D.C: Congressional Quarterly Press, 2001), 222. See also Morris Fiorina, *Divided Government* (New York: MacMillan, 1992).
33. John J. Coleman, "Unified Government, Divided Government, and Party Responsiveness," *American Political Science Review* 93 (December 1999): 821–35.
34. Jewell and Morehouse, *Political Parties and Elections in the American States*, 181. This percentage holds for individuals who both identified with a party and voted for a major party gubernatorial candidate. Jewell and Morehouse do not provide data on voting differences between strong and weak identifiers.
35. Postelection survey conducted by John McLaughlin and Associates. See Appendix. The party identification question in the postelection survey did not probe for the strength of respondents' partisanship.
36. For historical trends in the relationship between partisan identification and voting in presidential elections, see Paul Allen Beck, *Party Politics in America* (New York: Addison Wesley Longman, 1997), 156; Samuel J. Eldersveld and Hanes Walton, Jr., *Political Parties in American Society* (New York: St. Martin's Press, 2000), 95; Paul R. Abramson, John H. Aldrich, and David W. Rohde, *Change and Continuity in the 1996 Elections* (Washington,D.C.: Congressional Quarterly, 1998), 173.
37. Bibby, *Politics, Parties, and Elections*, 326.
38. Ibid.
39. Samuel J. Eldersveld and Hanes Walton, Jr., *Political Parties in American Society* (New York: St. Martin's Press, 2000), 95.
40. Jacobson, The Politics of Congressional Elections, 91–92.
41. Stephen Earl Bennett, "Changes in the Public's Perceptions of Governmental Responsiveness, 1964–1980." Paper prepared for delivery at the annual meeting of the Midwest Political Science Association, Milwaukee,

Wisconsin, 1982, 32. Bennett reported that 41 percent thought parties helped "a good deal" in 1964 but only 18 percent did so by 1980.

42. See Wattenberg, *The Decline of American Political Parties*; Stephen Craig, "The Decline of Partisanship in the United States: A Reexamination of the Neutrality Hypothesis," *Political Behavior* 7: 1 (1985): 57–58; Martin Wattenberg, "Do Voters Really Care About Political Parties Anymore? A Response to Craig." Paper delivered at the annual meeting of the American Political Science Association, Washington, D.C., August 27–31, 1986.

43. Sabato, *The Party's Just Begun*, 1st ed., 133.

44. Eighty-five percent of our respondents gave no answer to our open-ended inquiry for the Reform Party, and 81 percent offer no answer for the Green Party.

45. Sabato, *The Party's Just Begun*, 1st ed., 140.

5

Realignment: Reality or Reverie?

N O SUBJECT FASCINATES political observers quite as much as major party realignment. Have individual voters and groups changed partisan loyalties in sharp and durable ways? Have these shifts been sufficient to make the GOP the new dominant party in the United States? Have Democrats relinquished the majority status they secured at the onset of the New Deal in the 1930s? Of course, Republican analysts have been busily attempting to convince the political world of the reality of major realignment; most recently, they tout as evidence the Republican takeover of the House and Senate in 1994, maintenance of that majority in the House, significant gains in state houses, and President George W. Bush's electoral college victory in 2000. Democrats have been equally preoccupied with touting their party's fortunes, insisting that the Republican claims are nothing more than wishful thinking and reverie. As evidence of Democratic party strength, Democrats point to presidential victories in 1992 and 1996, several high profile statewide victories in the South in 1998, gains in the House of Representatives in 1996, 1998, and 2000, defeat of four incumbent Republican U.S. Senators in 2000, and Democratic presidential candidate Al Gore's nationwide popular vote victory in 2000.

Clearly, major changes in the American electorate have occurred in the last 30 years. But election victories—the result of short-term

responses to issues and candidates as much as to long-term partisan pre-
dispositions—are not by themselves evidence of a long-term realignment of partisan attitudes in the electorate. Examining party coalitions
of the past four decades, this chapter explores the possibilities of realignment from both parties' perspectives and ultimately calls into question
the utility of party realignment theory to account for political trends in
an era of weakened party attachments among citizens.

REALIGNMENT AND CONTEMPORARY POLITICAL CONDITIONS

Major realignments—circumstances when relatively swift and permanent alterations in existing partisan alignments occur—are rare events in
American political life, with the last full-scale realignment happening in
the 1928–1936 period.[1] A major realignment is precipitated by one or
more critical elections, which may polarize voters around new issues and
personalities in reaction to crucial political, economic, or social developments. Three tumultuous eras in American history produced major party
realignments. First, during the period leading up to the Civil War, the
Whig party gradually dissolved, and the Republican party developed
and won the presidency in 1860. Second, the radicalization of the Democratic party in the 1890s enabled the Republicans to greatly strengthen
their majority status and make lasting gains in voter attachments. Third,
the Great Depression of the 1930s propelled the Democrats to power.
Popular Democratic programs led large numbers of voters to repudiate
the GOP and embrace the Democratic party. In each of these cases, fundamental and enduring alterations in the party equation resulted.

The major realignment that occurred during Franklin D. Roosevelt's
presidency has served as a hopeful model for Republicans. Beginning
the electoral phase of realignment in 1932, the electorate decisively
rejected the party previously in power. This dramatic vote of "no confidence" was followed by substantial changes in policy by the new president, who demonstrated, in fact or at least in appearance, that his
policies were effective. The people responded to his success, accepted
his vision of society, and ratified their choice of the new president's party
in subsequent presidential and congressional elections. This period saw
the emergence of the New Deal coalition: northern and western industrial workers and southerners. White southerners, solidly Democratic
since the end of Reconstruction, continued to feel at home in Roosevelt's
Democratic party because Roosevelt generally left southern racial
arrangements undisturbed. Simultaneously, the former majority party
reluctantly but inevitably adjusted to its new minority role. So strong

was the new Democratic partisan attachment for most voters that even when short-term issues and personalities that favored the minority party dislodged the majority party from power, the basic distribution of party loyalties did not shift significantly. Thus in 1952, 1956, 1968, and 1972, Republicans could win the presidency but the New Deal Democratic majority coalition could survive. These four examples of alignment-deviating elections can be contrasted to the alignment-maintaining elections of 1940, 1944, 1948, 1960, 1964, and 1976, when the New Deal coalition prevailed in the presidential contests. But in all ten cases, regardless of the party identity of the presidential winner, the underlying distribution of party affiliation was essentially the same.

Until recent times, at least, major realignments had been spaced about thirty-six years apart in the American experience. With the aid of catalytic circumstances, realignments are accomplished in two primary ways.[2] Some voters are simply converted from one party to the other by the issues and candidates of the time. New voters may also be mobilized into action: immigrants, young voters, and other previous nonvoters may become motivated and then absorbed into a new governing coalition. However vibrant and potent they may be at first, party coalitions age, tensions increase, and grievances accumulate. The original *raison d'être* of the majority fades; new generations do not remember the traumatic events that originally brought about the realignment, and they lack the stalwart party identifications of their ancestors. New issues arise, producing conflicts that can only be contained by a breakup of old alignments and a reshuffling of individual and group party loyalties. Viewed in historical perspective, party realignment has been a mechanism that ensures stability through the management of unavoidable change.

By no means is a critical realigning era the only occasion when changes in partisan affiliation are accommodated. In truth, every election produces realignment to some degree, since some individuals are undoubtedly pushed to change parties by events and by their reactions to the candidates. Indeed, some research suggests that major realignments are just extreme cases of the kind of changes in party loyalty registered every year.[3] While the term realignment is usually applied only if momentous events produce enduring and substantial alterations in the party coalitions, political scientists have long recognized that a more gradual rearrangement of party coalitions could occur.[4] Called *secular realignment*, this piecemeal process depends not on convulsive shocks to the political system but on slow, almost subterranean demographic shifts—the shrinking of one party's base of support and the enlargement of the other's, for example, or simple generational replacement. Of course, electoral trends during certain periods may be also characterized as much by *dealignment* as by (re)alignment; indeed, some political observers have described much of the contemporary political era as such. During periods of dealignment, more citizens consider themselves independents, voters shift with greater ease between the parties, and little permanence or intensity exists in identifications made and held so lightly.

By the early 1980s, trends in ticket-splitting, partisan independence, and voter volatility left little doubt that the United States had moved through a considerable dealigning period. Although each previous dealignment has been a precursor of realignment,[5] there is no immutable law that requires realignment to succeed dealignment—especially under modern conditions where parties play a less of a role in organizing citizen conceptions of politics. The question today, then, is whether the dealigning trends that began in the 1970s are an antecedent to a partisan realignment or the beginning of a new postalignment period in American politics.

REPUBLICAN GAINS AND DEMOCRATIC PERSISTENCE: REALIGNMENT WITHOUT A MAJORITY?

The past four decades have witnessed some dramatic changes in the makeup of each party's coalition of identifiers in the electorate. By far the most important of these changes—the massive long-term shift among white southerners, especially males, away from the Democratic party—has clearly benefited the GOP.[6] Still, any claims of a full-scale Republican realignment are probably overblown. In terms of net gains, the realigning forces of the recent past have produced only moderate GOP increases in partisan identification and relatively small Democratic losses. Indeed, despite GOP gains, Democratic identifiers in the electorate continue to outnumber Republican identifiers—even in the South. In addition, Democrats have regained some of the ground they lost in the 1994 congressional elections; by 2000, they had narrowed the partisan balance in the House even further and achieved parity with the GOP in the Senate. Although the last several decades have brought about a gradual shift in partisanship in the electorate, the shift has not produced a new majority party in American so much as it has produced a more competitive—and volatile—two-party politics.

As with all political alignments, the New Deal coalition's eventual demise was inevitable. Fueled by Depression-era problems, the coalition of southern conservatives and northern Democratic liberals could survive as long as economic issues were center stage and the South was left alone on matters of race. Once the nation's economic fortunes began to improve, however, the original *raison d'être* for the coalition faded and other issues came to the fore. Civil rights for African Americans was among the most important of these issues. The erosion of white Democratic party loyalties in the South can be detected as early as 1948,[7] when civil rights proposals sent by President Truman to Congress prompted South Carolinian Strom Thurmond, then a Democratic House member, to bolt the party and run as a Dixiecrat in the 1948 presidential election. Tensions between southern Democrats and the national party would only escalate in the early 1960s, when civil rights moved to center stage in American politics and polarized the nation. President John F. Kennedy's response to the national turmoil was a cautious one; he charted a moderate course between the strong civil rights legislation supported by most northern congressional Democrats and the status quo favored by most southern congressional Democrats. Ironically, Kennedy's successor, southerner Lyndon B. Johnson, repositioned the national Democratic party by aligning himself with northern congressional Democrats and pushing for strong civil rights legislation. Regional rifts on civil rights could be found in the Republican party as well. But the GOP's 1964 presidential nominee, Senator Barry Goldwater of Arizona, sided with southern conservatives and staunchly opposed civil rights legislation. Indeed, Goldwater was one of only eight nonsouthern Senators to vote against the 1964 Civil Rights Act.[8]

The national parties' positions on civil rights had a profound impact on electoral politics and on partisan attitudes in the electorate. In the 1964 presidential election, Goldwater won five Deep South states (including an astonishing 87 percent of the vote in Mississippi), as white southern Democrats, antagonized by Johnson's civil rights crusade, deserted the party's presidential ticket in droves. However, in a trend that would persist well into the 1980s, many white southern Democrats, although voting for GOP presidential candidates, continued to support Democratic candidates below the presidential level. Indeed, in the five southern states won by Goldwater, only seven of the thirty-seven congressional districts sent Republicans to the House. Fortunately for Democratic presidential candidates, losses among white southern conservatives brought on by the national party's position on civil rights were offset by considerable electoral gains among African Americans. Whatever support African Americans had shown for the GOP's presidential candidates up until then all but vanished by 1964.[9] Moreover, the 1965 Voting Rights Act, which brought thousands of southern blacks into the electorate, amplified African American support for national Democrats.

In addition to its immediate impact at the polls, civil rights produced significant long-term shifts in partisan allegiances in the electorate. After 1964, the percentage of white southerners who considered themselves Democrats declined sharply. Yet initially, the estrangement of white southern Democrats from the national party did not produce gains in GOP identifiers. Rather, white southern conservatives increasingly considered themselves independents—a label consistent with their growing propensity for split-ticket voting on election day.[10] For African Americans, in contrast, the movement toward Democratic partisanship was immediate, sharp, and lasting. Of African Americans who responded to the 1960 National Election Studies (NES) survey, 50 percent considered themselves Democrats. By 1964, this figure jumped to 82 percent; in 1968 it increased again to 91 percent.[11] Clearly, by the mid-1960s, African Americans had become the Democratic party's most loyal and consistent partisans, while white southern conservatives were left, so to speak, without a national party.

Several political scientists have wisely cautioned against viewing race as the sole cause of changes in party identification during the 1960s. Although the issue of civil rights clearly played a pivotal role in galvanizing white southern conservatives to reconsider their partisan allegiances, other issues loomed large as well—especially as the 1960s progressed. As the influence of southern Democrats on the national party waned during the 1960s, Democratic party positions on national issues became increasingly liberal. Johnson's Great Society programs, as well as the national Democratic party's increasingly liberal positions on the economy, foreign policy, and issues of law and order, simply did not sit well with southern conservatives.[12] The modernization of the southern economy also contributed to decreases in Democratic partisanship in the South, as a newly emerging southern middle class found GOP positions attractive for the same reasons that northern middle class citizens did.[13] More generally, political scientist Paul Allen Beck shows that, ironically, the success of the Democratic party's New Deal programs in ushering working class Americans into the middle class made it increasingly less likely that these Americans (and especially their children) would find the Democratic party's message appealing.[14]

The tumultuous years between 1965 and 1980 produced volatility at the ballot box and further destabilization of partisan attitudes among Americans. In the 1968 election, against a backdrop of civil rights issues, the Vietnam War, urban unrest, and wide-scale political protests on college campuses, Democratic presidential candidate Hubert Humphrey received only 31 percent of the southern popular vote—a significant drop from the 50 percent of the southern vote that Johnson received just four years earlier. Disaffected southern conservatives instead cast their presidential ballots for either Republican Richard Nixon or American Independent Party candidate George Wallace—the flamboyant proseg-regation governor of Alabama who, asserting there wasn't "a dime's worth of difference" between the two major parties, carried five south-ern states (and also attracted some support outside of the South). Fol-lowing the 1968 election, Democratic presidential fortunes continued to lag in the South. Paralyzed by a would-be assassin's bullet, Wallace called off his 1972 presidential bid, and Nixon absorbed much of Wal-lace's electoral support, pulling 70 percent of the southern popular vote.[15] While clearly rejecting Democratic presidential tickets, southern conservatives continued to provide considerable support for Democrats at the state, local, and congressional level. Indeed, the 1972 election saw new heights of ticket-splitting in the South, with Nixon carrying all 108 southern congressional districts but Republican House candidates elected in only thirty-four of them.[16] In the wake of the Watergate scan-dal that rocked the nation and ended Nixon's presidency, Georgia Gov-ernor Jimmy Carter's successful presidential bid in 1976 helped stem the persistent tide of "white flight" from the Democratic party in the South—but only temporarily.[17]

As appealing as Republican presidential candidates became to southern conservatives during this period, Republican success at the polls translated only slowly into long-term gains in GOP partisan iden-tifiers. Between 1956 and 1980, the number of white southern males who considered themselves Democrats had declined by nearly half. (The decline was less extreme among white southern women.) But there was no immediate movement to the GOP among disaffected southerners.[18] Rather, the number of white southern males who considered themselves independents grew, increasing from 2.3 percent in 1952 to a record high of 21.5 percent in 1974. Clearly, southern conservatives were still with-out a partisan home.

The turning point for the GOP was the Reagan presidency. Although Carter carried ten of the eleven southern states in 1976, he lost all but his home state of Georgia to GOP presidential victor Ronald Rea-gan in 1980. Reagan was, as political scientist Warren Miller points out, the only unabashed conservative partisan to win the presidency in the postwar era.[19] Across a host of economic, foreign, and social policy issues, Reagan staked out unequivocally conservative positions and cared little for bipartisan compromise. His unyielding conservatism gal-vanized an increasingly combative partisan politics at the national level. As the Reagan presidency progressed, congressional Democrats—led first by Speaker Tip O'Neill (D-Mass.) and then by Speaker Jim Wright

(D-Tex.)—circled the wagons and unified against the Reagan Administration's conservative initiatives. Indeed, Speaker Wright went so far as to offer a Democratic agenda at the start of the 1987–1988 session of Congress—a brash move for a Speaker in the pre-Gingrich era. In Congress, the number of party votes skyrocketed, and cohesion within the parties increased markedly. (See Chapter Three.) The Reagan presidency thus accelerated a trend in American politics whereby both parties were becoming more ideologically homogenous—the GOP more uniformly conservative and Democratic Party more uniformly liberal.

With fewer and fewer issues cutting across partisan lines, citizens more easily discerned differences between the parties.[20] Indeed, in 1976, 47 percent of the respondents interviewed in the NES survey saw important differences in what the parties stood for; by 1984, this figure had jumped to 63 percent.[21] The impact of polarized politics on partisan allegiances in the electorate was sharp. Southern conservatives, long since voting for Republican presidential candidates, began considering themselves Republicans. The movement towards the GOP was especially notable in younger southern conservatives—the children of conservative southern Democrats—who rejected their parents' Democratic party attachments in favor of the more ideologically compatible GOP.[22] Northern professionals relocating to the South also helped make the region more Republican, as they brought with them their traditional GOP allegiances.[23] Compounding the Democrats' problems, young voters across all regions were identifying with the Republican Party over Democrats.[24] By 1988, 41 percent of respondents polled in the NES survey considered themselves Republicans or leaning Republican—a higher number of GOP identifiers than ever reported in the history of the survey.

Not surprisingly, gains in GOP identifiers slowly but surely began translating into election victories below the presidential level. As old-school southern conservative Democrats in the South began to retire, voters replaced them with conservative Republicans. By 1990, many southern states had elected Republican governors more than once.[25] Even Alabama elected its first Republican governor in 1986, though Mississippi would wait until 1991. Changes in state legislatures came more slowly. During the 1980s, for example, Mississippi Republicans held, on average, only nine percent of the state's legislative seats. The GOP was becoming more competitive in non-southern states as well—states such as Pennsylvania, New Jersey, and Michigan. Still, by the end of the Reagan presidency, more states could be reasonably categorized as Democratic than Republican.[26]

The GOP ascendancy continued into the 1990s. Although some of the GOP gains in partisan identification made during the Reagan years were reversed during the Bush presidency, the setback proved to be temporary.[27] Indeed, Democrats surely celebrated breaking the GOP's twelve-year lock on the presidency in 1992, but they were no doubt alarmed at having *lost* nine House seats to Republicans in the same election. Moreover, without the need to support a moderate GOP president willing to compromise with Democrats, the increasingly influential conservative wing of the congressional GOP was free to define the party in its own (very conservative) terms. Firebrand conservatives such as Newt Gingrich (R-Ga.), Bob Walker (R-Pa.), and Dick Armey (R-Tex.) assumed leadership positions in the Republican conference with increasing frequency. Able and willing to employ hardball tactics on the House floor, these leaders rejected compromise with Democrats and sought to delineate further the GOP's policy positions from those advocated by national Democrats.[28] Gingrich, elected minority whip in 1989, played an especially important role in furthering the GOP rise to power during the 1990s. A committed partisan—he played an instrumental role in forcing Democratic Speaker Jim Wright's resignation from Congress in 1989—Gingrich used his leadership PAC (GOPAC) to finance and groom a growing number of conservative state legislators ready to compete for a congressional seat when the opportunity presented itself. In 1994, Gingrich took the unprecedented step (at least for a House minority leader) of organizing a national campaign centered around the "Contract With America"—a ten-item manifesto of conservative campaign promises signed by almost three hundred House GOP candidates. Led by Gingrich, and aided by public frustration with President Clinton, the GOP produced results that were nothing short of earth shattering, gaining fifty-two seats in the U.S. House and giving the GOP majority control of the House for the first time since 1955. Republicans also won back control of the U.S. Senate by taking eight seats from Democrats. Yet perhaps most impressive was the GOP tide at the state level. In addition to gaining eleven governorships, Republicans gained more than five hundred state legislative seats in 1994.[29] The political earthquake was especially damaging to Democrats in the South. Indeed, Republicans gained 133 seats in southern state legislatures. Moreover, for the first time since Reconstruction, Republicans held a majority of southern governorships, U.S. Senate seats, and U.S. House seats.[30] Clearly, the heady days of Democratic dominance were gone.

The decisive GOP victory at the polls in 1994 was reinforced by trends in partisan attitudes in the electorate. Republican party affiliation, down under the Bush presidency, rebounded to its 1988 level of 41 percent.[31] Importantly, 1994 brought increases in GOP identifiers among almost every conceivable demographic category, though gains within some of these groups were clearly short-lived responses to immediate political circumstances. Consistent with trends leading up to 1994, GOP gains in partisan identification were strongest in the South—and, within the South, among southern white males. Indeed, a record-breaking 55 percent of white southern males identified themselves as Republicans in the 1994 NES survey, while only 35 percent of southern white males— a record low—considered themselves Democrats.[32] Moreover, GOP increases among southern conservatives were clearly the most durable of Republican gains. Although partisan identification among southern white males has ebbed and flowed slightly since 1994, the numbers remain solid and represent nothing short of a long-term shift in southern partisan loyalties.

Still, in terms of both election outcomes and partisan attitudes, the years since the 1994 Republican tsunami have witnessed not an increasingly dominant Republican party but rather a more competitive two-party politics. To be sure, the Republican party continued to make noteworthy gains at the state level. Following the 2000 elections, party control of state legislatures was fairly evenly balanced, with Republicans controlling both chambers in 17 states, Democrats controlling both chambers in 17 states, and 15 states split.[33] The GOP also holds the majority of governorships, though the Democrats picked up one governorship (West Virginia) in the 2000 elections. But Democrats have just as surely regained ground since 1994, especially at the national level. In 1996, Democratic President Bill Clinton was reelected to the presidency, racking up an impressive 379 electoral votes (carrying 31 states and the District of Columbia) and nearly capturing a majority of the popular vote in a three-way contest. Notably, Clinton even won four southern states: Arkansas, Florida, Louisiana, and Tennessee. And while Democrats lost two additional seats in the U.S. Senate in 1996, they gained nine seats in the U.S. House. Aided by public perceptions of GOP overzealousness in handling the Clinton impeachment crisis, Democrats continued to regain ground in the House in 1998 by winning yet another five seats—the first time in 60 years that the president's party picked up seats in the House in a midterm election.[34] (The partisan balance remained unchanged in the Senate.) What's more, Democratic challenger John Edwards' victory over incumbent Senator Lauch Faircloth in North Carolina, as well as Democrat Don Siegelman's defeat of Republican Governor Fob James in Alabama, illustrated that Democrats were still capable of competing on a statewide basis in the South.

The extraordinary 2000 elections, of course, provided further evidence of relentlessly competitive two-party politics. After weeks of legal wrangling in Florida, George W. Bush finally won the presidency, despite losing the national popular vote to Democrat Al Gore. At the presidential level, the South returned solidly to the GOP, with Bush winning every southern state—including Gore's home state of Tennessee. Meanwhile, Democratic gains in the Senate produced a 50–50 party split—the first even split in the Senate since 1881.[35] (Five months into the 107th Congress, however, Vermont Senator Jim Jeffords' defection from the GOP gave Democrats control of the Senate.) Despite smaller than expected gains in the House, the Democrat's two-seat net gain moved that chamber closer to partisan parity as well.[36] If there is a majority party in the United States, it certainly couldn't be discerned from the 2000 election results.

Measured in terms of partisan identifiers, changes over the past thirty years have been nothing short of spectacular; and indeed, some political scientists argue that such changes constitute a secular realignment. Yet if a realignment has occurred, it has been an unconventional one—indeed, one that has not produced a new majority party in the United States, as past realignments have.[37] Certainly, Republicans have made substantial gains in partisan identifiers, most notably in the South and especially among men. But GOP boosters cannot escape several sobering realities. First, as of 1998, Democratic partisans continue to outnumber Republican partisans—and this remains true even in the South. Second, Democrats have sustained their considerable advantage over the GOP in partisan identification among women. Erosion of Democratic loyalties was simply never as severe among women as among men. Third, African Americans are more firmly than ever in the Democratic camp. Indeed, as political scientist Paul Allen Beck points out, any talk of GOP gains in the African American community must be tempered by the realization that the GOP had more African American identifiers in 1964—the year the party's presidential candidate opposed the 1964 Civil Rights Act—than it had in 1998.[38] Finally, the ideological foundations of the Republican realignment—political conservatism—may make it difficult for the GOP to attract new partisans from the relatively large group of moderate independents that continue to populate the American electorate.[39]

REALIGNMENT'S RELEVANCE IN AGE OF WEAKENED PARTY TIES

Every election offers a new test of realignment theories, and political observers will no doubt interpret the 2000 election through the lens of realignment theory. The truth is, unfortunately, that the election probably does not herald any new era at all. For real realignment to occur—for a large percentage of the population to change parties—people must believe that political parties really matter and that partisan affiliation is a vital element of their lives. In fact, there is little evidence that much of the electorate cares much about parties, as we have discussed in previous chapters. The reality is obvious: Most citizens do not appreciate the role that political parties play in running government, organizing elections, or stabilizing society. Moreover, they do not see much if any party connection to their everyday lives. As long as the parties remain irrelevant to the public's view of the political world, ticket-splitting will flourish, volatility in the electorate will be the norm, and shifts between party identification and independence or "leaning" status will be mere casual responses to the personalities and issue fads of the day. Further, the concept of realignment itself may become obsolete, both because voters will not take parties seriously enough to adopt a new label with any permanency and because realignments under these conditions can be nothing more than lightly held, easily changeable, seesaw associations—transient adjustments to the candidates and circumstances of the moment.

As engaging as the realignment debate may be to political observers, it is not pertinent to the central question at hand: how to strengthen and maintain the tie between the voter and the party. Only when partisan loyalty at the individual level is strengthened will realignment be possible and the full benefits of a vibrant party system (as described in Chapter One) be realized. It is to that critical task that we now turn in the concluding chapters.

NOTES

1. On the subject of realignment, see V. O. Key, Jr., "A Theory of Critical Elections," *Journal of Politics* 17 (February 1955): 3–18; Walter Dean Burnham, *Critical Elections and the Mainsprings of American Politics* (New York: W.W. Norton, 1970); Kristi Andersen, *The Creation of a Democratic Majority* (Chicago: University of Chicago Press, 1979); Robert S. Erikson and Kent L. Tedin, "The 1928–1936 Partisan Realignment: The Case for the Conversion Hypothesis," *American Political Science Review* 75 (1981): 951–962; Jerome M. Clubb, William H. Flanigan, and Nancy H. Zingale, *Partisan Realignment* (Beverly Hills: Sage, 1980); James L. Sundquist, *Dynamics of the Party System: Alignment and Realignment of Political Parties in the United States* (Rev. ed.) (Washington, D.C.: The Brookings Institution, 1983); Stanley Kelley, Jr., "Democracy and the New Deal Party System," Project on the Federal Social Role, Working Paper No. 10, Democratic Values (Washington, D.C.: National Conference on Social Welfare, 1986); John R. Petrocik, "Realignment: New Party Coalitions and the Nationalization of the South," *Journal of Politics* 49 (May 1987):

347–375. Warren E. Miller, "Party Identification and the Electorate of the 1990s," in L. Sandy Maisel, ed., *The Parties Respond: Changes in Parties and Campaigns*, 3rd ed. (Boulder, Colo.: Westview Press, 1998). Alan I. Abramowitz and Kyle L. Saunders, "Party Polarization and Ideological Realignment in the U.S. Electorate, 1976 to 1994," in Maisel, ed., *The Parties Respond*, 3rd ed. Paul Allen Beck, "The Changing American Party Coalitions," in John G. Green and Daniel M. Shea, eds., *The State of the Parties: The Changing Role of Contemporary American Parties* (Lanham, Md.: Rowman & Littlefield, 1999).

2. See especially Andersen, *The Creation of a Democratic Majority*; Clubb et al., *Partisan Realignment*; and Sundquist, *Dynamics of the Party System*.

3. See Charles H. Franklin and John E. Jackson, "The Dynamics of Party Identification," *American Political Science Review 77* (1983: 957–973); Morris Fiorina, *Retrospective Voting in American National Elections* (New Haven, Conn.: Yale University Press, 1981).

4. See, for example, Key, "A Theory of Critical Elections."

5. See Paul Allen Beck, "The Dealignment Era in America," in Russell J. Dalton et al., *Electoral Change in Advanced Industrial Democracies: Realignment or Dealignment?* (Princeton, N.J.: Princeton University Press, 1984), 264. See also Philip M. Williams, "Party Realignment in the United States and Britain," *British Journal of Political Science* 15 (January 1985): 97–115.

6. Miller, "Party Identification and the Electorate of the 1990s," 111; Abramowitz and Saunders, "Party Polarization and Ideological Realignment in the U.S. Electorate, 1976 to 1994"; Beck, "The Changing American Party Coalitions."

7. Indeed, 1944 was the last presidential election in which Democrats would win every state in the South. Total dominance over the South in presidential contests ended when the Democratic party adopted a stance on civil rights, galvanizing South Carolinian Strom Thurmond to bolt the party and run as a Dixiecrat in the 1948 presidential election.

8. Sundquist, *Dynamics of the Party System*, 356.

9. Ibid., 362. Earl Black and Merle Black, *Politics and Society in the South* (Cambridge, Mass.: Harvard University Press, 1987), 270-271.

10. NES Cumulative Data File, 1948–1998. See also Beck, "Changing American Party Coalitions," 32.

11. NES Cumulative Date File. See also John H. Aldrich, *Why Parties? The Origin and Transformation of Party Politics in America* (Chicago: University of Chicago Press, 1995), 246.

12. Black and Black, *Politics and Society in the South*. Miller, "Party Identification and the Electorate of the 1990s," 111.

13. Beck, "The Changing American Party Coalitions," 34; Black and Black, *Politics and Society in the South*, Chapter 3.

14. Paul Allen Beck, "A Socialization Theory of Partisan Realignment," in *The Politics of Future Citizens*, ed. Richard G. Niemi (San Francisco: Jossey-Bass, 1974).

15. Black and Black, *Politics and Society in the South*, 263.

16. Sundquist, *Dynamics of the Party System, 373*. (Individual-level NES data confirms heightened ticket-splitting among southerners.)

17. Miller, "Party Identification and the Electorate of the 1990s."

18. NES Cumulative Data File. See also Beck, "Changing American Party Coalitions," 32.
19. Miller, "Party Identification and the Electorate of the 1990s," 124.
20. Ibid., Abromowitz and Saunders, "Party Polarization and Ideological Realignment in the U.S. Electorate, 1976 to 1994."
21. NES Cumulative Data File.
22. Miller, "Party Identification and the Electorate of the 1990s," 111. Abromowitz and Saunders, "Party Polarization and Ideological Realignment in the U.S. Electorate, 1976 to 1994." Beck, "The Changing American Party Coalitions." Paul Allen Beck, "Partisan Dealignment in the Post-War South," *American Political Science Review* 71 (1977): 477–96. Paul Allen Beck, "Realignment Begins? The Republican Surge in Florida," *American Politics Quarterly* 10 (1982): 421–438.
23. Black and Black, *Politics and Society in the South*, 245.
24. Paul Allen Beck, *Party Politics in America* (New York: Addison Wesley Longman, 1997), 150.
25. Malcolm E. Jewell and Sarah M. Morehouse, *Parties and Elections in American States*, 4th ed. (Washington, D.C.: Congressional Quarterly Press, 2001), 34.
26. Beck, *Party Politics in America*, 37.
27. Miller, "Party Identification and the Electorate of the 1990s," 126.
28. William F. Connolly, Jr., and John J. Pitney, Jr., *Congress' Permanent Minority? Republicans in the U.S. House* (Lanham Md.: Rowman & Littlefield, 1994).
29. Jewell and Morehouse, *Parties and Elections in American States*, 36.
30. Ibid.; Beck, *Party Politics in America*, 150.
31. NES Cumulative Data File, 1948–1998.
32. Ibid.
33. The Senate is tied in Arizona, Maine, and South Carolina, and we counted these states as having split control of the legislature. Suzanne Dougherty, "GOP Primed for Redistricting," *Congressional Quarterly Weekly Report* (11 November 2000), 2671. Louis Jacobson and John Maggs, "Meanwhile, Back in the States," *National Journal* (11 November 2000): 3604–3608. See also Karen Hansen, "The New Political Parity," *State Legislatures* (December 2000): 12–15.
34. Paul S. Herrnson, *Congressional Elections: Campaigning at Home and In Washington*, 3rd ed. (Washington, D.C.: Congressional Quarterly Press, 2000), 27.
35. See Andrew Taylor, "Democrats' Pitch for Parity," *Congressional Quarterly Weekly Report* (9 December 2000), 2802–2804.
36. On the other hand, Republican gains at the state level promise to create headaches for Democrats in post-2000 legislative redistricting.
37. Beck, "The Changing American Party Coalitions." Abromowitz and Saunders, "Party Polarization and Ideological Realignment in the U.S. Electorate, 1976 to 1994." It is also worth noting that any such realignment has not been accompanied by heightened voter turnout, as have past realignments. Burnham, *Critical Elections and the Mainsprings of American Politics.*
38. Beck, "The Changing American Party Coalitions."
39. Ibid.

6

Toward Party Renewal, American Style, Part I

Despite the enthusiasm in the party organizational literature, party decline does not end until the voters return to the party.

—JOHN J. COLEMAN[1]

POLITICAL SCIENTISTS HAVE been at once pessimistic and hopeful about the future of the political parties. The reality is that Americans evidence relatively little fealty to their party identifications, while the personalities of individual candidates continue to be at the center of the nation's electoral show. The deeply rooted bias of individualistic Americans against parties often combines with vested (if shortsighted) interest of candidates and officeholders who treasure their independence from party leaders and thus prefer that parties remain in a weakened state. The parties, too, have not done much to help their own cause. The destructive, personal bitterness between the two parties that has pervaded Washington politics in recent years (a far cry from the policy-based, constructive partisanship that political scientists favor), as well as the parties' increasing reliance on six-figure soft money contributions to finance their activities, surely obscures the benefits that strong parties provide to the American political system and may well strain the bond between parties and voters.[2]

Yet room for optimism remains. There seems to be at least some appreciation of the role parties can play—an appreciation that must be fostered by the parties themselves in ways that will be described next. Certainly, most political scientists remain committed to healthy political parties as the anchor of stable democracies, and more than a few influential

153

journalists do as well.[3] Candidates and officeholders have also surely benefited from the revolution in party-sponsored services and campaign technologies. The voters, too—as survey data presented later in this chapter and the next one will suggest—appear receptive to strong political parties in at least some ways.

At least among political scientists, the commitment to healthy parties can likely be attributed to fear of the consequences of party decline. Political fragmentation, elections without majority winners, additional emphasis on candidates' personalities to the exclusion of broader issue themes, a still greater empowerment of the news media—all could become reality in the absence of sufficiently strong parties. Whereas the Progressive impulse to dismantle and restrict the parties no doubt continues to thrive in American politics, most political scientists uniformly line up on the side of strong parties and caution reformers about the consequences of party atrophy.

But the parties will have to take the initiative themselves. Not only are remedies requiring governmental action usually slow in coming, but they inevitably will be compromised by partisan politics, the ambitions of elected officials, and lingering public mistrust of centralized parties. Luckily, both national parties have demonstrated the resolve and the institutional capacity necessary to enact at least some of the internal reforms proposed in this chapter. And a few of the government-sponsored changes to be discussed in Chapter Seven are more than pipe dreams as well.

Governing our choice of proposals are ten attributes that we believe strong parties ought to display in the American context:[4]

1. *Equity and Legitimacy*: The appearance and the reality of equity and legitimacy in the eyes of the electorate, which are absolutely essential to the public acceptance of the parties' role in democracy.

2. *Electoral Appeal*: A broad-based electoral appeal that enables a party to mobilize support, aggregate power, unify disparate groups and interests, and provide stability to representative democracy.

3. *Participation and Education*: Internal mechanisms that encourage participation by voters in the party and educate voters about the party's candidates and ideas.

4. *Accountability*: Internal mechanisms that help to hold party leaders and officeholders accountable to the party and its supporters for their actions.

5. *Conflict Control*: Sufficient power to control, contain, or successfully arbitrate dissension, conflict, and fragmentation in the party ranks.

6. *Resources*: Sufficient resources (money, people, technology, etc.) to accomplish important party goals and perform party functions well.

7. *Autonomy*: The autonomy and power to make fundamental decisions and choices about party structure, organization, method of nomination, and so forth.

8. *Policy Capacity*: The capacity to formulate, refine, and promote its philosophy, policies, ideas, and issues.

9. *Incentives*: The possession of enough rewards, incentives, and penalties to enable the party to induce cooperation from its officeholders and partisan activists—cooperation not only with the party but with each other in government so as to project a coherent image and to produce a solid record of accomplishments.

10. *Candidate Assistance*: The ability to assist its candidates to win elections in substantial, sophisticated, and effective ways.

We would argue that each of the proposals contained in this chapter and in Chapter Seven shores up or fulfills one or more of these crucial "strong-party attributes." (Those attributes reinforced by each proposal will be designated following every reform subtitle.) In selecting and promoting ideas for party renewal, we were also guided and motivated by a fundamental belief in the case for parties that was made in the opening chapter. *So crucial is their role that the two major parties deserve what we might term "most favored nation" status in our laws and political practices.* Since the two-party system manifestly assists in preserving the stability of American democracy, we should make every effort to enable the parties to perform their functions better.

AN AGENDA FOR PARTY RENEWAL: PARTY-INITIATED ACTIONS
Ombudsman/Mobile Office Provision
Build modern grassroots parties on an old-style model by designating party "ombudsmen" in key constituencies and establishing mobile party offices. Strong-party attributes:

EQUITY AND LEGITIMACY

PARTICIPATION AND EDUCATION

RESOURCES

Compared to European parties or even American parties of a century ago, United States political parties today maintain remarkably little personal contact with average voters. In a poll conducted for the first edition of this book, fully 77 percent of the electorate reported that they have never "been helped with a problem by a member of a political party."[5] Additionally, the survey revealed that only a small percentage of citizens would contact a party official if they had a problem or concern with the government.[6]

There should be no surprise here. Party officials and scholars alike have long noted the decline of this kind of activity by many local party organizations. Even when the local party committee rosters are at full strength and providing services to candidates, relatively few of the individual committee members tend to be active or particularly well known in the precinct they are charged with organizing. The rewards (social and political) for energetic service are often too small or nonexistent to encourage any other kind of behavior; committee posts are unpaid and there are generally no sanctions (save expulsion) to be levied for indolence. The result, of course, is that the party becomes invisible in the community, and people fail to see a useful connection between their party and their lives. Precisely this disjunction is cited by some scholars to explain the growing estrangement between voter and party.[7]

The question might reasonably be asked: do people really want the parties to strike out in the direction of community involvement, and would it make much difference to voters' partisan loyalties if the parties did adopt an activist posture? An historical answer is certainly provided by the big-city machines of old; their devotion to their constituents' daily needs made them a dominant element of urban life and was richly rewarded at election time with votes from grateful beneficiaries.[8] But modern public opinion also supports increased party activism. In a survey conducted for the first edition of this study, respondents were asked this question:

> It has been suggested that there be a basic change in the role played by political parties in America. Some people want political parties to be more active as social and civic organizations to help people deal with government and better their communities. Do you believe that such a change should happen, or should political parties stay the way they are now?

As Table 6.1 indicates, a substantial majority (58 percent) favored a shift in party activity, and the proposal was popular among all major segments of the population. Interestingly, Americans who live in the sprawling suburbs—the least organizable demographic unit, where parties are least in evidence—were the most supportive of change, signaling both their desire for visible party assistance and an opening for the parties to appeal to them. Perhaps most importantly, the idea of a party role change appealed particularly to segments of the electorate who were more alienated from the parties and the political system: the unreg-

TABLE 6.1. BASIC CHANGE IN PARTY ROLE.

Selected Subgroup	Change in Party Role[a]	
	% Favor	% Oppose
National sample	58	36
Northeast	64	31
Midwest	52	39
South	59	37
West	62	33
Democrats	60	34
Republicans	55	40
Independents	60	34
Men	53	42
Women	63	30
African American	67	31
White	59	35
18–34	58	37
35–49	64	31
50+	52	41
Executive/professional	58	37
Other white collar	58	35
Blue collar	58	38
City dweller	62	32
Suburban	63	30
Small town	55	38
Rural	58	38
More committed to party[b]	57	38
Less committed to party	67	28
Registered to vote[c]	58	36
Not registered to vote	65	28

Source: Larry J. Sabato, *The Party's Just Begun: Shaping Political Parties for America's Future* (Glenview, Ill.: Scotts, Foresman and Company, 1988): 181.

[a]See text for question wording.

[b]Respondents with any party identification or leaning were asked: "Would you say you are more committed or less committed to your political party today than you were five years ago?"

[c]Self-reported unregistered N = 330.

istered and those who admitted having become "less committed" to their political party in the five years that preceded the survey. This finding suggests at least the possibility that the least involved, most party-neutral citizens might establish or strengthen their partisan loyalties if a party tangibly contributed to their lives.

The abstract concept of greater civic involvement by the parties is certainly attractive to many, then, but how could the idea be practically applied? One appealing way would be the designation of certain party precinct or ward committee persons as "community ombudsmen." As a designated "red tape cutter," the ombudsman's job would be akin to the ward heeler of old: to keep in touch with his or her neighbors, to be alert to their needs, and to act as their advocate when problems arise. From getting potholes filled to organizing "crime watch" neighborhood security programs, ombudsmen could perform valuable services for voters who surely would be grateful and perhaps more receptive to their benefactor's party as well. As offensive as it may be to political purists, there is nothing inherently wrong with the time-honored, pragmatic American tradition of "votes given for favors done"; it is, in fact, the operating premise of the constituency service operations so carefully nurtured by incumbent members of Congress. Undoubtedly, volunteer spirit and party fealty alone will not be enough to spur the designated ombudsmen to energetic action. They should receive a stipend commensurate with such part-time work, perhaps several thousand dollars a year. In many states and localities, parties are in a better financial position than ever to pay for such efforts.

A less expensive alternative to the ombudsman program—or, more grandiosely, a supplement to it—would be the establishment of party "mobile units" that would travel from precinct to precinct and locality to locality on a regular schedule. Staffed by both volunteers and paid workers, these mobile units could raise the party's profile in nonelection seasons, assist residents with governmental problems, and serve as a field base for party operations such as canvassing. If these units sound suspiciously like the mobile offices many members of Congress send throughout their districts, they are intended to be. In fact, one of the purposes of these units should be to provide service competition to incumbent members of Congress, and the party's mobile offices should be used heavily in marginal districts controlled by the opposition party. (The mobile units will probably of necessity be restricted to these kinds of districts, given limited resources and the objections that would be raised by same-party incumbents who would see the party units as unwarranted intrusion and unwanted competition.) At present, incumbent legislators are essentially "unopposed" in their delivery of assistance to voters, using several hundred thousand dollars of taxpayer funds each year to do it—a fact that surely accounts in part for a House incumbent reelection rate that regularly exceeds 90 percent and neared 98 percent in 2000.[9] Such massive reelection rates are delightful for officeholders, but of questionable value to citizens in a system where arguably the best government results from strong two-party competition. Using mobile units may be one way for parties to help themselves as well as the voters *and* to inject more competition into congressional politics. Granted, incumbent members of Congress will still have a decided advantage in service delivery and reelection, given their large staffs and their unmatched ability to get the attention of bureaucrats and the press. But some added competition is surely better than none at all, and there are subsidiary benefits to the party in terms of voter mobilization. The attractiveness of both the ombudsman scheme and the mobile units stems from the opportunities they give to build the parties in the only way likely to prove enduring: person to person, from the bottom up.

Services to Party Members

Strengthen solidarity between the party organization and its activists and adherents by providing nonpolitical services and other rewards. Strong-party attributes:

PARTICIPATION AND EDUCATION

INCENTIVES

E. E. Schattschneider was among the first to recognize that party organizations do not own the allegiance of their partisans. He understood that, much as individual politicians, interest groups, and even commercial institutions do, the voter must be "courted" by a political party.[10] Other scholars have long acknowledged the importance of nonpolitical social and personal motivations for party involvement.[11] That, combined with the fact that most Americans are not vitally concerned with politics, leads to another suggestion for party renewal: Why not offer party-sponsored services and preferments to party activists, contributors, and identifiers?

The AFL-CIO and several other interest groups provide helpful models. The AFL-CIO has a series of "Union Privilege" programs that provide union members with a broad variety of money-saving services and benefits. Incentives for membership include access to low-interest credit cards and loans, low-cost insurance, savings on prescription drugs and health care, cut-rate legal and financial services, college scholarships, and a plethora of other individual benefits.[12] One credit card offered is designed specifically for union members who need to establish or repair credit ratings. The labor federation understands that it often takes more than collective benefits to build union membership, and it skillfully provides the individual benefits mentioned above as a means of enticing new members.[13] Several other interest groups offer similar incentives for joining. The American Association of Retired Persons (AARP) provides an especially prodigious array of benefits for members,[14] as does the Association of Trial Lawyers of America (ATLA).[15] Naturally, given its mission, the Sierra Club provides access to hundreds of worldwide nature outings as an enticement to join.[16]

Whether the parties make a profit or not on the transactions—and they should be encouraged to do so as long as the party members also benefit from discounted interest charges—there is no reason why the political parties should not undertake innovative service arrangements that help their partisans while strengthening party-voter ties. People join and stay active in organizations for many different reasons, and it is a fiction to believe that party membership can be enhanced and expanded by issues and ideology alone. In a culture that devalues politics as ours does, parties should employ every reasonable incentive to interest citizens in their groups. Before a congregation can be inspired and uplifted, it must be enticed to enter the church doors.

Expansion of Party Fundraising, Campaign Services, and Volunteer and Candidate Recruitment

Expand parties' fundraising capacities, services to the political campaigns of their nominees, and party efforts to recruit candidates and volunteer workers. Strong-party attributes:

> EQUITY AND LEGITIMACY
>
> ELECTORAL APPEAL
>
> PARTICIPATION AND EDUCATION
>
> ACCOUNTABILITY
>
> RESOURCES
>
> INCENTIVES
>
> CANDIDATE ASSISTANCE

As Chapter Three discussed, there has been no more substantial change in political parties than their newfound role as provider of services. Candidates now depend on the parties for useful advice, training, and technologies. As the link between party and nominee grows, so too does the connection between party and elected officeholder. To the extent possible, each party can and must further expand its capabilities to recruit candidates who share its basic philosophy, to train and instruct them and their staffs in the art of campaigning, and to make available the maximum financial assistance, expertise, and campaign technology. The more outstanding the party's candidates, staffs, and campaigns, the more appealing the party will appear in the eyes of the voter. (Unavoidably, the party's shine will always be in part reflected glory from its successful nominees.)

How the parties should go about raising the funds necessary to continue financing these activities is a difficult question. Although soft money—funds not subject to federal contribution restrictions—has been instrumental in helping the parties finance their activities, the controversial nature of these funds (they can be raised in unlimited sums from individuals, unions, corporations, and other interest groups) and the intense press scrutiny of party soft money operations threaten to undermine public support for the parties. In an ideal world, the parties would raise the bulk of their funds through small, hard money contributions; and in fact, the national parties do raise considerable sums of money through such contributions.[17] The parties should continue to expand their grass-roots donor bases—with the Internet potentially serving as a fruitful vehicle for such expansion. Even given an expanded grassroots donor base, however, hard money contributions will probably not suffice to finance the extensive range of desirable campaign activities presently being underwritten by the parties—especially the national committees. In Chapter Seven, we propose several regulatory changes to help parties maintain their vital presence in American political campaigns without resorting to an even greater reliance on image-tarnishing soft money. These changes include substantial increases in the sums of hard money that individuals and PACs may contribute to parties, tax-deductions for small individual contributions to parties, and a generous menu of public subsidies for the national parties.

While both parties deserve praise for expanding their portfolio of campaign services to candidates, neither party has earned many kudos for volunteer recruitment. But effective political parties need people no less than they need sophisticated campaign technologies. Voters respond best to a personal contact; television, direct mail, and literature, for all their advantages, are poor cousins.[18] The more that citizens can be attracted to participate in a party's activities, the more the party's candidates will gain and the more that the party itself will benefit from the expansion of its cadre.

Although very few Americans volunteer for political campaigns,[19] there is at least some untapped potential for party volunteer recruitment in the United States. In the August 2000 survey conducted for this study, 16 percent of respondents reported that they would be interested in becoming active with a political party at the local level.[20] Given the minuscule level of current participation, these survey figures are heartening, even after discounting for "good intentions." If even half of those who expressed interest could truly be mobilized by the parties, politics could be revolutionized. Here again, precinct "ombudsmen" could act as intermediaries, identifying and involving volunteers. In order to keep volunteers interested once they are signed up, the parties must also offer incentives and rewards. Patronage and honorary appointments (discussed in the next chapter) are certainly useful here, but the value of regular communication and social meetings should not be underestimated either. Periodic newsletters (sans fundraising pitch), issue forums, and relatively nonpolitical entertainment functions all build the solidarity from which real, lasting commitment is made. One thing is certain: the parties' current preferred vehicle for "voter contact," direct mail, is a one-way channel. It may provide for mass financial contributions but it is not the basis for mass action. Grassroots loyalty and two-way communication must be produced by other means.

Interestingly, there seems to be a valuable opportunity for local parties to reach out to citizens on an issue-oriented basis. A remarkable 87 percent of respondents to our survey agreed with the statement that "Local political parties should become more active in getting people involved in local issues."[21] While certainly the exception, policy-driven local parties are by no means unprecedented. Indeed, political scientist Samuel Eldersveld's masterful study of politics in Ann Arbor, Michigan, shows the powerful—and indeed, beneficial—impact that policy-driven local parties can have on local politics and policymaking.[22]

Party Institutional Advertising and Other Generic Party Building Efforts

Make party institutional advertising and other generic party building activities a permanent component of campaigns. Strong-party attributes:

> ELECTORAL APPEAL
>
> PARTICIPATION AND EDUCATION
>
> ACCOUNTABILITY
>
> RESOURCES
>
> POLICY CAPACITY
>
> CANDIDATE ASSISTANCE

Candidate-specific activities financed by a party surely help its candidates compete at the ballot box, but such activities do less to shore up the party's label among voters. The overwhelming majority of party-financed issue-advocacy ads run in 1998, for example, made no reference whatsoever to party labels.[23] Although candidate-specific activities are essential to the parties' central mandate of contesting and winning elections, the parties—especially the congressional and state legislative campaign committees—ought to devote more money than they presently do to activities that benefit the entire party ticket and bolster party identification in the electorate.

Generic party institutional advertisements (as described in Chapter Three) provide an effective way for parties to promote the party ticket.[24] In recent years, though, generic party advertising has gradually given way to issue-advocacy attack ads, most of which are virtually identical to candidate-sponsored ads and in fact are designed specifically to help or hurt specific candidates.[25] And while some issue-advocacy ads contain both generic and candidate-specific components, most are decidedly candidate-centered.[26] Parties will no doubt continue to use issue-advocacy ads to influence the outcome of specific contests, but such ads should not completely crowd out the use of more party-centered advertising campaigns. Generic party advertising permits the party to participate in setting the campaign or governmental agenda; it nationalizes key themes, thus making politics a bit more comprehensible for the voters while drawing its candidates and officeholders together (willing or not) around common ideas and—most importantly—around the party label itself. Survey research on the effects of party institutional advertising demonstrates that it can have a salutary impact on both the party and its nominees: recognition and understanding by the voters of a party's approach and philosophy increase, and (depending on the quality and context of the advertising) substantial gains can be registered for a party's ticket.[27]

Both parties ought to make institutional advertising a permanent aspect of the political landscape, and not just at campaign time. Why not air party commercials during the intervals between campaigns in support of or opposition to a president's initiatives or mistakes, or Congress's actions (assuming Congress is controlled by one party)? State and local parties should also produce institutional advertising for campaigns at their level, or in support of or opposition to governors, mayors, state legislatures, and city councils. Of course, air time is notoriously expensive, though radio is a relatively cheap and often overlooked alternative. Ideally, free time should be provided to the parties each year—campaign years and noncampaign years alike—by all television and radio stations, as proposed in more detail in Chapter Seven.

In allocating their resources, the parties must strike a healthy balance between candidate-specific and generic party-building activities. This applies especially to the congressional and state legislative campaign committees, which have typically lagged behind their nonlegislative party counterparts in underwriting important generic party-building efforts that benefit the entire party ticket and shore up party allegiances in the electorate.[28] Ultimately, as political scientist Daniel Shea points out, healthy parties are more than mere election-driven machines concerned about immediate electoral victory. "They are concerned as much about controlling branches of government as capturing more seats in any one of them, long-term party development as well as immediate electoral success, and what goes on in communities as well as in legislative districts."[29]

Party Policy Formulation

Increase the parties' capacities for policy formulation by empowering policy commissions for presidential interregnums. Strong-party attributes:

ELECTORAL APPEAL

PARTICIPATION AND EDUCATION

POLICY CAPACITY

American parties compete in elections partly by developing and marketing policy ideas. The need to win does not eclipse the task of proposing policy. Quite the contrary—electoral victory requires successful policy formulation and articulation by the parties. As the most broadly based political institutions in the United States, the parties must constantly develop and refine at least a generalized philosophy of government that differentiates one party from the other and presents voters with a rational choice.

Political scientists for decades have urged the parties to present well-publicized, specific, and comprehensive policy programs devised in representative fashion. In the late 1940s, a blue-ribbon committee of the American Political Science Association (APSA) urged not only that parties develop clear policies, but that only candidates who supported the policies be nominated and that parties insure that the pledges were enacted after the election.[30] To a very limited extent, the APSA's conditions have been met. The party platform, after all, is drawn up every four years after platform committee members—who are usually broadly representative of the party's key constituencies—hold dozens of hearings and take thousands of pages of testimony. As we saw in Chapter One, the platforms are not just the pablum they are frequently presented as being, and they do sharply differentiate the parties on many vital issues. Occasionally, as in 1936, the platforms contrast dramatically and set forth sharply defined alternatives.

And yet, American parties are fundamentally pragmatic and not strongly ideological (although they have become more ideological in recent years).[31] The European model of ideological parties simply does not and cannot fit the American experience, any more than a rigid, unitary parliamentary system could comfortably replace our nation's fluid separation-of-powers arrangement. The remarkable diversity of interests in the United States, combined with only two parties to organize the nation's political conflict, ensures that American parties remain pragmatic and flexible rather than ideological and rigid. At the same time, there is a public yearning for the parties to have between them "more than a dime's worth of difference"—to use George Wallace's 1968 indictment of the two-party system. The public certainly wants the parties to represent a choice,[32] though not an extreme one. And while voters hardly want to see officeholders become puppets of their parties, strictly bound to every nuance contained in the platform, there is a desire that officials be somewhat accountable to the parties that nominated them. In a poll conducted for the first edition of this book, 67 percent of the respondents favored "having candidates be more accountable to their political party and its policies or issues."[33]

A useful possibility may be for the parties to offer more policy guidance to officeholders on a regular basis. As the brief history of parties presented in Chapter Two suggested, such efforts must be carefully designed to avoid offending congressional sensibilities (as permanent policy councils have sometimes done) or producing ideologically extreme results that could damage a party's electoral chances (as midterm mini-conventions always threaten to do). But useful models of policy formulation do exist. In 1985, for example, the Democratic party established the Democratic Policy Commission, a forum chaired by Utah Governor Scott Matheson and designed to generate alternatives to policies being touted by the GOP.[34] After more than a year's hearings and deliberations, the Policy Commission in 1986 issued a thoughtful and well-conceived report[35] that appealingly and perceptively presented Democratic ideas and alternatives to Reagan administration policies. The commission achieved consensus without losing all substance, and it suggested worthwhile proposals for the party's congressional leadership and presidential contenders to consider. If free television time or institutional advertising had been available, the report could have done much more to communicate to a broader audience the Democratic party's policy goals. It is unlikely that the party controlling the White House would undertake such an exercise, since the administration, in effect, articulates the policies of the president's party. But it would be a productive innovation if the "out" party formed such a policy commission during each four-year cycle and effectively used free and paid media to disseminate the product. To avoid the unpleasant side effects mentioned earlier, the commission's membership should always include a wide sampling of elected leaders from Congress, the statehouses, and the local level; should be temporary and appointed for a fixed period after the midpoint of a presidential term; should try to produce issue research useful to gestating presidential campaigns; and should have a clear mandate to arrive, where possible, at a party consensus on the most critical areas of concern.

More Unpledged, Unbound Delegates

Increase the number of unpledged and unbound delegates to the presidential nominating conventions of both parties. Strong-party attributes:

ELECTORAL APPEAL

CONFLICT CONTROL

The presidential nominating conventions of both parties need the leavening provided by the participation of large numbers of elected officials. Having stood for office, these individuals understand what it takes to satisfy an electoral majority, and most know that compromise is an essential ingredient of political success in a diverse democracy. Moreover, they frequently are well acquainted with the potential nominees and can share this experience and knowledge with the other delegates. Besides the benefit of "peer review," elected officials—generally having the respect accorded their positions—are in a position to broker a tumultuous conclave and smooth over conflict in some circumstances. Their presence at a nominating convention, given sufficient numbers, may increase the legitimacy of the convention as the electorate observes it, improve the public image of the party, and assist in the nomination of more moderate, electable candidates. In keeping the party's most crucial political decision out of the hands of ideologically extreme firebrands, the elected officials will help the party maintain credibility with mainstream America, just as their participation draws them closer to their own political party.

All of this is widely acknowledged, yet for years—particularly in the Democratic party—the proportion of key elected officials attending the presidential convention was permitted to decline.[36] By 1980 only 14 percent of Democratic U.S. senators and 15 percent of Democratic House members participated in the party's presidential convention. (By contrast, 61 percent of Democratic senators and 32 percent of Democratic House members had served as delegates at the 1968 Democratic national convention.[37]) More appallingly, 38 percent of the Democratic National Convention delegates held no public or even party office in 1980.[38] The decline in elected officials serving as convention delegates signified officials' reluctance to declare early preferences in the presidential contest and to compete against their party constituents for delegate slots—disincentives that resulted from 1972 changes to delegate selection rules.[39]

Fortunately, the Democrats took steps to remedy this situation. In 1984 a prestigious bloc of 566 delegates was created specifically for party and elected officials. By and large, these "superdelegates" were permitted to be free agents and to vote for the candidate of their choice, regardless of the results of their state's primary or caucus.[40] This new contingent was in addition to a 1980-mandated bloc of 10 percent of each state delegation that was set aside for state and local Democratic politicians; unlike the superdelegates, however, these individuals were obligated to reflect the results of primary or caucus voting. By 1988, the Democrats expanded both categories of official representation. Seats at the convention were reserved for an additional 75 superdelegates and about 150 more "pledged" leaders in each state delegation.

By 2000, Democratic party rules designated as superdelegates all 450 or so members of the Democratic National Committee, all Democratic House members and Senators, all Democratic governors, and an array of former Democratic elected officials—presidents, vice presidents, senate leaders, House speakers, House minority leaders, and DNC chairs.[41] These unpledged delegates made up approximately 17 to 18 percent of the Democratic party's 4,370 total delegates. "What is remarkable," political scientists Nelson Polsby and Aaron Wildavsky wryly note, "is that special arrangements should have to be made to bring party officeholders back into the conventions or to allow the people who probably know most about the candidates to support whomever they think best."[42] Nevertheless, the gradual inclusion of greater numbers of Democratic elected and party officials at the presidential nominating convention is heartening.

But more can reasonably be done. The superdelegate proportion of the convention total ought to be expanded from its current rate to about a quarter of all delegates, perhaps by including other statewide Democratic leaders (e.g., lieutenant governors, attorneys general, etc.), state Democratic legislative leaders, and big-city mayors. GOP delegate selection rules, which are less confining than Democratic rules, make it relatively easy for Republican public officials to become delegates.[43] Republicans have therefore been fairly successful in attracting elected officials even without a "superdelegate" mandate. Both parties, though, would certainly gain from encouraging the states not to bind permanently any delegate (public official or otherwise) to the results of the state primary or caucus.[44] Political conditions, like the weather, can change drastically from a winter primary season to a summer convention, and delegates ought to be able to shift allegiances as circumstances warrant.

"Small d" democrats have no reason for alarm at such a proposal, for it would hardly result in a return to the "smoke-filled room." A candidacy christened by party hacks in a back room at today's nationally televised conventions would be doomed from the start. Or as Leon Epstein observed in reference to the superdelegates: "Only a most astonishingly bold group of politicians would in our time nominate someone other than the already acclaimed popular preconvention choice"[45] Rational delegates could be expected to select the popular choice save for a startling shift in the political winds after the conclusion of the primary process. All delegates should be free to shift with those winds in the interest of their party's electoral fortunes.

Greater Party Concern for Long-Term Public Support

The parties need to strike a better balance between the short-term goal of winning the next election and the long-term goal of building and maintaining support among the American public. Strong-party attributes:

EQUITY AND LEGITIMACY

ELECTORAL APPEAL

PARTICIPATION AND EDUCATION

In this section, we return briefly to a point we made at the conclusion of Chapter Three. Although parties in the United States exist primarily to contest and win elections, the parties need to do a much better job of ensuring that the short-term quest for electoral victory doesn't undermine the long-term goal of building stronger party ties in the electorate. As political scientist John Coleman writes in an insightful essay,

> Intended or not, party behavior through campaigning or governing are public acts that may produce public discontent. Parties ignoring this discontent because 'it's not our problem' have a history of being deformed through reforms. Public opinion matters.[46]

The normative corollary of Coleman's observation is that parties need to campaign and govern in ways that shore up, rather than undermine, party ties in the electorate and public support for the party system. One obvious area of concern is campaign finance. The "success" of the parties' soft money operations will count for little if, in the long run, the public finds such fundraising objectionable. The parties should thus make every effort to shore up their small donor programs. In addition, they should support campaign finance reform that imposes reasonable fundraising limits, providing such limits allow for a healthy degree of organizational strength. (We suggest a proposal in Chapter Seven.) In the absence of campaign finance reform, the parties should institute their own self-imposed limits on soft money contributions. Indeed, the DNC did precisely this after the Clinton/Gore fundraising scandals came to light at the end of the 1996 election, though the limits were too high and the effort was short lived.

The parties could also do better job of governing in ways that encourage stronger party ties. Party emphasis on policy and philosophy encourages a meaningful and enduring connection to the parties by illustrating the relevance of parties to people's lives. By contrast, party emphasis on destroying the political opposition obscures that relevance. The parties, then, would do well to keep the focus on policy differences and curb the scorched-earth politics of personal attack that have so poisoned the political environment in the past decade and a half. While perhaps effective at rallying committed party stalwarts around election time, the take-no-prisoners brand of attack politics surely leaves a significant portion of the electorate wondering how the parties are relevant to their lives. The media, of course, could help by curbing its propensity to focus on the personal and petty dimensions of party politics and by instead providing an account of party conflict that:

> emphasized the policy agendas underlying the fierce rhetoric as something intrinsically meaningful, not just labels for identifying the political players; ... that treated party divisions as a healthy reflection of different perspectives rather than as a sign of institutional weakness; ... that saw in the ongoing process of negotiating interests a manifestation of democratic problem solving rather than a scorecard for who is temporarily in vogue in some short-term political sweepstakes.[47]

Procedural fairness by the majority parties in Congress can probably also go a long way toward creating a constructive partisan environment. Floor rules that shut out the minority party from meaningful participation, as well as committee ratios that fail to reflect the overall partisan balance of the chamber, too often poison the political atmosphere by cutting off channels of legitimate political opposition for the minority party. Especially when the partisan balance in Congress is razor thin, majority parties should recognize that it is in their self-interest to treat the minority party with fairness, since a shift of a few seats in the next election might well find the majority back in the minority (facing a majority party bent on exacting revenge). Such procedural fairness can help foster the kind of meaningful partisanship that political scientists have long since advocated—where the minority party plays the loyal opposition, critiquing majority party programs and putting forth its own policy alternatives. And such partisanship, the optimist hopes, can help bring about parties that play a more useful role in organizing citizen perceptions of politics.

The party-initiated actions set forth in this chapter comprise an ambitious internal agenda for the American political parties to tackle, and the implementation of most or all of these proposals would go a long way toward generating the kind of partisan renewal that this study has advocated. Yet even successful adoption of all these measures may prove insufficient to achieve the desired goal. The laws and practices of states and nation can be altered to supplement the efforts of the parties themselves, and the final chapter of this volume suggests how.

NOTES

1. John J. Coleman, "Resurgent or Just Busy? Party Organizations in Contemporary America," in John C. Green and Daniel M. Shea, eds. *The State of the Parties: The Changing Role of American Parties,* 2nd ed. (Lanham, Md.: Rowman & Littlefield, 1996), 382.
2. Political scientists Jeffrey Cohen and Paul Kantor suggest that the parties' excessive reliance on soft money is a double-edge sword — strengthening parties organizationally but possibly discouraging strong party ties in the electorate. See Jeffrey E. Cohen and Paul Kantor, "Decline and Resurgence in the American Party System," in Jeffrey E. Cohen, Richard E. Fleisher, and Paul Kantor, eds., *American Political Parties: Decline or Resurgence* (Washington, DC: Congressional Quarterly Press, 2001), 258-259. Attack politics turns off mainly nonpartisans. See, for example, Stephen Ansolabehere and Shanto Iyengar, *Going Negative: How Political Advertisements Shrink and Polarize the Electorate* (New York: Free Press, 1995), 110. As a result, attack politics surely limits the parties' abilities to attract new adherents from the ranks of independents.
3. The most notable among journalists is David Broder, who has often lamented the weakening of American political parties. See, for example, David S. Broder, *The Party's Over: The Failure of Politics in America* (New York: Harper and Row, 1972).
4. This list of ten is not exclusive, but it certainly contains the most important items. For a somewhat different accounting of strong-party attributes, see David E. Price, *Bringing Back the Parties* (Washington, D.C.: Congressional Quarterly Press, 1984), 123.
5. See Larry J. Sabato, *The Party's Just Begun: Shaping Political Parties for America's Future* (Glenview, Ill.: Scott, Foresman and Company, 1988), 179.
6. Ibid.
7. See, for example, Jack Dennis, "Public Support for the American Party System," in William J. Crotty, 2nd ed., *Paths to Political Reform* (Lexington, Mass.: D.C. Heath, 1980), 43.
8. See, for example, William L. Riordon, ed., *Plunkitt of Tammany Hall* (New York: E.P. Dutton, 1963).
9. On constituency service, see Morris P. Fiorina, *Congress: Keystone of the Washington Establishment,* 2nd ed. (New Haven, Conn.: Yale University Press, 1989); George Serra, "What's in it for Me? The Impact of Congressional Casework on Incumbent Evaluation," *American Politics Quar-*

terly 22 (1994): 403–420. Glenn R. Parker and Suzanne L. Parker, "Correlates and Effects of Attention to District by U.S. House Members," *Legislative Studies Quarterly* 10 (May 1985): 223–242. The incumbency reelection rate for 2000 comes from Gregory L. Giroux, "GOP Maintains Thin Edge," *Congressional Quarterly Weekly* (11 November 2000): 2652–2654.

10. E. E. Schattschneider, *Party Government* (New York: Rinehart, 1942), 61.
11. Paul Allen Beck, *Party Politics in America,* 8th ed. (New York: Addison Wesley Longman, 1997), 107–111.
12. Information from http://www.unionprivilege.org/benefits/index.htm. (December 6, 2000.)
13. See http://www.unionprivilege.org/organize/whenorg.htm. (December 6, 2000.)
14. http://aarp.org/memberguide. (December 6, 2000.)
15. http://atlanet.org/members/affinity.html. (December 6, 2000.)
16. http://www.sierraclub.org. (December 6, 2000.)
17. Paul S. Herrnson, "National Party Organizations at the Century's End," in L. Sandy Maisel, ed., *The Parties Respond: Changes in Parties and Campaigns,* 3rd ed. (Boulder, Colo.: Westview Press, 1998), 59.
18. Daniel M. Shea, *Campaign Craft: The Strategies, Tactics, and Art of Political Campaign Management* (Westport, Ct.:Praeger, 1996), Chapter 13.
19. In 1998, for example, only 2 percent of respondents in the 1998 NES survey reported working for one of the parties of a candidate.
20. August 2000 survey conducted for this study by John McLaughlin and Associates. See Appendix. In the poll conducted for the first edition of this book, 13 percent of the respondents replied that they had "a great deal of interest" in working for a political party and 41 percent had "some interest." See Sabato, *The Party's Just Begun,* 186.
21. August 2000 survey conducted for this study by John McLaughlin and Associates. See Appendix.
22. Samuel J. Eldersveld, *Party Conflict and Community Development: Postwar Politics in Ann Arbor* (Ann Arbor, Mich.: University of Michigan Press, 1995).
23. Jonathan Krasno and Daniel Seltz, *Buying Time: Television Advertising in the 1998 Congressional Elections* (New York: New York University Law School, 2000).
24. Paul S. Herrnson, *Party Campaigning in the 1980s* (Cambridge, Mass.: Harvard University Press, 1988), 60; Anthony Corrado, "The Politics of Cohesion: The Role of the National Committees in the 1992 Election," in John C. Green and Daniel M. Shea, eds., *The State of the Parties: The Changing Role of American Parties* (Lanham, Md.: Rowman & Littlefield, 1996), 81; Anthony Corrado, *Paying For Presidents: Public Financing in National Elections* (New York: Twentieth Century Fund Press, 1993), 75.
25. Paul S. Herrnson, *Congressional Elections: Campaigning at Home and In Washington* (Washington D.C.: Congressional Quarterly Press, 2000), 112; Paul S. Herrnson and Diana Dwyer, "Party Issue Advocacy in Congressional Election Campaigns," in John C. Green and Daniel M. Shea, eds., *The State of the Parties: The Changing Role of American Parties,* 2nd ed. (Lanham, Md.: Rowman & Littlefield, 1999).
26. Herrnson, *Congressional Elections,* 112; Herrnson and Dwyer, "Party Issue Advocacy."

27. Larry J. Sabato, *The Rise of Political Consultants: New Ways of Winning Elections* (New York: Basic Books, 1981), 293, 300–301 n. 73.
28. See, for example, Daniel Shea, *Transforming Democracy: Legislative Campaign Committees and Political Parties* (Albany, N.Y.: SUNY, 1995).
29. Ibid., 171–172.
30. Committee on Political Parties of the American Political Science Association, *Toward a More Responsible Two-Party System* (New York: Rinehart, 1950).
31. See Louis Hartz, *The Liberal Tradition in America* (New York: Harcourt Brace, 1955).
32. Jack Dennis, "Public Support for the American Party System," in William J. Crotty, editor, *Paths to Political Reform* (Lexington, Mass.: D.C. Heath, 1980), 49–51.
33. See Sabato, *The Party's Just Begun*, 192.
34. See Philip Klinkner, *The Losing Parties: Out-Party National Committees, 1956–1993* (New Haven, Conn.: Yale University Press, 1994), 186.
35. See the Democratic Policy Commission, "New Choices in a Changing America" (Washington, D.C.: Democratic National Committee, September 1986).
36. Nelson Polsby, *Consequences of Party Reform* (New York: Oxford University Press, 1983), 114.
37. Price, *Bringing Back the Parties*, 202.
38. Ibid., 201–202.
39. Ibid., 202.
40. The rule changes were crafted by the DNC's Hunt Commission in 1982. See Price, *Bringing Back the Parties*, 166–171.
41. Democratic National Committee, *Delegate Selection Rules for the 2000 Democratic National Convention*, May 9, 1998.
42. Nelson Polsby and Aaron Wildavsky, *Presidential Elections: Strategies and Structures of American Politics*, 10th ed. (New York: Chatham House, 2000), 149.
43. See John F. Bibby, *Politics, Parties, and Elections* (Belmont, Calif.: Wadsworth, 2000), 228.
44. There is now no national party rule binding delegates to the primary/caucus choice (though the Republicans had one in 1976 and the Democrats did so in 1980). But the vast majority of primary states—36 of 39 in 1992, for example—bind their delegates to the election outcome. For an excellent discussion of presidential nomination rules, see Elaine Ciulla Kamarck and Kenneth M. Goldstein, "The Rules Do Matter: Post-Reform Presidential Nominating Politics," in L. Sandy Maisel, ed., *The Parties Respond: Changes in Parties and Campaigns*, 2nd ed. (Boulder, Colo.: Westview Press, 1994), 169–195.
45. Leon Epstein, *Political Parties in the American Mold* (Madison, Wisc.: University of Wisconsin Press, 1986), 107.
46. Coleman, "Resurgent or Just Busy? Party Organizations in Contemporary America," 372.
47. Matthew Robert Kerbel, "Parties in the Media: Elephants, Donkeys, Boars, Pigs, and Jackals," in L. Sandy Maisel, ed., *The Parties Respond: Changes in Parties and Campaigns*, 3rd ed. (Boulder: Westview Press, 1998), 258.

7

Toward Party Renewal, American Style, Part II

Parties are the central intermediate and intermediary structure between society and government.

—*GIOVANNI SARTORI*[1]

There are few nations on earth whose diversity and complexity rival that of the United States. If political parties serve as the "central intermediary" wherever they exist, then their job is both more requisite and more exacting in an unbridled democracy, such as the United States, that teems with different peoples and beliefs. As the introductory chapter explained, the American people and their government have a stake in well-functioning strong parties; therefore, the people, acting through their government, should assist the parties in the effort to reform, renew, and advance.

Undoubtedly, the party-initiated actions set forth in Chapter Six comprise the most hopeful part of our agenda for party renewal since the political parties need nothing but their own resolve to accomplish them. But there are other changes that require the cooperation of government, and, occasionally, private enterprise and the public directly. It is to this more difficult, yet still essential, part of the agenda that we now turn.

AN AGENDA FOR PARTY RENEWAL: GOVERNMENT-ASSISTED REFORMS
Deregulation of Parties

Deregulate the parties and permit them to devise their own rules of operation to the greatest extent possible. Strong-party attributes:

> EQUITY AND LEGITIMACY
>
> CONFLICT CONTROL
>
> AUTONOMY
>
> INCENTIVES

Leon Epstein uses the phrase "public utilities" to describe the treatment of parties under state law, since the state exercises governmental regulatory control without ownership and management of the organization—much as electric companies are treated in the United States.[2] Granted, some state control of parties is both necessary and desirable; for example, state statutes on ballot access help to assure the continuity and legitimacy of the two major parties even in the face of minimal electoral success.[3] And as Malcolm Jewell has noted, only judicial regulation and congressional intervention eliminated some of the odious discriminatory practices of Democratic parties in the South.[4] Still, American political parties should be accorded unbegrudgingly their right of free association as guaranteed by the First and Fourteenth Amendments to the Constitution. Within the broadest possible state legal framework—designed only to insure that equality and other fundamental democratic values are not violated—the parties ought to be permitted to set up their own structures and rules of operation as they see fit. After all, extensive state regulation of parties began mainly as a reaction to the excesses of America's post-Civil War, boss-controlled parties.[5] Conditions today are completely changed, and in the post-Tammany media age, parties will design open, fair, and inclusive procedures because it is in their own interests to do so; any significant moves that smack of bossism are sure to draw ire from the news media and retribution from the voters.

In this era when "less government" is the premiere political mantra, it is striking to discover how overregulated the parties are in most states. In fact, the United States has the dubious distinction of hosting the most governmentally fettered parties in the democratic world.[6] Often the parties are treated little better, or worse, than any garden-variety political action committee or special interest group.

The most recent compilation of state regulations on parties was conducted by a team of political scientists led by Andrew Appleton and

Daniel Ward.[7] Table 7.1, which summarizes the findings of these researchers, indicates just how mistrustful of the parties some states are.[8] Based on Appleton and Ward's data, 17 states can reasonably be classified as light party regulators, 18 as moderate regulators, and 15 as heavy regulators.[9] At the deregulated end stands Alabama—which regulates parties in none of the areas defined in Table 7.1. New Jersey state parties, in contrast, are the most highly regulated in the nation, with laws on the books dictating party action in every area examined by Appleton and Ward's team.

States in a mood to clear statutory deadwood ought to start with their political party laws. The parties ought to be left completely free to organize and conduct themselves in any reasonable manner without state interference. In addition to deregulating the parties, the states ought to pass a number of measures (to be discussed in subsequent sections) to assist parties. Even simple allowances can be of enormous help. A number of states currently restrict the parties' access to voter registration lists.[10] This nonsensical regulation inhibits the parties' mobilization of supporters, raising of revenue, and communication with the voters. Finally, Congress should resist all impulses to federalize party rule-making in the presidential nominating process. Proposals for mandated national and regional presidential primaries, for instance, represent an unwarranted invasion and usurpation of state party prerogatives in this vital arena.

There would normally be little cause for optimism that states would suddenly cede regulatory authority back to the parties, save for several encouraging Supreme Court decisions in the last decade and a half. In 1986, for example, the Court ruled in *Tashjian* v. *Republican Party of Connecticut* that states may not require political parties to hold "closed" primary elections (where only registered party members may vote).[11] Such laws, said the Court, unconstitutionally burden the parties' First Amendment freedom of association rights. Justice Thurgood Marshall, writing for the majority, explained that, while the Constitution grants states the power to prescribe the "times, places, and manner" of holding elections, "This authority does not extinguish the state's responsibility to observe the limits established by the First Amendment rights of the state's citizens." Connecticut's badly outnumbered Republican party had wanted to allow registered Independents to vote in its primary in an attempt to broaden its base, but the GOP had been stymied by a Democratic legislature and governor intent on denying them that opportunity.

Incidentally, the Connecticut case is a double-edged sword for strong party advocates. While they joyously welcome the judicial recognition of party rights, they note with dismay that Connecticut Republicans are using

TABLE 7.1. STATE PARTY REGULATIONS.

State	Mandate selection of state committee	Mandate central committee meetings	Mandate composition of central committees	Regulate leadership of party orgs.	Forbid party nominating conventions	Forbid preprimary endorsements	Mandate open primary
Light Regulators							
AL							
AK					X		
DE					X		
GA					X		
KY					X		
MN					X		
OK					X		
UT				X			
VA							X
AR	X				X		
CT					X[a]		X
HI				X	X		
KS					X[b]		X
NB		X			X		
NC					X		X
PA	X				X		
WI			X		X		
Moderate Regulators							
FL					X	X	X
MS	X			X	X		
MT	X		X				X
NM	X			X			X
NY	X			X			X
SC	X		X	X			
WY	X		X	X			
ID	X	X	X		X		
IL	X	X	X	X			
IA	X		X		X		X
ME	X			X	X		X
MA	X		X	X	X[c]		
MI	X		X	X	X[d]		
NH	X		X	X	X		
OR	X			X	X		X
RI				X	X	X	X
TX	X		X	X	X		
WV	X		X	X	X		
Heavy Regulators							
CA	X		X	X	X		X
IN	X	X	X	X	X[e]		

(continued)

TABLE 7.1. Continued

State	Mandate selection of state committee	Mandate central committee meetings	Mandate composition of central committees	Regulate leadership of party orgs.	Forbid party nominating conventions	Forbid preprimary endorse-ments	Mandate open primary
MD	X	X		X	X		X
MO	X	X	X	X	X		
NV	X		X	X	X		X
SD	X		X	X	X^f		X
TN	X		X	X	X^g		X
VT	X	X	X	X	X		
WA	X	X	X		X		X
AZ	X	X	X	X	X		X
CO	X	X	X	X	X^h		X
LA	X	X	X	X	X		X
ND	X	X	X	X	X	X	
OH	X	X	X	X	X	X	
NJ	X	X	X	X	X	X	X

Source: Compiled from Andrew M. Appleton and Daniel S. Ward, *State Party Profiles: A 50-State Guide to Development, Organization, and Resources* (Washington, D.C.: Congressional Quarterly Press, 1997), Appendix. Used by permission. Categorization scheme from Paul Allen Beck, *Party Politics in America*, 8th ed. (New York: Addison Wesley Longman, 1997), 67-68.

[a]Connecticut allows for conventions to nominate statewide candidates but gives candidates who receive at least 15 percent of the convention votes the right to call for a primary.

[b]Minor parties (those that received less than 5 percent of the votes cast for governor in the previous election) are exempt from Kansas's prohibition on nominating conventions.

[c]Massachusetts makes primary ballot access conditional on a threshold vote at the convention.

[d]In Michigan, the prohibition on convention nominations applies only to governor.

[e]In Indiana, the prohibition on convention nominations applies to governor and U.S. senators; candidates for other statewide offices are nominated by conventions.

[f]In South Dakota, primaries are required for federal offices and governor; candidates for other offices are nominated by convention.

[g]Tennessee's prohibition on convention nominations applies to a range of offices U.S. House and Senate seats, general assembly seats, the governor, and the public service commission.

[h]Colorado makes primary ballot access conditional on a threshold vote at the convention. (Candidates may also petition for primary ballot access.)

their newfound grant of authority to open a "closed" primary, diluting their own partisans' control over the nominating process. The dilemma of this case was best captured by Gerald Benjamin: "Should parties be allowed to do as they wish, or should they be required to do what's good for them?"[12] The danger in deregulation is that the political equivalent of Gresham's law might hold true, with "bad" nominating practices (e.g., open primaries) driving out "good" ones (e.g., closed primaries). There are risks involved, certainly, but they are probably worth taking. Connecticut Republicans may not be acting in the best interests of their party, but that is properly their determination. On the whole, if deregulated, we believe that parties will make the right decisions most of the time, will learn and adjust from their mistakes, and will be much the stronger for it all.

Other recent judicial decisions have clearly put the states on the defensive in justifying regulation of political parties. In 1989, the Supreme Court further championed the cause of party autonomy with its ruling in *Eu, Secretary of State of California* v. *San Francisco County Democratic Central Committee*.[13] In *Eu*, the Court struck down onerous California statutes that limited state party chairs to two-year terms, required state party chairmanships to be rotated between northern and southern Californians, and banned party endorsements in primaries. As Andrew Appleton and Daniel Ward note, some of the regulations on state parties (see Table 7.1) may well be inconsistent with the Court's ruling in *Eu*,[14] and states may be hard-pressed to enforce them. New Jersey, for example, has not enforced its regulations prescribing state party structure since the *Eu* decision.[15]

The Court's defense of party autonomy did not end with the *Eu* ruling. In June 2000, the U.S. Supreme Court handed parties another stunning victory by striking down California's law mandating blanket primaries—contests in which all candidates are listed by party label on a single ballot, all voters are eligible to participate (regardless of party affiliation), and the two-party candidates receiving the most votes face off in the general election.[16] In its 7–2 decision, the Court ruled that California's blanket primary law trampled on parties' freedom of association rights by preventing parties from controlling their nominating processes. Notably, the Supreme Court has also recently given its imprimatur to states seeking to reinforce the two-party system. In *Timmons* v. *Twin Cities New Party* (1997), the Court ruled that the Minnesota State Election Commission could prohibit fusion balloting—a practice that aids minor parties by permitting them to nominate candidates already nominated by one of the major parties.[17] The Court's 6–3 ruling left little doubt that states are free to promote two-party politics. As Chief Justice William Rehnquist wrote in the Court's majority opinion, "The Constitution permits the Minnesota Legislature to decide that political stability is best served though a healthy two-party system."[18]

More Conventions and Caucuses, Fewer Primaries

Leave the choice of nominating method to the parties, which should choose to hold more caucuses and conventions and fewer primaries. If primaries must be held, preprimary endorsing conventions should be convened, and the preference should be for "closed" party primaries, not "open," "blanket," or "nonpartisan" ones. In states that conduct presidential primaries, select convention delegates in separate party caucuses following "beauty contest" primaries. Strong-party attributes:

ELECTORAL APPEAL
PARTICIPATION
ACCOUNTABILITY
CONFLICT CONTROL
AUTONOMY

Political scientists favoring stronger parties find it easy to criticize popular primaries and to wax eloquent about the merits of caucuses and conventions as a preferred nominating method. Primaries may attract far more participants, but this quantity is more than matched by the quality of caucus participation. Compared to unenlightening minutes spent at the primary polls, caucus attendees spend several hours or more learning about politics and the party, listening to speeches by candidates or their representatives, and taking cues from party leaders and elected officials. While primaries measure only first choices, conventions and caucuses permit brokering and compromise that can result in the nomination of a "second choice" acceptable to most; thus, conventions can often dampen factionalism and promote party unity where primaries can exacerbate the divisions. Similarly, a convention can engineer the nomination of a "balanced slate" of candidates representing all the party's major constituency groups; such a slate can emerge only by fortunate accident in a primary. Conventions and caucuses also provide for a "peer review" of candidates by other elected officials; are useful for party recruiting of volunteers and funds; generally cost less for the candidates than primary elections; and keep candidates and officeholders tied more closely to their party by requiring them first to woo party regulars before paying their attentions to the general electorate. If these advantages are not enough, caucuses and conventions offer an important incentive for involvement in the party: a major voice in the selection of potential governors, senators, and presidents. And by generally limiting participation to party loyalists, they greatly reduce cross-party voter raiding (voters of one party participating in the primary of the other party, presumably in some cases to choose the weakest nominee, but meddling, whatever the motive), a problem that can plague primaries. Finally, one could also contend that caucuses and conventions, since they are normally limited to relatively informed partisans with a keen interest in politics, limit the power of the news media and of wealthy candidates whose money and advertising can sometimes sway the votes of the less involved.

With all of these wonderful arguments to recommend caucuses and conventions, why is it that the vast majority of nominations are made by primary? The amusing explanation may be that no one listens to political scientists, but the more immediate cause is the popular affection for pure democracy. As the late Tom McCall, former governor of Oregon, once put it: "The people, if you gave them their choice, would like to elect everything clear down to dogcatcher."[19] The poll conducted for this study certainly confirms his observation. We frankly tried to construct a survey question that might attract a sizeable number of voters to the caucus standard. Since the terms *caucus* and *convention* tend to be associated with *boss control* in the public's mind, we substituted "open meetings of party activists." (The word *open* in itself usually prompts higher approval from a "freedom of information"-conscious electorate.) And we emphasized that *party* candidates were being nominated, with the hope that respondents might make the connection between purpose and power. But it was for naught. To the question, "Would you favor or oppose having a party's candidates for office chosen in open meetings of party activists rather than by primary elections?" survey respondents gave a resounding no, 60 to 33 percent.[20] Other polls have also demonstrated lopsided support for primaries over caucuses.[21] Some national surveys have even shown that a large majority want to eliminate the party presidential nominating conventions in favor of a national primary election to select presidential and vice-presidential nominees.[22]

There are a couple of supplementary reasons for the predominance of primaries today. In the Democratic party, complicated party rules on the choice of presidential convention delegates (enacted in the early 1970s) led many party leaders to push for primaries as the simplest method of selection and the one least open to challenge. Primaries also offered a way to separate the tumultuous presidential process from the conduct of other party business.[23] Then, too, the news media played a role by giving inordinate coverage to primaries and all but ignoring many state presidential caucuses.[24] Implicit in the news media's coverage was their view of primaries as open, democratic, and conflict oriented, and caucuses as closed, suspiciously party dominated, and sometimes consensual in nature.[25] For both the news media and the people, therefore, the primary is "an institutionalized means for pursuing [candidate-centered] politics in a civic culture that is broadly hostile to party organizational control."[26]

The state legislatures have, by and large, given the people what they wanted, though there are important variations. Not a single state relies completely on the convention system of nomination. Two southern states—Alabama and Virginia—at least permit each state party to choose the method of nomination every year,[27] though only Virginia parties have opted for the convention option in recent years. A few other states use conventions in limited fashion. Iowa provides for a postprimary convention if no candidate receives more than 35 percent of the vote in a primary.[28] Michigan and Indiana rely on conventions to nominate statewide candidates for offices below U.S. Senator and governor.[29] In addition, six states—Colorado, Delaware, New Mexico, New York, North Dakota, and Utah—hold preprimary screening conventions, and Connecticut employs a "challenge primary" in which convention runners up who receive at least 15 percent of the convention vote may challenge the convention winner in a primary.[30] The remaining states, though, rely exclusively on the direct primary for making state and congressional nominations.[31]

Not only do most states nominate almost all offices by primary, but the type of primary frequently employed is not conducive to building strong parties. Twenty states use "open" primaries, whereby voters may participate in either party's primary, regardless of their partisan affiliation.[32] In nine of these states, the voter is not even forced to divulge in which party's primary he or she is choosing to cast a ballot; the selection is made in secret. In three other states, the antiparty conditions of primary voting are still worse. Alaska and Washington employ a "blanket" primary where people can simultaneously vote in both Democratic and Republican primaries for different offices. (As noted above, California also mandated a blanket primary in 1998 but was rebuffed by the Supreme Court in 2000 when the state parties challenged it.) Worst of all is Louisiana whose primary is completely "nonpartisan"; all Democratic and Republican candidates are listed together on the same ballot, with the general election "runoff" sometimes held between candidates of the same party! "Closed" primaries limited to registered party voters are obviously preferable, if strong parties are the goal, since there is greater incentive and reward for a voter's identification with a party, and the party itself is guaranteed that its nominees truly represent its constituency. Evidence has also been offered by Malcolm Jewell to suggest that states requiring closed primaries have higher party identification levels among the public.[33] In other words, voters who are encouraged to make a real choice between parties in the registration and primary voting processes are more inclined to admit allegiance to a party.

Presidential nominations are also largely decided through primary elections rather than caucuses. Democratic party delegate selection reforms of the early 1970s (see Chapter Six)—which produced highly complex rules for delegate selection through party caucuses—had the effect of encouraging states to select delegates through primaries.[34] The GOP was also impacted by these reforms, since many Democratically-controlled state legislatures seeking to comply with new national party rules rewrote state presidential nomination laws for both parties.[35] The result has been a sharp increase in the number of presidential primaries for both parties. In 1968, for example, 17 Democratic state parties held presidential primaries, and these primaries selected 38 percent of the total delegates to the Democratic National Convention. By 1992, 39 Democratic state primaries chose 79 percent of the delegates to the Democratic national convention.[36] (The number of Democratic presidential primaries decreased somewhat in 1996.[37]) GOP reliance on presidential primaries to nominate presidential candidates has been even more pronounced. By 1996, Republicans held presidential primaries in 43 states, and these events produced 85 percent of the total delegates to the 1996 Republican National Convention.[38] In 2000, the number of primaries held by both parties remained similar to that for 1996. [39]

In the best of all party worlds, presidential primaries would either be eliminated in favor of caucuses or would be reduced to "beauty contests," nonbinding affairs held prior to separate caucuses as an indication of popular sentiment for caucus participants to consider. The idea of eliminating primaries or making them purely advisory is, of course, a pipe dream. Though the United States is almost alone among the world's democracies in insisting upon mass participation in party nominations as well as general elections, Americans prefer it that way. They have never accepted E. E. Schattschneider's assertion that "democracy is not to be found *in* the parties but *between* the parties."[40] They have not cared that, as Austin Ranney writes, "the direct primary has not only eliminated boss control of nominations but party control as well."[41] Recognizing popular sentiment, party leaders often have not exercised their right to hold a caucus even where the state properly cedes to the party committees at each level (statewide, congressional district, and local) the option of selecting the nominating method they desire each year.

So, reluctantly conceding the inevitable, if primaries must be the preferred method of nomination, then at least they should be closed party affairs; open primaries are inimical to strong parties, and blanket and nonpartisan arrangements are particularly offensive. And if primaries are to select all the individuals who will bear the party standard, then the parties ought to be allowed, and encouraged, to bestow preprimary endorsements at state, district, and local conventions. Ideally, the endorsed candidates should be designated as such on the primary ballot as a useful guide to voters, and the candidates should be listed in order of finish at the convention, since there is probably some slight electoral advantage to being first on the ballot. Further, candidates' access to the ballot should be restricted to those who can muster at least 20 percent support among the convention delegates. If any candidate is able to muster an extraordinary majority of delegates (say, 70 percent), he or she should be declared the nominee and no primary should be held.[42]

The advantages of this system are many, and similar in many respects to the enticing qualities of caucuses and conventions generally. Potential and incumbent officeholders must campaign first among party loyalists, thus forcing the candidates to develop a rationale for carrying the party standard as well as the office title. The party's power and legitimacy are augmented considerably as a result, and politically interested citizens are given a greater incentive to become involved in the party. All primary voters, involved or not, are handed a valuable voting cue—a kind of "personnel review" by the candidates' peers. Preprimary endorsements seem to help a party manage disputes and resolve conflicts in a more controlled environment than an open primary, thereby helping to reduce party fragmentation. Indeed, this was certainly true in the contest for the 2001 Democratic gubernatorial nomination in New Jersey. When U.S. Senator Robert Torricelli announced that he would challenge front runner Jim McGreevey for the Democratic nomination, county party leaders—whose preprimary endorsement secures for the endorsee the official party line on many county primary ballots—threw their support behind McGreevey, forcing Torricelli to withdraw his candidacy and avoiding a fractious Democratic primary.[43] Those who are concerned about candidates "buying" elections should also favor this reform. Money is of less value in this setting because participants are normally well informed and less subject to easy manipulation by media advertisements; a candidate's qualifications, proposals, and general election chances tend to weigh more heavily with savvy party activists than with average voters.

The Supreme Court's decision in *Eu* upheld the right of political parties to make preprimary endorsements, so no state may legally prohibit this activity. At present, seven states (Colorado, Connecticut, New Mexico, New York, North Dakota, Rhode Island, and Utah) have laws providing for preprimary endorsements.[44] In addition, nine state parties (California, Delaware, Illinois, Massachusetts, Michigan, Minnesota, Ohio, Pennsylvania, and Virginia) make extralegal preprimary endorsements at least some of the time, and New Jersey's county parties often endorse candidates.[45] Political scientists Malcolm Jewell and Sarah Morehouse demonstrate that the primary success rate for party-endorsed candidates—at least at the gubernatorial level—has declined somewhat during the past two decades.[46] Nevertheless, a large majority of party activists involved in party endorsing conventions believe that their parties should continue to endorse candidates.[47] The most important reasons why, according to these activists, are that such endorsements enhance the party's grassroots character and help strengthen the party.[48]

Needless to say, all parties should take advantage of their right to endorse candidates and do so regularly for all state and local offices.

Public Financing Provisions

Allow citizens to make small contributions to parties by means of an add-on or check-off device on their federal and state income tax forms. Additionally, Congress should reestablish at least a 50-percent federal tax credit for small contributions to parties, and preferably make it a 100-percent credit. Strong-party attributes:

> PARTICIPATION AND EDUCATION
>
> RESOURCES
>
> CANDIDATE ASSISTANCE

The special role played by political parties in democracies justifies providing them with at least partial public subsidies. Although some legislators—especially conservatives—find public funding objectionable, two minimally controversial means exist for generating public monies for parties. One way is through a tax "add-on" that permits citizens to make small contributions to the party of their choice by checking the appropriate box on their income tax returns. Seven states (Alabama, Arizona, California, Maryland, Massachusetts, Montana, and Virginia) presently have some form of add-on to provide money for parties,[49] and the device could easily be implemented at the federal level. Since the contributions are over and above one's tax liability, the federal budget would not be impacted.[50] Moreover, the voluntary nature of this self-imposed tax should appeal to conservatives. The public, too, seems to favor the idea: in a survey conducted for the first edition of this book, a solid majority of respondents approved of it.[51] In its ideal form, the federal 1040 (short and long form) would include an add-on provision that gives a taxpayer the opportunity to contribute a gift of $2, $5, $10, $25, $50, or $100 to the national party he or she designates. Will any significant number of taxpayers give money using this device? Sadly, taxpayer participation rates in the states that use add-on programs have declined since 1980.[52] Still, while giving to the political parties will doubtless never become the rage among beleaguered taxpayers anticipating a refund, it is possible that the presently small percentage of participation could be augmented by a joint two-party educational advertising campaign undertaken at tax time.

An alternative means of generating public funds for the parties is through the use of tax "check-off" programs. Unlike add-on programs— in which participation involves making a contribution over and above one's tax payment—tax check-off programs permit taxpayers to earmark a small percentage of their tax liability to a political party. Thirteen states currently employ some variant of the tax check-off, though some of these states provide public subsidies only to candidates and not to parties.[53] Not surprisingly, given that no additional money comes out of the taxpayer's pocket, state tax check-off devices have been more successful in attracting participants than have state tax add-on programs.[54] A federal check-off provision for the national parties could reap significant sums of small contributions for them. As with tax add-on programs, tax check-off devices should appeal even to political conservatives. After all, taxpayer participation is purely voluntary, and indeed, check-off programs constitute a rare opportunity for citizens to designate how their tax dollars are spent![55] John Green and Daniel Shea note that this type of party support program, enacted in Ohio in 1987, has helped fuel party renewal in that state.[56]

Tax credits and deductions for political contributions are an indirect type of public funding. Congress should reestablish at least a 50 percent federal tax credit for small contributions to parties, and preferably make it a 100 percent credit. Before landmark tax reform legislation was passed in 1986, federal taxpayers were granted a 50 percent tax credit for all contributions to candidates, PACs, parties, and political committees of up to $50 for an individual and $100 on a joint return. Unfortunately, this credit was eliminated in the tax revision, and currently there is no federal credit for political gifts. It will not come as a surprise to this volume's readers if we recommend the restoration of the credit not only to the 50 percent level, but all the way to 100 percent. Such a move would clearly encourage small donations that have few if any real strings attached; the parties not only would remain less encumbered by the perceived debts that come with large contributions, but both parties would have an exceptionally valuable tool to use in expanding their donor and membership base. Seven income-taxing states (Arizona, Hawaii, Minnesota, Montana, North Carolina, Ohio, Oklahoma, and Oregon) presently provide tax deductions or credits for political contributions.[57] Indeed, Minnesota currently provides a 100 percent refund for individual contributions to parties and candidates up to $50. In this era of projected national budget surpluses, there is no excuse for not restoring the federal tax credit for small political contributions.

It ought to be mentioned here that the universe of potential contributors to the parties, while not enormous, is often underestimated. As the national parties have demonstrated with direct mail, millions of Americans are willing to give small and medium-size amounts to parties, if the right stimulus is applied. The more parties can develop closer personal contact with their partisans, and the more they can promote the funding options at their disposal, the higher will be their yield. The fundraising potential is great for creative and energetic parties with the ability to cultivate grassroots loyalty. Tax check-off and add-on provisions—two reforms to which it is difficult to imagine serious objection—allow governments to help parties fulfill their financial potential. "These programs," note political scientists Michael Malbin and Thomas Gais, "put the state into the role of facilitator for small contributions to parties."[58]

Laws establishing virtually full public funding for legislative elections have recently been passed in Arizona, Maine, Massachusetts, and Vermont.[59] (All except Vermont's were passed through statewide ballot initiatives.) By and large, the plans passed by these states are all modeled after the "Clean Money Campaign Reform" (CMCR) plan devised by Public Campaign, a Washington-based campaign finance reform advocacy group.[60] In a nutshell, the CMCR plan provides full public funding for primary and general election candidates who meet ballot access requirements, raise a threshold number of $5 "qualifying" contributions, and voluntarily agree to spend no more than a nominal sum of seed money on their campaigns. The plan also provides additional funds for candidates who are outspent by nonparticipating opponents or targeted by independent expenditure campaigns. Although it's too early to judge the performance of the CMCR plan, one thing is certain: the plan includes no public monies for the political parties and no provision for parties to give direct financial assistance to their candidates.[61] By weakening the link between parties and candidates, the CMCR model threatens to advance the institutionalization of candidate-centered elections and, in the process, further undermines responsible party government. It also promises to amplify the importance of party issue-advocacy campaigns, as parties, statutorily sidelined in their own candidates' campaigns, seek influence in the election process.

Lawmakers and citizens should reject any public funding reform plan that fails to preserve a healthy electoral role for the political parties. At the very least, parties must have a legal right to provide adequate sums of direct financial assistance to any candidates they choose to support (including candidates who participate in public funding programs). Moreover, any comprehensive public funding plan should include direct public subsidies to the parties themselves for carrying out generic party-building activities (such as voter mobilization drives and party institutional advertising) and for financing overhead and administrative expenses. There is even a strong argument for giving parties a role in allocating the public monies designated for candidates. Public funding schemes that allocate equal amounts to all candidates are highly inefficient. Obviously, safe incumbents in one-party legislative districts need far less than candidates in two-party marginal districts. Although every party candidate should certainly be guaranteed a "floor" amount, the parties should have the authority, within reason, to concentrate public resources where they can do the most good.[62]

Free Television and Radio Time

Require all television and radio stations to make available to each major state and national political party an hour of free time every calendar year, in five-minute, sixty-second, and thirty-second advertising segments with at least half the allocations in prime time. In the absence of such a mandate, at least require stations to charge parties their lowest unit rates and to guarantee that at least some substantial, choice time will be made available for purchase. Strong-party attributes:

  PARTICIPATION AND EDUCATION

  RESOURCES

  POLICY CAPACITY

  INCENTIVES

  CANDIDATE ASSISTANCE

It is easy to become outraged when reviewing the political time policies of America's broadcast industry. No network—and virtually no television and radio station—regularly offers any free advertising time to political candidates or parties. Media advertising costs are consuming an increasing portion of all candidates' budgets,[63] and the commercial spot charges have risen far more quickly than the rate of inflation. In the 1971 Federal Election Campaign Act (FECA), Congress mandated that media stations give federal candidates the lowest unit advertising rate (LUR), as well as guarantee them reasonable access to advertising time, in the forty-five days preceding a primary election and the sixty days before a general election.[64] Unfortunately, no such laws exist for political parties.[65] As a regular practice, the media networks charge political parties full, undiscounted rates, and parties can have difficulty buying advertising time during peak, prime-time periods.[66] At the very least, then, Congress should extend the FECA's LUR mandate to the political parties as well.

Ideally, though, Congress ought to go much further and provide free media time to political parties. The justifications for this mandate are straightforward. First, the public, not the stations, owns the airwaves; we merely lease the airwaves for limited durations to the station proprietors.

Consider also, as political scientist Anthony Gierzynski points out, that the major television networks were recently the beneficiaries of a "multimillion dollar giveaway" from the federal government "in the form of frequencies for high definition television."[67] Even cable television stations should be required to provide free air time to parties; as Paul Herrnson writes, "much of what is viewed on cable television passes through the public airwaves or over publicly maintained utility poles."[68] The commercial media industry, easily among the most lucrative enterprises in the United States, can surely afford to provide a small portion of advertising time in return for the substantial benefits they accrue from the government. Yet, the United States remains one of the few major democracies in the industrialized world that does not allow the public to reclaim a little of its own air time for the most vital rituals (elections) and instruments (the parties) of democracy.

As a condition of license renewal, and without providing any tax credits or other taxpayer-financed subsidies to an already wealthy industry, every television and radio station should be required to make available an hour of free time every year to each of the two major national parties *and* each of the state party organizations in the station's primary viewing or listening area. The time should be granted in two-minute, sixty-second, and thirty-second spots. (Like it or not, Americans prefer their political advertisements to be short and sweet; the "tune-out" factor is likely to be devastating for political commercials that are lengthier than two minutes.) The parties should also be offered a wide variety of time slots, with at least half the allocations in weekday evening prime time.

The broadcasting industry ferociously fights proposals such as this one, of course. One of their favorite arguments is that many metropolitan stations' media markets stretch over dozens of congressional districts, while others incorporate only one or a few. A free time requirement, they insist, would unfairly deluge the metropolitan stations with demands for free time, that, if met, would virtually eliminate other commercial spots from the air during election seasons. Their claim is valid if time is given to individual candidates, but a free time grant to parties rather than candidates neatly solves the problem, since all stations would be accommodating just two entities. Party leaders should have wide discretion in determining the uses to which the time is put. For instance, they may choose to focus some spots on one or a few specific candidates, probably those in marginal races. (Discretion of this powerful sort can only reinforce the party's efforts to draw its nominees more closely to it.) Party officials may wish to conserve all the time for the general election, or they may allocate a few spots to the party's primary or convention candidates to assist their efforts to become better known before the party nominees are selected. In any event, every candidate would still be free to make whatever additional purchases are necessary and available to promote his or her own individual candidacy. Realistically, free media time for political parties is unlikely to curb individual candidates' reliance on television advertising (and thus is unlikely to relieve any of the fundraising pressure on politicians). This reform is nonetheless worthwhile because parties will so clearly benefit and voters will gain much useful campaign information presented in a party context.

No mention has been made here of third parties. As advocates of a strong two-party system, we see nothing wrong in discriminating against third parties in the provision of privileges such as free media availability and public financing. In our view, it is in our nation's interest to support and gird the two-party system that provides such stability and continuity to American democracy, and we shouldn't encourage fragmentation by building in incentives for third-party formation and promotion. At most, minor parties should be allotted slots based on the percentage of the vote they received in the prior election (with 5 percent of the vote a minimum threshold). New parties without electoral track records would simply have to wait until the next round for free time.

While awaiting congressional action on free media time—probably a lengthy biding—the parties should aggressively pursue opportunities for free broadcasts on the nation's thousands of cable and public access channels.[69] Audience ratings are surprisingly high for many of these community-based stations, and any channel that can televise live the entire proceedings of the local city council and school board—as many apparently do[70]—can surely afford to make moderate amounts of time available to the parties.

Changes in Federal Campaign Finance Law

Increase substantially the federal limits on hard money contributions to the parties and prohibit the national parties from raising unlimited soft money contributions. Repeal the FEC's decision allowing state parties to use unregulated soft money to finance the nonfederal portion of generic party activities that benefit federal and state candidates.Raise significantly the limits on party contributions to and coordinated expenditures on behalf of its federal nominees. Strong-party attributes:

PARTICIPATION AND EDUCATION RESOURCES

INCENTIVES

CANDIDATE ASSISTANCE

The revisions in campaign finance law that immediately followed the Watergate scandals were not especially conducive to strong political parties. Yet a combination of favorable judicial and FEC rulings, as well as some skillful innovation and adaptation by the parties themselves, have allowed political parties to carve out for themselves a new and influential role in American political campaigns. The parties' organizational revival has not been without its problems, however. Reform advocates, as well as the press and the public, are increasingly troubled by the national parties' growing addiction to soft money and the use of these funds to finance issue-advocacy campaigns (see Chapter Three). The challenge, therefore, is to propose changes to federal campaign finance law that both preserve party strength and bolster public confidence in the parties. Although this is a difficult standard to meet, it is a standard well worth striving for. The public, after all, has an interest in maintaining healthy parties, and the parties have an interest in maintaining public support.

The first reform we suggest constitutes a compromise between reformers and deregulation advocates: prohibit the national parties from raising soft money while substantially increasing the limits on hard money that individuals and interest groups may contribute to the parties. The present $20,000 annual limit on individual hard money contributions to the national parties, as well as the $15,000 annual limit that presently applies to PACs, should both be doubled and indexed annually for inflation. Additionally, the FEC ought to repeal its decision allowing state parties to use unregulated soft money to finance the nonfederal portion of generic party activities that benefit federal and state candidates.[71] State party-sponsored campaign activities that benefit federal candidates ought to be financed entirely with hard money (raised under the newly increased contribution limits), even if state candidates share in the benefit from the party activity. (In fact, this was the FEC's original ruling on this matter).[72] Taken together, these proposals would achieve the twin goals of preserving party strength and bolstering public confidence in the parties. The new contribution limits would not be overly burdensome for parties, yet they would halt the image-tarnishing torrent of unregulated money presently flowing into the national committees. Moreover, the reforms would ideally be accompanied by the party-fortifying initiatives of public funding and free-media time presented above, which would help make up for party funds lost due to the soft money prohibition. (Our plan stands in contrast to the McCain-Feingold campaign finance reform legislation which was being considered by Congress at the time this book went to press. The McCain-Feingold bill would prohibit the national parties from raising soft money but does not provide for meaningful increases in the limits on hard money donations to the parties.)

All political parties—national, state, and local—should be permitted to spend unlimited sums of hard money on all generic party activities such as voter mobilization drives and party institutional advertising.[73] Permitting parties to spend hard money without limit on generic party activities is justified by the fact that these activities benefit the party ticket as a whole and boost citizen participation in elections. As a practical matter, the political parties now also have the right to make unlimited independent expenditures of hard money to expressly advocate the election or defeat of specific federal candidates.[74] The only requirement is that such expenditures be made completely independently of a federal candidate's campaign. So far, the parties have not relied much on these expenditures.[75] But without soft money, parties would have few incentives to run "issue advocacy" ads (see Chapter Three) and would likely begin to make greater use of independent expenditures. Reformers may fret about this development, but they should take solace in the fact that—unlike party issue-advocacy ads—party independent expenditures must be financed entirely with regulated hard money.

Congress should also substantially raise the limits on party contributions to and coordinated expenditures on behalf of its federal nominees. The present—and absurdly low—$5,000 per election limit on direct party contributions to federal candidates ought to be increased to at least $15,000 and indexed for inflation. The present coordinated expenditure limit ought to be at least doubled.[76] These reforms would allow parties to keep up with the increasing costs of campaigns and guarantee them a healthy role in their candidates' election efforts.

Raising the limits on party contributions and coordinated expenditures is especially important when we consider how political parties offset the incumbent-based contribution strategies of most political action committees. PACs, which provide a significant portion of the money spent in congressional campaigns, contribute lavishly to incumbents and sparingly to challengers. In the 1998 elections, for example, only four percent of contributions to House candidates by corporate PACs (the largest category of PACs) went to challengers. It's no mystery why PACs spurn challengers. Many PACs, especially those sponsored by corporations and trade associations, contribute to campaigns not for broad ideological purposes but to curry favor with incumbents who preside over their narrow legislative interests. Not surprisingly, few PAC directors are willing to alienate incumbents by supporting their opponents. The result is that even highly qualified challengers have difficulty attracting PAC money, while entrenched incumbents raise more PAC dollars than they know what to do with. This scenario greatly diminishes the level of competition in congressional elections, no doubt causing many would-be challengers to opt out all together.

Political parties, however, offset the incumbent-driven strategies of PACs. Parties make campaign contributions not to curry favor with candidates but to maximize the number of party-held seats in Congress. Since defeating opposition-party incumbents is one way to accomplish this goal, parties are significantly more motivated than interest groups to support challengers. Indeed, House Republican challengers received 50 percent of the hard dollars distributed in 1998 by the National Republican Congressional Committee (NRCC), the main party fundraising unit for House Republicans. Similarly, many House Democratic challengers were generously supported in 1998 by the Democratic Congressional Campaign Committee (DCCC), the GOP's Democratic counterpart in the House. Electoral competition is the hallmark of a vibrant democracy, and parties encourage this competition by supporting the campaigns of well-qualified challengers. Emasculating the parties will only increase the power of special interests and inflate the overwhelming advantage already enjoyed by incumbents.

Universal Straight-Party Lever

Add a straight-party voting mechanism in all states, and list candidates of the same party in a column on every ballot. Strong-party attributes:

ELECTORAL APPEAL

ACCOUNTABILITY

INCENTIVES

Students are always surprised to learn that the form and structure of the ballot alone can influence the results of elections. Perhaps they prefer to believe that all voters are purely rational, well-informed, and issue-oriented, but for better or worse the truth is quite different. There is no doubt that the presence of a straight-party voting mechanism—a lever to pull or a box to check that casts the voter's ballot for all candidates of the same party simultaneously—can, in and of itself, increase straight-party voting.[77] Similarly, a *party-column* ballot, where all candidates of each party are listed together in a vertical column, results in more party voting than the office-block ballot that groups candidates separately according to the office they seek.[78]

The incidence of straight-party levers began to decline with the onset of the anti-boss Progressive Era, and just seventeen states retain it today.[79] The party-column ballot is somewhat more popular, currently used in twenty-six states.[80] As one would expect, there is significant overlap: many of the states that employ the party-column ballot offer voters the chance to use a straight-party lever.[81] Both party aids are valuable cues to voters. A straight-party lever actually reduces the tendency of some voters to skip races further down on the ballot, a phenomenon called "ballot fatigue."[82] Besides increasing voter participation for lesser offices, a straight-party mechanism and the party-column ballot increase the value of the party label by lengthening "coattails" and encouraging unity among the party's candidates and officeholders.

The thirty-three states without a straight-party lever should add one, and the twenty-four states not using the party-column ballot should adopt it. Despite the advantages of these reforms for the party, however, most voters apparently remain unconvinced of their usefulness. When our poll respondents were asked whether they favored "making it easier to vote for all the candidates of one party by pulling a single lever or making a single mark on the ballot," a 52–42 percent majority was opposed."[83] Clearly, the spirit of the Progressives lives on in America—and often to the detriment of the parties.

Universal Party Registration

Require in all states that voters express and enroll a party preference (Democrat, Republican, or Other/Independent) when registering to vote. Strong-party attributes:

EQUITY AND LEGITIMACY

ELECTORAL APPEAL

PARTICIPATION AND EDUCATION

More than half of the states already require registration by party, and the others should do so, too. By linking the act of registering to vote with a choice of party, this procedure encourages and reinforces partisanship and perpetuates the party system.[84] Research shows that individuals who reside in states with party registration are considerably more likely to identify as partisans than are individuals who reside in states without this requirement.[85] Moreover, party registration (or enrollment, as it is sometimes called) is also a necessary precondition for holding the closed form of primary advocated earlier in this chapter.

Like the straight-party lever, this reform will not be easy to enact, due to a lack of public support. Perhaps resenting perceived invasion of privacy, a 60-percent majority of our poll respondents opposed requiring voters "to name a party affiliation when they register to vote.[86]

More Partisan Elections

Identify all candidates who are the nominees of a party by their party label, and reduce the number of nonpartisan elections. Strong-party attributes:

EQUITY AND LEGITIMACY

ELECTORAL APPEAL

PARTICIPATION AND EDUCATION
ACCOUNTABILITY

The modern decline of American political parties should be traced not from the advent of television in the 1950s but from the adoption of the Australian (or secret) ballot from 1880 to 1900.[87] Prior to the secret ballot, voters selected a party ballot at the polling places to mark and place in boxes.[88] Since the parties or candidates printed these ballots and they were usually distinctively colored, a voter essentially made his party preference publicly known simply by choosing a ballot. Casting a split ticket was impossible under these conditions.

The Australian ballot radically changed the act of voting, because it listed candidates from all parties on a single government-printed ballot form, thus guaranteeing the voter privacy of choice but also permitting ticket-splitting for the first time and eliminating an important public display of partisanship.

No one seriously advocates a return to party balloting. Voter intimidation was widespread with its practice, and outright vote-buying was facilitated since a voter could publicly fulfill his part of the bargain. Employers, landlords, and creditors were sometimes able to control the votes of their employees, tenants, and debtors as well.[89]

But a secret ballot need not result in a nonparty ballot. Until 2001, Virginia included no party labels on the ballot except for presidential Electoral College slates; voters were thus denied the most revealing voting cue of all, and the candidates were separated from their party identity. The same is still true in Nebraska where the state legislature is technically "nonpartisan," though almost all legislators' party affiliations are informally known by the press and political activists.[90] (Only the voters are left in the dark.) Moreover, a large majority of local municipal elections are officially nonpartisan, and regrettably the proportion is growing. While in the 1960s, 65 percent of all municipalities used nonpartisan ballots, the percentage had grown to about 75 by the late 1990s.[91] A product of reforms in the late nineteenth and early twentieth centuries, nonpartisan elections make parties irrelevant at the expense of responsible politics. Voters are denied a vital piece of information that brings order out of the chaos of personality politics. Elected officials lose a crucial link with their peers, a tie that helps them to work together on a common agenda. And the power taken from party elites is simply transferred to other entities. Wealthy candidates, the news media, and incumbents all gain power because they can buy or confer or possess "name identification" to substitute as a voting cue for lost party identification. Are any of these agents more worthy of our trust than the parties?

Ingrained political habits stubbornly persist, and it will be exceedingly difficult to convince states or localities to convert from nonpartisan to partisan elections. Yet the attempt should be made wherever possible. While the antiparty spirit of the Progressive age has endured in the popular mind, it is at least somewhat encouraging that our poll respondents favored "requiring all candidates for political office to be identified by party label on the ballot" by a margin of 62 percent to 29 percent.[92] Indeed, even 64 percent of the self-identified Independents were approving.[93]

Consolidation of Elections and Governmental Structure

In order to strengthen party unity and foster responsible party government, consolidate elections to increase the potential coattail effect and restructure state governments to favor the governorship. Strong-party attributes:

ACCOUNTABILITY

CONFLICT CONTROL

INCENTIVES

As we pointed out in the discussion on straight-party levers, the coattail effect—whereby candidates at the top of the party ticket can attract votes to those at the bottom—draws all of the party standard-bearers together since their fates are intertwined. It gives party officeholders a strong incentive to push for the strongest possible party nominees for president and governor, since these top-of-the-ballot candidates can sink or save their electoral chances. Similarly, all the party's legislators have a stake in seeing the executives succeed, once in office, so that at reelection time the party can boast a successful record.[94] Given these political ground rules, it makes sense to consolidate elections so that the coattail effect is magnified. Gubernatorial and state legislative elections should be held simultaneously with presidential elections, for example, and both houses of the state legislature should be elected at the same time as the governor.

Of course, what seems sensible to a party builder seems ludicrous to an elected official bound and determined to preserve his public office in a bad year for his party. Officeholders prefer to control their own fates, and, as a consequence, events have been moving in precisely the opposite direction to the course desirable for the good of the parties. In 1952, 30 states elected their governors in presidential years, but by 2000, the number had declined to 11.[95] Five states (Kentucky, Louisiana, Mississippi, New Jersey, and Virginia) insulate gubernatorial elections by setting them in odd-numbered years when neither the presidency nor Congress is contested,[96] and all of these states except Kentucky do this with legislative elections as well.[97] Additionally, most states elect only half of their state senate in the gubernatorial year, and in four states (Kentucky, New Mexico, South Carolina, and Virginia), the entire upper house is permanently immune from gubernatorial coattail influence since it is always elected at the midpoint of the governor's term.[98]

On the other hand, conditions in state governments have improved dramatically, empowering the governors and enabling them to exert strong party leadership in most of the states.[99] In 1950, twenty-one states had a short two-year gubernatorial term that often prevented bold executive action and long-range planning. By 2000, only two states (New Hampshire and Vermont) retained the outmoded short term; all other states had lengthened the tenure to four years. In like fashion, thirteen states (most of them in the South) restricted their governor to a single consecutive term in 1950, but by 2000 only Virginia did. One reform that has been widely advocated is that of reducing the number of elected statewide officials, thereby creating state governments that are more rationally structured and easier for governors to lead.[100] "Team election" of the governor and lieutenant governor, similar to the way the nation's top team is elected as a unit, has become the practice in twenty-two states—an ultimate form of coattail that potentially gives the chief executive much more influence over the second-in-command. Unfortunately for the governor and the parties, there are still far too many separately elected statewide officials—an average of 10.2 per state—a situation that often promotes factionalism within the governing party, split-party rule (with both parties controlling some executive offices), and diluted gubernatorial authority.[101] So there remains ample room for improvement in this area.

"Sore Loser" Provisions

Enact statutes in all states prohibiting losing party primary or convention candidates from launching Independent general election bids. Strong-party attributes:

ACCOUNTABILITY

CONFLICT CONTROL

INCENTIVES

One of the oldest and most revered rules of good sportsmanship demands grace in defeat. This attractive standard of human conduct should apply to all candidacies for party nomination. A candidate who loses a bid for nomination should not be able to file as an independent in the general election. So-called sore loser laws are already in effect in twenty-three states,[102] and all states ought to have them. To the extent possible, the laws also should be applied to presidential candidates, so that individuals (such as John Anderson in 1980) would be prevented from running in a party's primaries and caucuses and then launching an autumn Independent candidacy.

Not just good sportsmanship but the prevention of electoral chaos warrants these reforms. Without them, the party nomination potentially becomes "Round One" preceding a free-for-all in the fall. In these circumstances, candidates can use the primary merely as a warm-up exercise, building up name identification in the process. A party can sponsor an "Independent" in the general election drawn from the other party's ranks in order to split the opposition vote. As a result, voters can be faced with a confusing welter of candidates on the general election ballot, and election winners can be denied the clear mandates and majorities necessary to govern effectively.

This pro-party reform is surely distasteful for reformers sounding the siren call for easier ballot access. But sore loser provisions are instrumental in protecting the integrity of the two parties and preserving a rational electoral process.

More Patronage

Expand the number of patronage positions available to reward party workers, with appropriate safeguards to guarantee competence in public service. Strong-party attributes:

EQUITY AND LEGITIMACY

ELECTORAL APPEAL

PARTICIPATION AND EDUCATION

ACCOUNTABILITY

CONFLICT CONTROL

RESOURCES

INCENTIVES

CANDIDATE ASSISTANCE

Patronage—the use of appointive government jobs as a reward for party work—is one of the dirty words of American politics, thanks to the efforts of a century's worth of reformers. The mere mention of the term is enough to raise the eyebrows of an enormous majority of the American public. Citizens are simply unpersuaded by the central party-building argument used by patronage's advocates, as the results of one of our survey questions indicate:[103]

> *Which of the following statements comes closer to your own personal opinion?*
>
> When a candidate for governor wins the election, (s)he should be able to give the majority of appointed state government jobs to people who work for or support his or her political party.   6%
>
> For most appointed state government jobs, people should be hired based on their skills and experience alone, and the political party they belong to should not matter.   83%

It was not always this grim for patronage. In the last century, patronage was an accepted part of the party system and the electoral process. Beginning with the era of Presidents Andrew Jackson and Martin van Buren in the 1830s, the operating premise of politics became, "to the victors belong the spoils." Not until the Pendleton Act, establishing the first professional civil service system, was passed by the federal government in 1883 did the theory of "neutral competence" and the practice of competitive, standardized civil service examinations begin to supplant patronage. The Progressive movement accelerated the pace of change, and the big-city political machines began to suffer the consequences—though not silently. George Washington Plunkitt of New York's Tammany Hall machine well expressed the fighting spirit of his party contemporaries:

> This civil service law is the biggest fraud of the age. It is the curse of the nation. There can't be no real patriotism while it lasts. How are you goin' to interest our young men in their country if you have no offices to give them when they work for their party?... I have good reason for sayin' that most of the Anarchists in this city today are men who ran up against civil service examinations.... I see a vision. I see the civil service monster lyin' flat on the ground. I see the Democratic party standin' over it with foot on its neck and wearin' the crown of victory. I see Thomas Jefferson lookin' out from a cloud and sayin' "Give him another sockdologer; finish him." And I see millions of men wavin' their hats and singin' "Glory Hallelujah!"[104]

Plunkitt's vision was not to be, and, gradually, civil service came to dominate government at all levels. While there perhaps remain a few exceptions to the rule, patronage has been reduced to a mere shadow of its former self. Even Chicago's vaunted Democratic machine, which under Mayor Richard Daley was believed to control some 35,000 government jobs, has fallen victim to civil service rulings and court decisions inimical to patronage.[105] At the national level, only a tiny portion of federal jobs—less than 1 percent—can still be classified as patronage.[106] All states now have merit systems that cover at least some state workers, and 35 states have comprehensive merit systems that extend to nearly every state employee.[107] What few patronage plums remain are often used by public officials to reward their own personal followers and staff members rather than longtime party workers. Thus, these patronage appointees serve an individual officeholder, not the needs of the party, and they reinforce the advantages of incumbency, not the exigencies of party organization.

The Supreme Court can also take some credit for the modern decline of patronage. In *Elrod* v. *Burns* (1976),[108] *Branti* v. *Finkel* (1980),[109] and *Rutan* v. *Republican Party of Illinois* (1990),[110] the Court used the First and Fourteenth Amendments to rule against the hiring, firing, transfer, recall, and promotion of governmental employees on the basis of party affiliation. (The only government positions spared were those for which partisan affiliation is essential to job performance.) In the first case, *Elrod* v. *Burns,* a majority of the justices said that a newly elected Democratic sheriff in Cook County, Illinois, could not fire the Republican appointees of his GOP predecessor just because they were not of his party. Political tests for employment, decreed the Court, would only be valid for policymaking positions, not lesser posts. In the *Branti* case, the Court added that patronage firings were only valid when partisan affiliation was a necessary condition for satisfactory job performance. In *Rutan,* the Court extended its rulings in *Elrod* and *Branti* to promotions, transfers, and recalls.

Given these judicial decisions, there would seem to be little hope of broadening the patronage base for bottom-level jobs, even if the public would acquiesce in an expansion of patronage. Where there is room for legitimate maneuver is at the top, in the policymaking posts recognized by the Court. Presidents, governors, and mayors should be given appointive powers for policymakers as broad as court rulings and public opinion will allow. Another way to increase patronage is through executive-initiated creation of more honorific posts (blue-ribbon commissions, watchdog committees, advisory boards, etc.). While nonpaying, these positions bring prestige and public recognition—not insignificant prizes, especially for middle-class party workers who already enjoy full-time employment elsewhere. The point here is not that we should return to bygone days of governments run by rank amateurs whose sole qualifications were party work and a willingness to kick back a portion of their public salaries to the party treasury. Rather, there is a serious need to involve more people in the party organizations. This can be accomplished by delivering help and service (ombudsman assistance and so on), but also by offering rewards of patronage employment and honors.

CONCLUDING REMARKS

The premise of this book is that healthy political parties provide an array of desirable benefits to the American political system. Accordingly, the reform agenda put forth in Chapters Six and Seven is designed to strengthen parties as electoral organizations, as governing units, and—ultimately—as enduring cues that anchor the electorate politically. While some of the proposals admittedly have a more realistic chance of being enacted than others, all of the proposals, we hope, have provoked readers to contemplate the limits of and prospects for party vitality in America.

America's constitutional structure and political culture have always placed real limits on party strength, and modern features of American life and governance have only added to these limits.[111] Only for a relatively brief period in American history (from the 1830s to the 1890s) did parties dominate American political life.[112] And certainly, modern American parties cannot compete with their European counterparts in terms of organizational discipline and voter fealty. Efforts to bolster the parties, then, do not sit easily in the American context. As political scientist Leon Epstein observes, "Parties can be maintained and strengthened but only within a well-established political culture that is hostile to both the revival of older American party organizational forms and the emergence of European-style parties."[113]

Yet as this book makes clear, there is ample room for healthy political parties in American political life even within the parameters imposed by the American political setting. As Chapter Seven illustrates, governmental reforms can go a long way toward facilitating party strength even as they respect America's tradition of progressive reform. State laws facilitating pre-primary endorsements, for example, empower parties while at the same time acknowledging primary elections as Americans' preferred means of nominating candidates. Moreover, American parties can do much to help themselves within the limitations posed by the American context. They can campaign and govern in a manner that more adequately illustrates their relevance to people's lives, and they can find unobjectionable ways to make themselves a more integral part of community life. Because the parties' roots in the nation's political history are so extensive, their prospects for survival remain good. But the extent to which parties can be truly vital components of American political life depends on how well they can respond to the needs of the American public while working within the constraints posed by the American political tradition.

NOTES

1. Giovanni Sartori, *Parties and Party Systems: A Framework for Analysis*, vol. 1 (New York: Cambridge University Press, 1976), ix.
2. Leon Epstein, *Political Parties in the American Mold* (Madison, Wisc.: University of Wisconsin Press, 1986), 156–157.
3. Gerald M. Pomper, ed., *Party Organizations in American Politics* (New York: Praeger, 1984), 149; John F. Bibby, *Politics, Parties, and Elections* (Belmont, Calif.: Wadsworth, 2000), 132.
4. Malcolm Jewell, "Political Parties and the Nominating Process," *Comparative State Politics Newsletter* 7 (February 1986): 14.
5. Epstein, *Political Parties in the American Mold*, 158.
6. Ibid.
7. Andrew M. Appleton and Daniel S. Ward, eds., *State Party Profiles: A 50-State Guide to Development, Organization, and Resources* (Washington, D.C.: Congressional Quarterly Press, 1997).
8. Researchers asked seven questions regarding party regulation: Does state law mandate the manner of selecting members of the parties' state central committee? Does state law mandate the timing of central committee meetings? Does state law mandate the composition of central committees? Does state law regulate leadership of party organizations? Does state law forbid nominating conventions for statewide office? Does state law forbid preprimary endorsements by the party? Does state law require an open primary for statewide office? The researchers also asked a series of questions designed to measure state *support* for parties—for example, does a state allow for straight party voting mechanism?—and we address these measures at varied places in this chapter.
9. Light regulators are defined as states that regulate in 0–2 of the 7 areas; moderate regulators are defined as states that regulate in 3–4 of the 7 areas, and heavy regulators are states that regulate 5–7 in the 7 areas.
10. Advisory Commission on Intergovernmental Relations, *The Transformation in American Politics* (Washington, D.C.: ACIR, (1986), 128–132, 135–136.
11. 107 S. Ct. 544 (1986).
12. Correspondence with Larry J. Sabato dated February 18, 1986.
13. 109 S.Ct. 1013 (1989).

14. Appleton and Ward, *State Party Profiles*, 372.
15. Stephen A. Salmore and Barbara G. Salmore, "New Jersey," in Andrew M. Appleton and Daniel S. Ward, eds., *State Party Profiles: A 50-State Guide to Development, Organization, and Resources* (Washington, D.C: Congressional Quarterly Press, 1997), 218.
16. *California Democratic Party* v. *Jones*, No. 99–401 (2000).
17. In this case, the Minnesota state election commission prohibited Minnesota's New Party from nominating a state legislative candidate already nominated by the state Democratic party.
18. As quoted in Paul S. Herrnson and John C. Green, "Making or Repeating History? American Party Politics at the Dawn of a New Century," in Herrnson and Green, eds., *Multiparty Politics in America* (Lanham, Md.: Rowman & Littlefield, 1997), 16.
19. Personal interview with Larry J. Sabato, as quoted in Sabato, *Goodbye to Good-Time Charlie: The American Governorship Transformed* (Washington, D.C.: Congressional Quarterly Press, 1983), 66.
20. Seven percent didn't know or refused to answer the question. August 2000 poll conducted for this book by John McLaughlin and Associates. See Appendix 1. One cause for optimism is that these numbers are more favorable to caucuses than are those reported in the first edition of this book, where 67 percent of respondents opposed replacing primaries with caucuses. See Sabato, *The Party's Just Begun*, 207.
21. Surveys taken in Arkansas and Oklahoma—then both presidential caucus states—during the mid-1980s indicated that significant margins of citizens (67 percent to 14 percent in Oklahoma and 70 percent to 13 percent in Arkansas) wanted the parties to switch to primaries. Voters got their wish. Both Arkansas and Oklahoma now use presidential primaries. Both surveys were conducted by the Bailey survey organization and asked the following question to 655 adults in each state from December 11–18, 1985: "Thinking about presidential elections, some states select their delegates for presidential candidates by statewide party primary elections; other states, like Oklahoma/Arkansas, use the party caucus system to select delegates. Do you support the party caucus system, or would you prefer statewide party primary elections here in Oklahoma/Arkansas?" See Sabato, *The Party's Just Begun*, 207.
22. Thomas E. Patterson, *Out of Order* (New York: Vintage Books, 1994), 231. See also Jack Dennis, "Public Support for the American Party System," in William J. Crotty, ed., *Paths to Political Reform* (Lexington, Mass.: D.C. Heath, 1980) 55–56.
23. Andrew E. Busch, *Outsiders and Openness In the Presidential Nominating System* (Pittsburgh, Pa.: University of Pittsburgh Press, 1997), 12–13. David E. Price, *Bringing Back the Parties* (Washington, D.C.: Congressional Quarterly Press, 1984), 207.
24. Michael Robinson, "Television and American Politics: 1956–1976," *Public Interest* 48 (Summer 1977): 21.
25. Richard Rubin, *Press, Party and Presidency* (New York: W.W. Norton, 1981), 195.
26. Epstein, *Political Parties in the American Mold*, 155–156.
27. L. Sandy Maisel, Cary T. Gibson, and Elizabeth J. Ivry, "The Continuing Importance of the Rules of the Game: Subpresidential Nominations in 1994

and 1996," in L. Sandy Maisel, ed., *The Parties Respond: Changes in Parties and Campaigns*, 3rd ed. (Boulder, Colo.: Westview Press, 1998), 150. John F. Bibby, *Politics, Parties, and Elections* (Belmont, Calif.: Wadsworth, 2000), 170. Paul Allen Beck, *Party Politics in America*, 8th ed. (New York: Addison Wesley Longman, 1997), 199.

28. Maisel et al., "The Continuing Importance of the Rules of the Game, " 150; Beck, *Party Politics in America*, 199.
29. Ibid.
30. No primary is held in the absence of a challenge. Beck, *Party Politics in America*, 199; Bibby, *Politics, Parties, and Elections*, 170.
31. Beck, *Party Politics in America*, 199.
32. See FEC, "Party Affiliation and Primary Voting 2000," (http://www.fec.gov/votregis/primaryvoting.htm). See also Bibby, *Politics, Parties, and Elections*, 171; Maisel et al., "The Continuing Importance of the Rules of the Game, " 152.
33. Malcolm E. Jewell, "Democratic or Republican?: Voters' Choice of a Primary," a paper prepared for delivery at the annual meeting of the Southern Political Science Association, Birmingham, Alabama, November 3–5, 1983.
34. Busch, *Outsiders and Openness In the Presidential Nominating System*, 12–13.
35. Ibid.,16; Beck, *Party Politics in America*, 220.
36. Busch, *Outsiders and Openness In the Presidential Nominating System*, 15. Although the number of presidential primaries has increased sharply for both parties since 1968, the increase has not always been constant. For example, the number of Democratic primaries in 1984 fell to 24 from 33 in 1980, and the caucus total rose from 18 to 27. This was at least partly in response to the Democratic party's 1982–1983 Commission on Presidential Nomination, chaired by then-Governor Jim Hunt of North Carolina, which encouraged states and territories to employ caucuses instead of primaries where possible.
37. Ibid., 15. On the nominating rules for 1996, see also "Steps to the Nomination—Special Report: A State-by-State Guide to the Process of Choosing Presidential Candidates," *Congressional Quarterly* (19 August 1995).
38. By comparison, 16 GOP state parties held primaries in 1968, and these primaries produced only 34 percent of delegates to the 1968 Republican National Convention. Busch, *Outsiders and Openness In the Presidential Nominating System*, 15.
39. For a listing of the 2000 presidential primaries and caucuses, see John Kenneth White and Daniel Shea, *New Party Politics: From Jefferson and Hamilton to the Information Age* (Boston: St. Martin's Press, 2000), 127–128.
40. E. E. Schattschneider, *Party Government* (New York: Rinehart, 1942), 59–60.
41. Austin Ranney, *Curing the Mischiefs of Faction* (Berkeley: University of California Press, 1975), 129.
42. This model is similar to the nomination contest that Connecticut uses.
43. David Kocieniewski, "Torricelli, Opposed Within Party, Drops New Jersey Governor Bid," *New York Times* (1 August 2000): A1, B4.
44. Bibby, *Politics, Parties, and Elections*, 178.
45. Ibid.
46. Malcolm E. Jewell and Sarah M. Morehouse , *Political Parties and Elections in American States*, 4th ed. (Washington, D.C.: Congressional Quarterly Press,

2001), 109–110. See also Malcolm E. Jewell and Sarah M. Morehouse, "What Are Party Endorsements Worth? A Study of Preprimary Gubernatorial Endorsements," *American Politics Quarterly* 24 (1996): 338–362.

47. Jewell and Morehouse, *Political Parties and Elections in American States,* 116–117.

48. Ibid.

49. Michael Malbin and Thomas Gais, *The Day After Reform: Sobering Campaign Finance Lessons From the States* (Albany, N.Y.: Rockefeller Institute Press, 1998), 67. Maine used the tax add-on system until the Maine Public Funding Initiative was passed in 1996.

50. The tax add-on differs from a tax check-off program, in which a taxpayer can opt to "earmark" a small percentage of her tax liability to a political party.

51. Sabato, *The Party's Just Begun,* 213.

52. Malbin and Gais, *The Day After Reform,* 67.

53. Ibid.

54. Ibid.

55. Unlike donations from tax add-ons, dollars generated from tax check-offs impact government spending priorities by permitting taxpayers to divert a portion of their tax liabilities to public funding accounts.

56. John C. Green and Daniel M. Shea, "Ohio," in Appleton and Ward, *State Party Profiles,* 254–255.

57. Malbin and Gais, *The Day After Reform,* 61.

58. Ibid., 54.

59. Jennifer Drage, "Do Campaign Finance Laws Make a Difference?," *State Legislatures* (September 2000): 22–25.

60. For a detailed description of the Public Campaign model, see Public Campaign's web site at http://www.publicampaign.org/QA.html.

61. The plans have also been susceptible to judicial challenge. See Carey Goldberg, "Publicly Paid Elections Put to the Test in 3 States," *New York Times* (19 November 2000): 44. "Campaign-finance Limits Struck," *State Government News* (September 2000): 7.

62. Malbin and Gais, *The Day After Reform,* 54–55.

63. See Herrnson, *Congressional Elections,* 3rd ed., 73; Dwight Morris and Murielle E. Gamache, *Gold-Plated Politics: The 1992 Congressional Races* (Washington, D.C.: Congressional Quarterly Press, 1994), ch. 1.

64. The lowest unit advertising rate is defined as the lowest charge for the same class and amount of time given the station's best customers. See Larry J. Sabato, *Paying for Elections: The Campaign Finance Thicket* (New York: The Twentieth Century Fund, 1989), 40; Daniel M. Shea, *Campaign Craft: The Strategies, Tactics, and Art of Political Management* (Westport, Conn.: Praeger Press, 1996), 217.

65. Sabato, *Paying for Elections,* 41.

66. See ACIR, *The Transformation in American Politics,* 377–379; Sabato, *The Rise of Political Consultants,* 186–192, 326–328; Sabato, *Paying for Elections,* 41–42.

67. Anthony Gierzynski, *Money Rules: Financing Elections in America* (Boulder, Colo.: Westwiew Press, 2000), 122.

68. Herrnson, *Congressional Elections,* 3rd ed., 277.

69. ACIR, *The Transformation in American Politics,* 380–381.

70. Ibid.

71. For an explanation of these decisions, see Anthony Corrado, "Party Soft Money," in Anthony Corrado, Thomas E. Mann, Daniel R. Ortiz, Trevor Potter, Frank J. Sorauf, eds., *Campaign Finance Reform: A Sourcebook* (Washington, D.C.: Brookings, 1997), 171–172.

72. Ibid.

73. This is consistent with the 1979 FECA amendments, though those amendments were designed to help state and local parties. Corrado, *Party Soft Money*, 170–171.

74. *Colorado Republican Federal Campaign Committee* v. *Federal Election Commission*, 116 S. Ct. 2309 (1996).

75. Herrnson, *Congressional Elections*, 3rd ed., 111–112.

76. The U.S. Court of Appeals for the Tenth Circuit is presently considering a challenge to the federal limits on coordinated expenditures (*Federal Election Commission* v. *Colorado Republican Campaign Committee*). Although we support substantially raising coordinated expenditure limits, we also agree with the FEC—and with many party scholars—that Congress should retain the power to regulate coordinated expenditures. See the *amici curiae* brief submitted with the Court by the Brennan Center for Justice at New York University Law School and fourteen political scientists (November 2000).

77. Beck, *Party Politics in America*, 248; ACIR, *The Transformation in American Politics*, 152–153; Price, *Bringing Back the Parties*, 134–136; Angus Campbell et al., *The American Voter* (New York: Wiley, 1960), 276.

78. Ibid.

79. Appleton and Ward, *State Party Profiles*, 374–375; see also the Federal Election Commission's web site (http://www.fec.gov/pages/faqvday/eprocedures.htm).

80. Bibby, *Parties, Politics, and Elections*, 253.

81. Ibid.

82. See Jack L. Walker, "Ballot Forms and Voter Fatigue: An Analysis of the Office Block and Party Column Ballots," *Midwest Journal of Political Science* 10 (August 1966): 460.

83. Six percent didn't know or refused to answer. Survey conducted for this book by John McLaughlin and Associates. See Appendix.

84. See Steven E. Finkel and Howard A. Searrow, "Party Identification and Party Enrollment: The Difference and the Consequence," *Journal of Politics* 47 (May 1985): 620–642.

85. Barry C. Burden and Steven Greene, "Party Attachments and State Election Laws," *Political Research Quarterly* 53 (March 2000): 63–76.

86. Survey conducted for this book by John McLaughlin and Associates. See Appendix.

87. ACIR, *The Transformation in American Politics*, 124–126.

88. In the colonial period, a voter simply appeared before election officials and told them his preferences. But by the mid–1800s party ballots were standard.

89. V. O. Key, Jr., *Politics, Parties, and Pressure Groups*, 5th ed. (New York: Thomas Y. Crowell Company, 1964), 639.

90. Nebraska has had a "nonpartisan" legislature since 1935; Minnesota had one from 1913 until 1974.

91. Beck, *Party Politics in America*, 43; Epstein, *Political Parties in the American Mold*, 126–127.

92. Nine percent didn't know or refused to answer. Survey conducted for this book by John McLaughlin and Associates. See Appendix.

93. Ibid.

94. See Sarah McCally Morehouse, "Legislatures and Political Parties," *State Government* 59:1 (1976): 21.

95. Jewell and Morehouse, *Political Parties and Elections in American States*, 141.

96. Ibid.

97. Figures complied from Council of State Governments, *Book of the States*, vol. 32 (Lexington, Ky.: Council of State Governments, 1998–99): 151–158.

98. Ibid.

99. Larry J. Sabato, *Goodbye to Goodtime Charlie: The American Governorship Transformed*, 2nd ed. (Washington, D.C.: Congressional Quarterly Press, 1983), 57–96.

100. Thad Beyle, "Governors: The Middlemen and Women in Our Political System," Virginia Gray and Herbert Jacob, eds., *Politics in the American States*, 6th ed. (Washington, D.C.: Congressional Quarterly Press, 1996), 229.

101. Beyle, "Governors: The Middlemen and Women in Our Political System."

102. Appleton and Ward, eds., *State Party Profiles*, 374–375.

103. Ten percent didn't know or refused to answer. Figures don't add up to 100 percent because of rounding. Survey conducted for this book by John McLaughlin and Associates. See Appendix .

104. William L. Riordon, ed., *Plunkitt of Tammany Hall* (New York: E.P. Dutton, 1963), 11, 89.

105. Paul M. Green, "Illinois," in Appleton and Ward, eds., *State Party Profiles*, 88–95.

106. Beck, *Party Politics in America*, 108.

107. Ann O'M. Bowman and Richard C. Kearney, *State and Local Government*, 3rd ed. (Boston: Houghton Mifflin, 1996), 190.

108. 427 U.S. 347 (1976).

109. 445 U.S. 507 (1980).

110. 110 S. Ct. 2729 (1990).

111. For example, John J. Coleman argues that the postwar creation of the "fiscal state"—which limited party control over the economy—helped marginalize political parties in the postwar era. See John J. Coleman, *Party Decline in America: Policy, Politics, and the Fiscal State* (Princeton, N.J.: Princeton University Press, 1996).

112. Joel H. Silbey, "From 'Essential to the Existence of Our Institutions' to 'Rapacious Enemies of Honest and Responsible Government': The Rise and Fall of American Political Parties, 1790–2000," in L. Sandy Maisel, ed., *The Parties Respond: Changes in Parties and Campaigns*, 3rd ed. (Boulder: Westview Press, 1998).

113. Epstein, *Political Parties in the American Mold*, 343.

APPENDIX

Public Opinion Survey Questionnaires

AUGUST 2000 SURVEY

Methodology

John McLaughlin and Associates conducted a national random-sample telephone survey of 1000 American adults (18 years of age and older) exclusively for this study of political parties. All interviews were conducted between August 6 and August 11, 2000. Interview selection was random within predetermined units; these units were structured to correspond with regional adult populations nationwide. The survey has a margin of error of approximately ± 3 percent at a 95-percent level of confidence.

Survey Questionnaire

JOHN McLAUGHLIN & ASSOCIATES, INC.
NATIONAL POLL OF ADULTS
AUGUST 6–11, 2000

Introduction: Good evening. My name is _____ and I'm calling from John McLaughlin & Associates, a national public opinion firm. This evening we're conducting a short public opinion survey and we'd like to get your opinions.

1. Could you please tell me—is your age … **[READ CATEGORIES]**
   a. Under 18 **[TERMINATE]**
   b. Between 18 and 24 **[CONTINUE]**
   c. Between 25 and 29 **[CONTINUE]**

    d. Between 30 and 34 **[CONTINUE]**
    e. Between 35 and 39 **[CONTINUE]**
    f. Between 40 and 44 **[CONTINUE]**
    g. Between 45 and 49 **[CONTINUE]**
    h. Between 50 and 54 **[CONTINUE]**
    i. Between 55 and 59 **[CONTINUE]**
    j. Between 60 and 64 **[CONTINUE]**
    k. Between 65 and 69 **[CONTINUE]**
    l. 70 or Over **[CONTINUE]**
    m. DK/Refused **[TERMINATE]**

2. How likely are you to vote in the November election for President? If you are not registered to vote, just say so. Would you say you are …
[READ CHOICES]
    a. Very Likely
    b. Somewhat Likely
    c. Not likely
    d. Not registered voter **[DO NOT READ]**
    e. DK/Refused **[DO NOT READ]**

3. If you were to label yourself, would you consider yourself to be liberal, moderate, or conservative in your political beliefs?
[PROBE LIBERAL/CONSERVATIVE for VERY/SOMEWHAT]
    a. Very liberal
    b. Somewhat liberal
    c. Moderate
    d. Somewhat conservative
    e. Very conservative
    f. DK/REFUSED **[DO NOT READ]**

4. Do you feel things in this country are generally going in the right direction or do you feel things have gotten pretty seriously on the wrong track?
    a. Right direction
    b. Wrong track
    c. DK/REFUSED **[DO NOT READ]**

Please tell me if you have a favorable or unfavorable opinion of the following people. If you have no opinion or have never heard of each, just say so. **[PROBE FAVORABLE/ UNFAVORABLE FOR SOMEWHAT/VERY] ROTATE QUESTIONS Very favorable (vf), Somewhat favorable (sf), Somewhat unfavorable (su), Very unfavorable (vu), No Opinion (no), Don't Know/Refused (dk)**

5. Bill Clinton   vf / sf / su / vu / no / dk

6. Al Gore   vf / sf / su / vu / no / dk

7. Pat Buchanan   vf / sf / su / vu / no / dk

8. Ralph Nader   vf / sf / su / vu / no / dk

9. George W. Bush   vf / sf / su / vu / no / dk

Please tell me if you have a favorable or unfavorable opinion of the following organizations. If you have no opinion or have never heard of each, just say so. **[PROBE FAVORABLE/ UNFAVORABLE FOR SOMEWHAT/VERY] ROTATE QUESTIONS Very favorable (vf), Somewhat favorable (sf), Somewhat unfavorable (su), Very unfavorable (vu), No Opinion (no), Don't Know/Refused (dk)**

10. The Republican Party   vf / sf / su / vu / no / dk

11. The Green Party   vf / sf / su / vu / no / dk

12. The Reform Party   vf / sf / su / vu / no / dk

13. The Democratic Party   vf / sf / su / vu / no / dk

14. The Libertarian Party   vf / sf / su / vu / no / dk

15. Would you say you most favor a smaller government with fewer services, or a bigger government with many services?
    a. Smaller government
    b. Bigger government
    c. DK/Refused

16. In general, are you most concerned about economic issues such as taxes, government spending, and jobs; social issues such as education, health care, and the environment; moral issues such as abortion, school prayer, and promoting traditional values; foreign affairs issues such as our policies in Asia, the Middle East, and Europe; or local issues like crime, drugs, and welfare reform?
    a. Economic issues
    b. Social issues
    c. Moral issues
    d. Foreign policy issues
    e. Local issues
    f. DK/Refused

17. If the election for President were held today, and the candidates were Al Gore, the Democrat, George W. Bush, the Republican, Pat Buchanan, the Reform Party candidate, and Ralph Nader, the Green Party candidate, for whom would you vote?
    a. Al Gore
    b. George W. Bush
    c. Pat Buchanan
    d. Ralph Nader
    e. DK/Refused

18. If the election for Congress in your district were held today, would you be more likely to vote for the Republican candidate or the Democrat candidate?
    a. Republican
    b. Democrat
    c. DK/Refused

19. Looking ahead, do you think the economy of the United States will be better, about the same, or worse a year from today?
    a. Better
    b. About the same
    c. Worse
    d. DK/Refused

20. How would you rate Bill Clinton's job performance as president? Would you say he is doing an excellent, good, fair, or poor job.
    a. Excellent
    b. Good
    c. Fair
    d. Poor
    e. DK/Refused

21. Which one of the following is *most* important to you in deciding your vote for president? **[READ AND ROTATE CHOICES]**
    a. A candidate's ability to manage the economy effectively
    b. A candidate's ability to conduct foreign policy effectively
    c. A candidate's style and personality
    d. A candidate's political party affiliation
    e. A candidate's positions on domestic policy issues like health care, education, and the environment
    f. A candidate's honesty and character
    g. DK/Refused **[DO NOT READ]**

22. What word or phrase do you think best describes the "Republican Party"?

23. Which person—either from the past or present—do you associate most with the Republican Party"?

24. What word or phrase do you think best describes the "Democratic Party"?

25. Which person — either from the past or present — do you associate most with the Democratic Party"?

26. What issue or action do you most associate with the "Reform Party"?

27. What issue or action do you most associate with the "Green Party"?

Regarding political parties, please tell me whether you favor or oppose each of the following:

        Favor (f)   **Oppose (o)**   **Don't Know/Refused (dk)**

28. Having a party's candidates for office chosen in open meetings of party activists rather than by primary elections   f / o / dk

29. Requiring all voters to name a party affiliation when they register to vote   f / o / dk

30. Making it easier to vote for all of the candidates of one party by pulling a single lever or making a single mark on the ballot

    f / o / dk

31. Requiring all candidates for political office to be identified by party label on the ballot f / o / dk

32. Allowing people to vote in a party's primary election whether or not they are registered with that party f / o / dk

33. Which of the following statements comes closer to your own personal opinion? **[READ CHOICES]**
    a. When a candidate for governor wins the election, he or she should be able to give the majority of appointed state government jobs to people who work for or support his or her political party.
       [OR,]
    b. For most appointed state government jobs, people should be hired based on their skills and experience alone, and the political party they belong to should not matter.
    c. DK/Refused **[DO NOT READ]**

34. How active are you presently with a political party at the local level—that is, in your town, city, or county—would you say you are very active, somewhat active, or not active at all?
    a. Very active
    b. Somewhat active
    c. Not active at all
    d. DK/Refused
    [IF NOT ACTIVE AT ALL, ASK:]

35. Would you be interested in becoming active with a political party at the local level—again, in your town, city, or county?
    a. Yes
    b. No
    c. DK/Refused
    [CONTINUE TO ASK ALL RESPONDENTS:]

36. Do you agree or disagree with the following statement? "Local political parties should become more active in getting people involved in local issues."
    a. Agree
    b. Disagree
    c. DK/Refused

    Please tell me whether you agree or disagree with each of the following statements:

Agree (a)	**Disagree (d)**	**Don't Know/Refused (dk)**

37. I usually vote for the candidate who I think is best for the job, regardless of what party he or she belongs to. a / d / dk

38. If I don't know anything else about a candidate for public office, knowing the candidate's political party helps me decide whether or not to vote for him or her.   a / d / dk

39. Overall, it really doesn't matter which political party holds the most seats in the U.S. House and Senate.   a / d / dk

40. It's wasting my vote to vote for a candidate that is not a Republican or Democrat, since Republicans and Democrats almost always win anyway.   a / d / dk

41. The two major political parties we have now in America are enough; we don't need any new ones.   a / d / dk

42. There is little difference between the candidates and the policies of the Republican party and the candidates and policies of the Democratic party.   a / d / dk

Please tell me which political party you think would do a better job on the following issues—the Democratic Party, the Republican Party, the Reform Party, the Green Party, or the Libertarian Party.
   [DO NOT READ ALL/NONE] ROTATE SECTION
   Democrat(D)   Republican(Rep) Reform(Ref) Green(G)
   Libertarian(Lib)   All   None DK/Refused(DK)

43. Improving education
   D / Rep / Ref / G / Lib / All / None / DK

44. Managing the economy and creating jobs
   D / Rep / Ref / G / Lib / All / None / DK

45. Protecting the environment
   D / Rep / Ref / G / Lib / All / None / DK

46. Handling foreign policy crises
   D / Rep / Ref / G / Lib / All / None / DK

47. Restoring honesty and integrity to government and politics
   D / Rep / Ref / G / Lib / All / None / DK

48. Holding the line on taxes
   D / Rep / Ref / G / Lib / All / None / DK

49. Fighting crime and drugs
   D / Rep / Ref / G / Lib / All / None / DK

50. Cutting wasteful government spending
   D / Rep / Ref / G / Lib / All / None / DK

[PLEASE READ: "THERE ARE JUST A FEW MORE QUESTIONS FOR DEMOGRAPHIC PURPOSES"]

51. Generally speaking, do you usually think of yourself as a Republican, a Democrat, an Independent, or something else?
   [PROBE REPUBLICAN/DEMOCRAT FOR STRONG/ NOT VERY STRONG]

a. Strong Republican
b. Not very Strong Republican
c. Independent
d. Not very Strong Democrat
e. Strong Democrat
f. Other/Something else
g. No preference
h. DK/Refuse

[IF INDEPENDENT, OTHER, OR NO PREFERENCE, ASK:]

52. Which party do you normally support in elections, the Republican Party or the Democrat Party?
    a. Republican
    b. Democrat
    c. Both Equally **[DO NOT READ]**
    d. Other **[DO NOT READ]**
    e. DK/Refused **[DO NOT READ]**

[CONTINUE TO ASK ALL RESPONDENTS:]

53. For whom did you vote in the 1996 presidential election? If you did not vote in the 1996 presidential election, just say so.
    a. Bob Dole
    b. Bill Clinton
    c. Ross Perot
    d. Other
    e. Did not vote
    f. DK/Refused

54. What is your current employment status? Are you employed, unemployed (and looking for a job), retired, a student, or a homemaker? **[PROBE EMPLOYED FOR PRIVATE SECTOR/GOVERNMENT]**
    a. Employed in private sector
    b. Employed in government
    c. Unemployed
    d. Disabled
    e. Student
    f. Retired
    g. Homemaker
    h. DK/Refused

[IF EMPLOYED, ASK:]

55. Which of the following best describes your occupation?
    [READ CHOICES]
    a. Executive/professional/managerial
    b. Blue collar
    c. Service/retail/clerical
    d. Farming or agriculture
    e. Government (excluding military)
    f. Military
    g. Other **[DO NOT READ]**
    h. DK/Refused **[DO NOT READ]**

[CONTINUE TO ASK ALL RESPONDENTS:]

56. Are you, or is any member of your household, a member of a labor union or organized group of workers?
    a. Yes
    b. No
    c. DK/Refused

57. At work or at home, how often do you use a computer for e-mail or Internet access? If you don't own or use a computer, just say so.
    [READ CHOICES]
    a. Everyday
    b. Almost everyday
    c. Couple times a week
    d. Once a week
    e. Rarely
    f. Never
    g. DK/Refused **[DO NOT READ]**

58. What is your current marital status? Are you ... **[READ CHOICES]**
    a. Married
    b. Single
    c. Widowed
    d. Divorced or Separated
    e. DK/Refused **[DO NOT READ]**

59. Are there any children under 18 living in this household?
    a. Yes
    b. No
    c. DK/Refused

60. What was your last grade of formal education?
    a. Less than high school
    b. High school graduation
    c. Some college or tech school
    d. College graduate
    e. Graduate or Professional degree
    f. DK/Refused

61. What is your religion?
    a. Evangelical Protestant
    b. Fundamental Protestant
    c. Mainstream Protestant
    d. Catholic
    e. Jewish
    f. Morman
    g. Buddhist
    h. Islam/Muslim
    i. Atheist
    j. Other
    k. DK/Refused

62. Do you live in a city of more than 100,000 people, a suburban area outside of a city, small city or town, or a rural area?
    a. City
    b. Suburb
    c. Small city/town
    d. Rural area
    e. DK/Refused

63. And just to make sure we have a representative sample, could you please tell me your race? Most people classify themselves as African American, White, Asian, Hispanic, Native American, or something else.
    a. African American
    b. White
    c. Asian
    d. Hispanic
    e. Native American
    f. Other/Something else
    g. DK/Refused

64. Just for statistical purposes, can you tell me which one of the following categories best represents your family's total annual income? **[READ CATEGORIES; PUSH FOR RESPONSE]**
    a. Under $20,000
    b. Between $20,000 and $40,000
    c. Between $40,001 and $60,000
    d. Between $60,001 and $75,000
    e. Between $75,001 and $100,000
    f. Over $100,000
    g. DK/Refused

65. Gender **[BY OBSERVATION]**
    a. Male
    b. Female

66. Region: **[PRE-CODE]**
    a. New England
    b. Middle Atlantic
    c. East North Central
    d. West North Central
    e. South Atlantic
    f. East South Central
    g. West South Central
    h. Mountain
    i. Pacific

POSTELECTION SURVEY

Methodology

In addition to conducting the August 2000 survey for this book, John McLaughlin and Associates shared with us the data from their 2000 postelection survey of 1000 voters, to which we refer in various sections of the book. All interviews for the postelection survey were conducted on election night, November 7, 2000. Interview selection was random within predetermined units; these units were structured to correspond with actual voter turnout in a national presidential election. The survey has a margin of error of approximately ± 3 percent at a 95 percent level of confidence.

Post-Election Survey Questionnaire

JOHN McLAUGHLIN & ASSOCIATES, INC.
NATIONAL POSTELECTION SURVEY
NOVEMBER 7, 2000

Introduction: Good evening. My name is _____ and I'm calling from John McLaughlin & Associates, a national public opinion firm. This evening we're conducting a short public opinion survey and we'd like to get your opinions.

1. Did you vote in today's election for President?
   a. Yes **[CONTINUE]**
   b. No/All other responses **[TERMINATE]**

2. Did you vote in person today at a local election day polling place or did you vote in person on an earlier date before today? If you voted by a write-in vote or by an absentee ballot, just say so.
   a. Voted in person on election day **[CONTINUE]**
   b. Voted in person on an earlier date **[CONTINUE]**
   c. Voted by write-in or absentee **[CONTINUE]**
   d. DK/Refused **[TERMINATE]**

3. When you voted today, for whom did you vote for President, Al Gore, the Democrat candidate, George W. Bush, the Republican candidate, Ralph Nader, the Green Party candidate, Pat Buchanan, the Reform Party candidate, or someone else? If you did not cast a vote for President, but voted for other offices, just say so.
   a. Al Gore **[CONTINUE]**
   b. George W. Bush **[CONTINUE]**

c. Ralph Nader **[CONTINUE]**
d.Pat Buchanan **[CONTINUE]**
e. Someone else **[CONTINUE]**
f. Did not vote for President, but voted for other offices **[CONTINUE]**
g.DK/Refused **[TERMINATE]**

[IF RESPONDENT SAID AL GORE, ASK:]
4. Why did you vote for Al Gore for President?

[IF RESPONDENT SAID GEORGE W. BUSH, ASK:]
5. Why did you vote for George W. Bush for President?

[IF RESPONDENT SAID RALPH NADER, ASK:]
6. Why did you vote for Ralph Nader for President?

[CONTINUE TO ASK ALL RESPONDENTS:]
7. When did you decide how you were going to vote for President today? Was it: **[READ CHOICES]**
   a. Before Labor Day
   b.During the month of September
   c. During the first two weeks of October
   d.During the last two weeks of October
   e. During the last week before Election Day
   f. DK/Refused **[DO NOT READ]**

8. This year, which of the following was the most important factor in deciding your vote for President? **[READ CHOICES]**
   a. The issue differences between the candidates
   b.The personality and character of each candidate
   c. The philosophy of your political party
   d.DK/Refused **[DO NOT READ]**

[Q#'s 9–16 ONLY ASK RESPONDENTS IN THE FOLLOWING STATES: DE, IN, MO, MT, NH, NC, ND, UT, VT, WA, WV (GUBERNATORIAL STATES)]

9. In today's election for governor in your state, did you vote for the Republican candidate or the Democratic candidate?
   a. Republican candidate **[GO TO Q#10]**
   b.Democratic candidate **[GO TO Q#13]**
   c. Other candidate **[DO NOT READ] [GO TO Q#16]**
   d.Did not cast vote for governor **[DO NOT READ] [GO TO Q#17]**
   e. DK/Refused **[DO NOT READ] [GO TO Q#17]**

[IF RESPONDENT SAID REPUBLICAN, ASK:]
10. What was the single most important reason you voted Republican today for governor?

11. Was your vote for the Republican gubernatorial candidate more a vote for the Republican candidate or more a vote against the Democratic candidate?
    a. Vote for Republican
    b. Vote against Democrat
    c. DK/Refused

12. Which of the following statements is the better description of why you voted for the Republican today for governor?
    [READ AND ROTATE CHOICES]
    a. You voted Republican for governor more as a vote against President Clinton and Al Gore.
    b. You voted Republican for governor more as a vote of support for the Republican candidate in your state and the candidate's policies.
    c. DK/Refused **[DO NOT READ]**

[IF RESPONDENT SAID DEMOCRAT, ASK:]

13. What was the single most important reason you voted Democrat today for governor?

14. Was your vote for the Democratic gubernatorial candidate more a vote for the Democratic candidate or more a vote against the Republican candidate?
    a. Vote for Democrat
    b. Vote against Republican
    c. DK/Refused

15. Which of the following statements is the better description of why you voted for the Democrat today for governor? **[READ CHOICES]**
    a. You voted Democrat for governor more as a vote to support President Clinton and Al Gore.
    b. You voted Democrat for governor more as a vote of support for the Democratic candidate in your state and the candidate's policies.
    c. DK/Refused **[DO NOT READ]**

[CONTINUE TO ASK ALL RESPONDENTS IN THE FOLLOWING STATES: DE, IN, MO, MT, NH, NC, ND, UT, VT, WA, WV (GUBERNATORIAL STATES)]

16. When did you decide how you were going to vote today for governor? Was it: **[READ CHOICES]**
    a. Before Labor Day
    b. During the month of September
    c. During the first two weeks of October
    d. During the last two weeks of October
    e. During the last week before Election Day
    f. DK/Refused **[DO NOT READ]**

[Q#'s 17–18 ONLY ASK RESPONDENTS IN THE FOLLOWING STATES: MI, MO, MT, RI, OH, TN, WA, MN, UT, TX, VT, AZ, MS, IN, FL, DE, PA, ME, WY, HI, NM, NV, WV, ND, CA, MA, NE, WI, NJ, CT, NY, VA, MD (SENATORIAL STATES)]

17. In today's election for U.S. Senate in your state, did you vote for the Republican candidate or the Democratic candidate?
    a. Republican candidate
    b. Democratic candidate
    c. Other candidate **[DO NOT READ]**
    d. Did not cast vote for U.S. Senate **[DO NOT READ] [GO TO Q#19]**
    e. DK/Refused **[DO NOT READ] [GO TO Q#19]**

18. When did you decide how you were going to vote today for U.S. Senate? Was it: **[READ CHOICES]**
    a. Before Labor Day
    b. During the month of September
    c. During the first two weeks of October
    d. During the last two weeks of October
    e. During the last week before Election Day
    f. DK/Refused **[DO NOT READ]**

[CONTINUE TO ASK ALL RESPONDENTS IN ALL STATES]

19. In today's election for U.S. Congress, did you vote for the Republican candidate or the Democratic candidate?
    a. Republican candidate
    b. Democratic candidate
    c. Other candidate **[DO NOT READ]**
    d. Did not cast vote for U.S. Congress **[DO NOT READ] [GO TO Q#21]**
    e. DK/Refused **[DO NOT READ] [GO TO Q#21]**

20. When did you decide how you were going to vote for U.S. Congress today? Was it: **[READ CHOICES]**
    a. Before Labor Day
    b. During the month of September
    c. During the first two weeks of October
    d. During the last two weeks of October
    e. During the last week before Election Day
    f. DK/Refused **[DO NOT READ]**

21. If you were to label yourself, would you say you are a liberal, a moderate, or a conservative in your political beliefs?
    a. Liberal
    b. Moderate
    c. Conservative
    d. DK/Refused

Now, I am going to read you a list of names. Will you please tell me if you have a favorable or unfavorable opinion of each person? If you have no opinion or have never heard of the person, just say so.
FAVORABLE (f), UNFAVORABLE (u), NO OPINION (no), NEVER HEARD OF (nh)

22. Bill Clinton   f / u / no / nh

23. Hillary Clinton   f / u / no / nh

24. Al Gore   f / u / no / nh

25. George W. Bush   f / u / no / nh

26. Denny Hastert   f / u / no / nh

27. Overall, how would you rate the job Bill Clinton has done as President? Would you say he has done an excellent job, a good job, only a fair job, or a poor job?
    a. Excellent
    b. Good
    c. Fair
    d. Poor
    e. DK/Refused

28. Would you say you most favor a smaller government with fewer services or a larger government with many services?
    a. Smaller government
    b. Larger government
    c. DK/Refused

29. Generally speaking, regarding the issue of abortion, would you say that you are pro-life or pro-choice?
    a. Pro-life
    b. Pro-choice
    c. DK/Refused

30. In general, are you most concerned about economic issues such as taxes, government spending, and jobs; social issues such as education, health care, and the environment; moral issues such as abortion, school prayer, and promoting traditional values; foreign affairs issues such as our policies in Asia, the Middle East, and Europe; or social issues like crime, drugs, and welfare reform?
    a. Economic issues
    b. Social issues
    c. Moral issues
    d. Foreign policy issues
    e. Local issues
    f. DK/Refused

31. Do you approve or disapprove of George W. Bush's proposal for an across-the-board federal income tax cut? **[PROBE FOR STRONGLY/ SOMEWHAT APPROVE OR DISAPPROVE]**
    a. Strongly approve
    b. Somewhat approve
    c. Somewhat disapprove
    d. Strongly disapprove
    e. DK/Refused

32. With which political party are you affiliated?
    a. Republican
    b. Democrat
    c. Independent
    d. Other
    e. DK/Refused

33. For whom did you vote in the 1996 presidential election, Bill Clinton, the Democrat candidate, Bob Dole, the Republican candidate, or Ross Perot, the Independent candidate? If you did not vote for president in 1996, just say so.
    a. Bill Clinton
    b. Bob Dole
    c. Ross Perot
    d. Other **[DO NOT READ]**
    e. Did not vote for president in 1996
    f. DK/Refused

34. How do you usually vote? **[READ ANSWERS]**
    a. Always Democrat
    b. Usually Democrat
    c. Ticket Splitter
    d. Usually Republican
    e. Always Republican
    f. DK/Refused

35. At home, between the hours of 7 PM and midnight, do you mostly watch network TV at that time, or which of the following cable TV networks do you watch most often? **[READ CHOICES]**
    a. Mostly watch network TV
    b. ESPN/Sports Channel/MSG
    c. CNN/Headline News
    d. A&E/Arts & Entertainment Network
    e. TNT (Turner Network Television)
    f. Lifetime Network
    g. Nickelodeon/Nick at Nite
    h. TBS/Superstation

i. MTV (Music Television)/VH1 (Video Hits One)
j. CNBC
k. FOX News Channel
l. MSNBC
m. C-SPAN
n. USA Network
o. The Family Channel
p. TNN (The Nashville Network)/CMT (Country Music Television)
q. The Discovery Channel/The Learning Channel
r. Other [**DO NOT READ**]
s. None/DK/Refused

36. What is the last grade of formal education you have completed?
 a. Less than high school graduate
 b. High school graduate
 c. Some college
 d. College graduate
 e. Post graduate
 f. DK/Refused

37. What is your annual household income—is it under $20,000; between $20,001 & $40,000; between $40,001 & $60,000; or over $60,000?
 a. Under $20,000
 b. Between $20,001 & $40,000
 c. Between $40,001 & $60,000
 d. Over $60,000
 e. DK/Refused

38. What is your religion? [**READ CHOICES**]
 a. Evangelical Protestant
 b. Fundamentalist Protestant
 c. Mainstream Protestant
 d. Catholic
 e. Jewish
 f. Mormon
 g. Muslim/Islam
 h. Atheist/Agnostic
 i. Other (Specify)
 j. DK/Refused

39. What would you say is your main racial background?
 a. Hispanic
 b. African American
 c. Asian-American
 d. White
 e. Other
 f. Refused

40. What is your age?
    a. 18–25
    b. 26–40
    c. 41–55
    d. 56–65
    e. Over 65
    f. Refused

41. What is your current marital status?
    a. Single, never married
    b. Married
    c. Separated
    d. Divorced
    e. Widowed
    f. DK/Refused

42. Do you currently have personal investments of stocks, bonds, or mutual funds of $5,000 or more?
    a. Yes
    b. No
    c. DK/Refused

43. Gender:
    a. Male
    b. Female

44. Area: **[PRE-CODE]**
    a. New England
    b. Middle Atlantic
    c. East North Central
    d. West North Central
    e. South Atlantic
    f. East South Central
    g. West South Central
    h. Mountain
    i. Pacific

45. State (2-DIGIT NUMERIC CODE)

INDEX